PENGUIN BOOKS

THE BOOK OF WORLD CUISINES

Food and wine lover Howard Hillman has acquired unsurpassed knowledge of world cuisines through his million miles of travel to over one hundred countries. A graduate of the Harvard Business School in 1961, Mr. Hillman went on to be the author of dining guidebooks on New York City, Chicago, San Francisco, Miami, Honolulu, Boston, and Washington. He has written globe-trotting gastronomic articles for *The New York Times, Wall Street Journal, Business Week, Food & Wine,* and other publications. He has critically rated restaurants for America's largest newspaper, the *New York News*. His many books include *The Diner's Guide to Wines* and *The Food Bible,* as well as several popular books on non-culinary subjects, including *The Art of Winning Foundation Grants, The Complete New Yorker,* and *The Ins and Outs of Living in New York.* Mr. Hillman has served as president of the National Academy of Sports and as vice-president of the American Film Theatre. A skilled cook in his own right, he has personally researched and prepared more than five thousand different dishes from around the world. Mr. Hillman lives in New York City, where he maintains a food and wine reference library of several thousand titles.

HOWARD HILLMAN

The Book of World Cuisines

Coauthor: DANA SHILLING
Research-Editorial Assistant: CHERRY DUMAUAL

PENGUIN BOOKS

Penguin Books Ltd, Harmondsworth,
Middlesex, England
Penguin Books, 625 Madison Avenue,
New York, New York 10022, U.S.A.
Penguin Books Australia Ltd, Ringwood,
Victoria, Australia
Penguin Books Canada Limited, 2801 John Street,
Markham, Ontario, Canada L3R 1B4
Penguin Books (N.Z.) Ltd, 182–190 Wairau Road,
Auckland 10, New Zealand

First published 1979

LIBRARY OF CONGRESS CATALOGING IN PUBLICATION DATA
Hillman, Howard.
The book of world cuisines.
Bibliography: p. 257.
Includes index.
1. Cookery, International. I. Shilling, Dana,
joint author. II. Title.
TX725.A1H544 641.5'9 79-17504
ISBN 0 14 00.4989 4

Printed in the United States of America by
Offset Paperback Mfrs., Inc., Dallas, Pennsylvania
Set in Optima

To the growing number of diners and cooks who believe that the distinct cuisines of the world should be preserved, not internationalized

~~ CONTENTS

 # PREFACE

THE CUISINES IN THIS book didn't just happen. They are the result of evolution, an intermingling of forces over centuries or millennia. A national cuisine grows, develops, and changes as part of a living culture. Historical forces (possession of a particular territory, an aversion to the foods characteristic of an enemy), geography, geology, and climate (certain crops demand heavy rains, or sandy soil, or hot summers, or whatever), and technology (the digging stick or the tractor) help to determine which raw materials will be available to the cook. The same factors will influence the cook's use of raw materials. Certain foods or combinations of foods may be forbidden by religion or deplored by custom. Fuel may be plentiful (as in early America, a land covered by virgin forests) or extremely scarce (as in India or China). Northern Indians grow wheat and eat bread; southern Indians eat rice. These traditions developed as a result of geography and climate. If the entire *batterie de cuisine* is an iron caldron over a campfire, the cooking style will differ from that of a cook with two ranges and a microwave oven. It may be necessary to disguise the smell and taste of spoiled food or to preserve eighty-four pounds of plums for winter use. The cook may be open to, or distrustful of, outside influences. A scholar who understands a nation's history, geography, topography, and sociology can describe that nation's cuisine by projection from this knowledge, just as a paleontologist can reconstruct the appearance of a dinosaur from one bone. "Tell me what you are, and I will tell you what you eat" is as true as its converse.

Cuisines evolve, but not in a vacuum. Conquerors impose changes; merchants advertise them. The European discovery of the New World had an explosive impact on the European diet. Those vast tracts of land, so far uncultivated by Europeans, gave the promise of more and cheaper food. New foods were introduced: potatoes, sweet potatoes, tomatoes, corn, chilis, allspice, chocolate, turkey, and vanilla, among others. Can you imagine southern Italian cooking without tomatoes, Hungarian cuisine without paprika, Chinese Szechuan seasoning without hot chilis, Irish and German diets without potatoes? Nor did the migration of foods move in only one direction. Chicken, beef, lamb, pork, wheat, and many fruits and vegetables (apples and oranges, for example) were brought to the Western hemisphere; the importation of the horse revolutionized agriculture.

The exchange was beneficial. But today characteristic national cuisines are being homogenized. This amalgamation is good if cooks can add the best dishes of other cultures to their repertoire. The Japanese say that tasting a new food adds seventy-five days to one's life. The trouble starts when new dishes displace the old, disrupting rather than enriching a traditional pattern of cooking and eating, and when the foods adopted represent the lowest common denominator rather than the best in a cuisine. There's a McDonald's on the Champs Elysées, which is cause for rue not because American food is barbarous and unfit for the land of Carême and Escoffier, but because America has better food to offer. Americanization—or Anglicization or Germanization—per se is not bad; it just seems sad that other cultures are losing some of their culinary heritage, a treasure worth preserving.

PART I
Europe

 # AUSTRIA

COUNTLESS COOKING INFLUENCES HAVE penetrated the walls of the Austrian kitchen. This is especially evident in Vienna, once the capital of the Hapsburg domain, a territory which included Hungary, Czechoslovakia, and portions of Italy, Yugoslavia, Romania, Poland, and the Soviet Union. Austrian cuisine has also absorbed culinary flavors from its neighbor, Germany, as well as from its traditional enemy, Turkey.

The introduction of coffee from Turkey was instrumental in shaping Austrian culture. Especially in Vienna, the coffeehouse has traditionally been the center of endless social, political, and literary activities. One can find innumerable varieties of coffee there: served black, with milk, cream, spirits, ice cream, or Schlagobers.

Schlagobers is whipped cream, eaten in cake, on cake, in coffee, or even by itself. Its qualities of airiness and elaboration extend to Viennese music and architecture—though not to the theories or prose style of Sigmund Freud, one of Vienna's most famous citizens.

Zuckerbäckerei (sugar bakery) is a Viennese talent. Gugelhupf, a yeast cake baked in a fluted tube pan, is one of the plainest of these confections; Spanische Windtorte, a sculptured meringue shell filled with fruit and whipped cream, is one of the most elaborate.

Somewhere between falls Sachertorte, a chocolate sponge layer cake with an apricot filling and/or coating, topped with a bitter chocolate glaze. This delicacy was the subject of a controversy between two illustrious Viennese establishments, the pastry shop Demel's and the Hotel Sacher, who battled each other in court for seven years over the exclusive right to sell the authentic Sachertorte.

The assortment of other world-famous Viennese sugar-bakery treats includes: Faschingkrapfen, doughnuts stuffed with apricot jam, traditionally eaten during the pre-Lenten feast called Fasching; Indiánerkrapfen, plain cupcakes stuffed with whipped cream and drenched in chocolate; Linzertorte, a shell of pie pastry containing ground almonds filled with raspberry jam and topped with a lattice crust; Apfel Strudelfülle, paper-thin pastry filled and rolled with a sweet apple mixture, then baked; Haselnusstorte, a light and airy hazelnut cake; Doboschtorte, the Hungarian sponge cake featuring a brittle caramel icing; and Rehrücken, a chocolate cake shaped and decorated like a saddle of venison.

Also to be sampled is the Kipfel, a crescent-shaped breakfast roll that, according to lore, derives its form from the crescent emblem on the Turkish flag. The Kipfel became the croissant when it was brought to France by an unsuccessful Austrian export, Marie Antoinette.

It is traditional for Vienna's solid citizens (who become ever more solid on this regimen) to start the day with a light Continental breakfast. They follow this with the *Gabelfrüh-stück* (fork breakfast) at midmorning, a meat meal based on the Hungarian-inspired Gulasch or the Germanic sausage.

Mittagessen (midday dinner) usually features soup, most likely Rindsuppe, beef broth. There will be meat, poultry, or fish, dumplings and/or potatoes, perhaps a vegetable dish or salad. A *Mehlspeise* (flour dessert) of fruit dumplings, pancakes, sweet potato noodles, or some other classic sample of Viennese home cooking usually follows. One of the best-known *Mehlspeise* is Kaiserschmarrn, a fluffy, raisin-studded pancake that is torn apart in the skillet by the cook with a pair of forks.

The more elegant creations of the professional bakers are served at the midafternoon *Jause*. This snack of coffee and cake or pastry, accompanied by glasses of water, is often taken at a coffeehouse or *Konditorei* (pastry shop).

The evening meal is usually a light one. Then, unless they prefer to snack after the theater, on a visit, or before bed, the Viennese must fast until the morrow.

As with Germans, the centuries-old five-meals-a-day eating pattern is being forsaken by many members of the younger generation of Austrians who place a great value on thin waistlines.

FAMOUS VIENNESE DISHES

Backhendl Quarters of young chicken are coated—like Wiener Schnitzel—with flour, beaten eggs, and breadcrumbs, then fried. (The Viennese specialty predates its "twin sister," the American Southern Fried Chicken.) Backhendl used to be a more aristocratic dish than Schnitzel or Tafelspitz because, until recently, chicken was expensive.

Tafelspitz The most popular cut of beef for boiling is Tafelspitz. Boiled beef with horseradish sauce is the traditional weekday lunch of Vienna's middle class. Viennese butchers can produce two dozen different cuts of beef for boiling, each with a minutely different texture and flavor, each with a passionate group of devotees.

Wiener Schnitzel A thin cutlet (usually veal) dipped successively in flour, beaten eggs, and breadcrumbs, and then fried. The ideal Wiener Schnitzel is thin, crisp, and large enough to lap over the edges of the serving plate. According to local connoisseurs, it should also be dry enough to be sat on without creating a grease stain on one's clothing.

REGIONAL DISHES

The Tyrol, in western Austria, is famous for its Bauernspeck, bacon that has been soaked in brine then cold-smoked. This bacon can be served raw or combined with other ingredients in cooked dishes. Speckknödel, bacon dumplings, are a Tyrolean member of the great Austrian dynasty of Knödel.

Nockerln, tiny flour dumplings parboiled and gently sautéed, are also popular in this region. Fried calves' liver is a typical Tyrolean meat dish, fried onion rings a characteristic Tyrolean flavoring agent.

Salzburg, located in northwest Austria near the West German border, has contributed not only masterpieces in music, but masterpieces in cooking as well. The Salzburger Nockerl, a plain dessert soufflé, is one example.

Carinthia, in the south of Austria, borders on Italy, which may explain the popularity of meat-and-cheese-filled noodle squares. But Carinthian Nudeln are also served with poppy seeds and with fruit filling—both Central European idiosyncrasies.

In the east of Austria, Styria specializes in thick Falschsuppen, soups made without meat stock, and Steierisches Schweinernes, a thick stew of pork and root vegetables.

Austrians as a whole are not great consumers of simply cooked fresh vegetables; they prefer heavier root vegetables and more elaborate preparations. Chocolate, apricot, raspberry jam, and caramel are preferred over fresh fruits.

BEVERAGES

Besides adoring coffee, Austrians consume a lot of beer and wine. Beer is the reigning alcoholic drink in western Austria, wine is the favorite in the eastern part of the country.

Beer brewing follows the German tradition of offering a wide variety of sound products to satisfy all tastes. You can easily find beers with a light or dark color, a mild or strong hop flavor, a low or high alcohol content, and a short or lengthy storage period.

The best Austrian wines are white and made from the Riesling grape, the most famous of these being Gumpoldskirchen. They tend to be low in alcohol and should be drunk young if you wish to savor their delightful freshness. In order to enjoy Austrian wine under the happiest of circumstances, tour the Viennese countryside during the late spring or early summer when the *Heurige* is drunk. *Heurige* is "this year's" new wine, fresh from the barrel containing the wine made from the grapes harvested last autumn. Small- and large-scale wine growers set up roadside tables, front-yard cafés or more elaborate outdoor wine gardens (*Heurigers*) inviting you to drop by for a glass or two of their wine, perhaps served with a bite to eat.

BELGIUM

FROM A CULTURAL AND culinary viewpoint, Belgium can be divided into two distinct regions. The northern region is Flemish-speaking and cooks and drinks in a style reminiscent of neighboring Holland. The French-speaking Walloons of the south favor wine rather than beer and prepare food like the French, using slightly more seasoning than their Gallic counterparts.

Despite these differences, Belgians share many common tastes. Most love *fritures*, fried foods sold from small stands. Biftek et Frites ("steak" and fried potatoes) and Moules et Frites (steamed mussels and fried potatoes) are national favorites. The preferred condiment for the thin, double-fried Frites is a dollop of mayonnaise. A *biftek* is just about any piece of lean, boneless meat; it need be neither beef nor steak. But the mussels better be mussels, which the Belgians love steamed, baked with breadcrumbs (Moules au Gratin), or steamed and sauced with wine and herbs (Moules à l'Anversoise).

The rich flesh of eel is enjoyed by Flemish in Paling in 't Groen, and by Walloons in Anguilles au Vert. Both names identify the same mixture of eel slow-cooked in butter and wine (or beer), fresh green herbs, and egg yolk. The dish is often served cold, so that it provides its own aspic.

Eel is also an integral part of the famous Flemish Waterzooi, a soup-stew of eel and fish from the North Sea, cooked in wine with delicate vegetables. In the Walloon area, however, Waterzooi usually means a poached chicken soup-stew, its broth enriched by egg yolks and cream.

Belgians love vegetables, especially springtime *primeurs*, which are small, tender, and expensive. Asparagus, sorrel, and endive (*witloof* in Flemish; *chicon* or *chicorée de Bruxelles* in French) are especially prized. The endive is used as a base for main dishes as well as salads. And naturally, there are Brussels sprouts in Belgium—*choux de Bruxelles*. Chervil (Kerrelsoep is a favorite soup), tarragon, chives, bay leaf, and nutmeg are common seasonings. Les Jets de Houblon à la Crême are fresh hop shoots smothered in cream. With all that beer made and consumed, there are always plenty of hops for the cooking pot.

Thanks mainly to the Flemish, beer consumption in Belgium is high; one of the highest rates of consumption in the world. Much of the beer is light lager. Patersbier is hearty beer brewed by monks. Brussels makes a specialty of Kriek-Lambic, beer with fermented sour cherries.

Not all the beer goes down the hatch in liquid form; Vlaamse Karbonaden (Carbonnades Flamandes in French) is a thick stew of beef and onions braised in beer. Hochepot is a similar stew of meat and several vegetables cooked in broth rather than beer.

The mountainous Ardennes area in the far south is famous for its game. The cooks of Liége take full advantage of this plentiful resource, being noted for Oie à l'Instar de Visé, tender lean goose poached in wine, diced, coated in breadcrumbs, and fried. The pieces are served with a garlic-flavored sauce of eggs and butter. Rognons de Veau à la Liégoise, sautéed veal kidneys flavored with juniper berries, is also a Liége dish. Café Liégois is another specialty which the city claims; it is an ice cream sundae made with mocha ice cream, coffee syrup, and drifts of whipped cream.

Other desserts popular throughout Belgium are Dame Blanche, vanilla ice cream with fudge sauce, and Gaufres, or Gaufrettes, waffles eaten with butter and sugar, ice cream, or whipped cream.

The Belgian day usually begins with a light meal of milky coffee and bread; Pain d'Épices (gingerbread) is a favorite. The main meal traditionally comes at midday. However,

Belgians today are preferring to eat a *pistolet* (a roll or, by extension, a sandwich) for lunch and dine in the evening. Housewives meet at 4 p.m. for *goûter*, coffee and cake. Street stands are always prepared to sell Gaufres, Beignets (fritters), or Moules et Frites to hungry passersby.

 # ENGLAND

ENGLISH FOOD IS THE butt of numerous jokes. Most originated during World War II when Americans and other non-English people encountered a country at war, subsisting on rationed foods, with limited time to devote to the art of cooking.

Another reason why English cuisine has been so maligned by foreigners is that the dishes generally are not as rich with complicated sauces as those of France, a comparison frequently made owing to England's proximity to France. The English find no reason to disguise the inherent flavors of their high-quality vegetables, fruits, meat, fish, eggs, and dairy products. In other words, the English want their roast beef to taste like roast beef.

If English cooks are to be faulted at all, it should be for their penchant for overcooking.

By reputation, the English are great eaters of meat. "A cut off the joint and two veg" is a familiar phrase resounding through most English dining rooms every Sunday afternoon. The traditional roast-beef dinner, the most celebrated meal of the week, usually consists of boiled or browned potatoes, spring greens (boiled cabbage or Brussels sprouts), fresh horseradish sauce, simple pan gravy, and, most importantly, roast beef. Yorkshire Pudding, also featured, is an airily substantial concoction of flour, egg, and milk cooked in a pan set under the joint to absorb the dripping beef fat and juices.

The remains of Sunday dinner appear, like King Charles's head, at various times throughout the week. Bubble and Squeak is a fried mixture of leftover potatoes, onions, Brussels sprouts, cabbage, and meat, if available. Shepherd's Pie (also called Cottage Pie) is a blanket of mashed potatoes over leftover meat and gravy. Toad-in-the-Hole can envelop leftover meat in a Yorkshire Pudding cloak, but it is generally made with sausages.

Beef may be the most popular meat; however, mutton, lamb, ham, and streaky bacon add variety. England's extensive forest regions also help satiate the country's carnivorous appetite by supplying game such as venison and grouse (preferably hung to age until it develops the "high" flavor the British enjoy).

English sausage, Banger, appears on the menu in a variety of fashions. Heavy in starch content, the Banger may be served with mashed potatoes, a combination appropriately called Banger and Mash. Scotch Eggs are hard-boiled eggs swathed in Banger and breadcrumbs, then deep-fried. Both these dishes are often accompanied by a side order of Chips (deep-fried potatoes).

Chips reach their highest degree of fame when served with batter-dipped fried fish (usually cod, plaice, or haddock). The famous combo, known as Fish and Chips, is traditionally served in hand-fashioned cones made from yesterday's newspaper. A sprinkling of salt and a splash of malt vinegar are the classic condiments (the introduction of tomato ketchup is a bastardization of the folk custom).

Fish has always been popular in England: as a fasting-day food in Catholic England; an alternative on meatless days decreed by the Tudors to encourage fishing; and as a quick, cheap meal for factory or office workers. And since no point of this island nation is more than 100 kilometers from the sea, the fish has a good chance of being fresh.

Herrings are an important item in the English person's diet. Kippers are split, gutted herrings preserved by salting and smoking. Bloaters are salted herring, but appear ungutted, whole, and lightly smoked. Bloater Paste, familiar to readers of English detective stories, is a condiment made from mashed bloaters. Pilchards are a small variety of herring.

Another major saltwater fish is the Dover sole. It is

especially prized for its delicate flesh whose taste is best preserved when poached. Whitstable oysters rank number one in the shellfish category, while trout reigns as the best fish in the freshwater sector.

Finnan Haddie, that Scottish creation, is smoked haddock. When served creamed or combined with rice, hard-boiled eggs, and curry powder, it is called Kedgeree. This, like the spicy lentil soup Mulligatawny, and Country Captain (curried chicken), is a dish which evolved from the old British imperialist days in India.

Dried fish are a staple of the English breakfast, traditionally a hearty meal of porridge, kippers, bacon and sausage, fried eggs, cold toast, and plenty of tea.

The second meal of the weekday, lunch, is taken at noon. Pub lunches are perfectly geared for the consumption of beer. However, affluent businessmen wash down their lamb cutlets or chops with water, or even wine.

Teatime is another English custom that is celebrated by many who, like Cole Porter's lady who is a tramp, get too hungry for dinner at eight. The hot pot of refreshing brew is most probably made from a blend of black tea, imported from India or Sri Lanka. It is customarily served with lemon, lumps of sugar, and cold milk. Hot milk and cream are believed to spoil the taste. A tray of treats, which might include small watercress, cucumber, or chutney sandwiches, and cakes or biscuits, usually accompanies the tea service. Crumpets, thin, bubbly rounds of dough baked on a griddle, are delicious with tea. So are Brandy Snaps, dark, thin, brandy-flavored cookies, rolled and filled with whipped cream. Teatime is also a good time to sample Chelsea Buns, rolls of sweet dough sprinkled with sugar; Sally Lunn, a plain yeast cake served with whipped cream; and Bath Buns, a crunchy pastry flavored with caraway seeds and candied fruit peels, and tinted with saffron.

The addition of fish, egg, or meat dishes, or such English idiosyncrasies as spaghetti or canned baked beans on toast, results in High Tea. In some homes, this more substantial meal substitutes for dinner.

The middle- and upper-class dinner, served later than the

American but earlier than the Spanish, centers around the meat course (perháps lamb with mint sauce, or mutton chops) and the pudding. Sometimes the two dishes overlap: Steak and Kidney Pudding is made of pieces of beef and beef kidney, steamed in a casing of suet pastry. The same mixture, baked, is Steak and Kidney Pie.

In England the term "pudding" covers a spectrum of preparations. A pudding can be a savory main course or a sweet dessert dish, and it can be cooked by boiling, steaming, or baking.

Boiled puddings are wrapped in a cloth—this bulbous mass goes right into a pot of boiling water. Steamed puddings are planted in a ceramic pudding basin (which resembles a flowerpot), which is then placed in a pan partially filled with water, covered, and allowed to steam. Baked puddings are just that—they are baked in the oven.

The most famous of English puddings is Plum Pudding, a Dickensian Christmas favorite, rich in dried fruit and suet and devoid of plums, sometimes flambéed. Other well-known puddings include Roly-Poly, sweet pastry rolled with fruit or jam; Spotted Dog, white suet pudding with raisins; Summer Pudding, a shell of bread slices stuffed with fresh fruits; and Burnt Cream (Créme Brûlée), a caramel-glazed custard dessert.

Trifle is not exactly a pudding, but this dessert is not exactly anything else. It consists of a mixture of cake or ladyfingers splashed with fortified wine, coated with jam, and layered with custard, fruit, and whipped cream.

Not every English dinner ends with a pudding, or even a tart English apple pie. The final course is often a spicy dish called a Savory. Savories can be identified by their place in the meal, and by the square of toast on which they rest. Welsh Rarebit (or Rabbit) is a melted cheese dish. The equally sardonic name Scotch Woodcock is given to scrambled eggs and anchovies on toast. Angels on Horseback are bacon-wrapped oysters.

The final course may also consist of cheese and biscuits (crackers). Cheddar, a whole-milk cheese with a tangy flavor, is white or golden. Cheshire is a high-butterfat cheese, excellent for melting. Sometimes a Cheshire cheese becomes inoculated with mold; these blue Cheshires are highly cherished. Stilton, England's most prized blue cheese, is very creamy with a hard crust. Good Stilton should be sliced from the top in horizontal rounds, then cut into wedges. Above all, this cheese should not be scooped or mashed up with port or beer. Single Gloucester is a flat cheese, eaten young; Double Gloucester is thick, and is eaten after aging. Wensleydale has a fresh, tangy flavor when young, and develops musky overtones as it ages. Lancashire is a strong, soft cheese, best when melted. Leicester is tinted orange by annatto seed.

The cheese can be (and, in formal meals, is) accompanied by a red wine, preferably a vintage Porto, the fortified Portuguese wine. Next comes the final phase of the Victorian-style formal meal: the ladies depart politely for another room to talk idly about the weather and other niceties while the gentlemen remain for cigars, cognac, and cognitive chatter about the world's most pressing problems. Nowadays, more and more women demonstrate their intellectual equality by staying for the cognac and pontification sessions— a few even light up cigars.

The English most commonly quench their thirst with either beer (which includes ale) or cider. Most beer is served in pint and half-pint mugs at cellar temperatures (55°F or 13°C), which is warm by foreign standards. Bitter, the most popular beer, has a strong flavor of hops and yeast and a high alcohol content. Bitter is the color of dark honey and possesses very little carbonation. Mild beer has a less assertive flavor. Both of these beers are often mixed in equal proportion ("half and half"). Porter is a dark, sweet drink and Stout is a malt liquor that, to some visitors, looks like black coffee. All of these beers go well with bread, cheese, and pickled onions—a combination called a Ploughman's Lunch in pubs—and with other highly salted or spiced food.

Cider, the "wine" fermented from apples, is full-flavored, somewhat sweet, and noted for felling tourists who treat it as a soft drink. This beverage, served cold, can reach the 10- to 15-proof range.

REGIONAL ENGLISH SPECIALTIES

Scrumpy is the dialect name for cider in Somerset and Devon, located in England's southwest. This area is renowned for its Clotted Cream, a dairy product made by heating milk over a slow fire until a layer of thick cream separates.

Cornwall, in the extreme southwest, specializes in Pasties (the "a" is short), turnovers filled with meat, onions, potatoes, and turnips. Some Pasties are even made with layers of meat, vegetables, and fruit, so that a miner can carry a three-course meal in his pocket. Stargazy Pie is a Cornish dish of pilchards baked in a pie, with their heads protruding from the crust. The local inhabitants are also proud—as they should be—of their rich cream and the high-fat-content butter they manufacture from it.

Melton Mowbrays are pork pies, named after their native town in Leicestershire, England. York hams, from the northeast, are world famous. Northumberland, on the east coast, makes Singing Hinnies, griddlecakes raised with baking powder. Lancashire, in the northwest, is known for its Hot Pot, a stew of mutton or lamb, kidneys, and oysters, under a topping of sliced potatoes. The English dish Parkin is also credited to the cooks of Lancashire: a gingerbread enriched with oats and flavored with treacle (dark molasses), a favorite British sweetener.

 # FRANCE

CLASSIC FRENCH CUISINE IS one of France's greatest glories, but it is not the true cuisine of the country. Far less than 1 percent of the dishes eaten by the French are prepared according to the dicta of classic French cuisine. These rich and elaborate dishes are usually consumed in expensive gastronomic temples such as Grand Vefour, Lasserre, Maxim's, Taillevent, Tour d'Argent, and Vivarois, where the average French person simply cannot afford to dine.

True French cuisine, like most other national cuisines, is regional in character—and each local cooking style has its own set of rules, philosophies, and basic ingredients, often in marked contrast to those of other regions. For instance, what do the delicate butter-and-cream cooking of Normandy, the not-so-delicate Mediterranean-style garlic-and-oil cooking of Provence, and the hearty Bavarianlike sauerkraut-based dishes of Alsace have in common with one another, save the French name? In short, a distinct concept of French cuisine does not exist. Regional yes, national no. Even the vaunted classic French cuisine, as well as the so-called *nouvelle cuisine* and the *cuisine minceur* of Chef Michel Guérard, are basically no more than adaptations (though good ones) of regional cooking methods which were originally developed in peasant kitchens, then improved upon by the cooks employed in local bourgeois homes over the centuries. When we're eating Boeuf Bourguignonne, for instance, we should be thinking in terms of Burgundian food rather than French food. Likewise, when we're enjoying Shrimps Provençal, we are really eating Provençal food, not French food. Consequently, before we

29

explore the classic, *nouvelle*, and *minceur* cuisines, it seems fitting to examine·briefly some of France's major culinary regions.

ALSACE AND LORRAINE

The local populace—and especially the Alsatians—share a fondness with neighboring Germany for sauerkraut, pork, goose, sausages, and beer, among other hearty products. Even the Alsatian wines are close cousins to the Rhines and Mosels of Germany.

Choucroute Garnie (a sauerkraut, pork, and sausage casserole), and Coq au Riesling (chicken in white wine sauce) are noted regional mainstays. Alsace's most acclaimed specialty, however, is Pâté de Foie Gras—light and delicate and undoubtedly the best pâté in the world.

Lorraine is famous for its Quiche Lorraine, a flaky open-faced pastry tart filled with a bacon-and-cheese-flavored custard. This region, along with Alsace, also prepares countless other quiches and tarts, whether their principal ingredient be meat for a main dish or fruit for a sweet dessert tart.

The Alsatians tend to use pork and goose fat as cooking oil more so than do the Lorrainers—the reverse is true when it comes to butter.

Cabbage, be it white or red, is the most popular regional vegetable and is more often than not pickled into *choucroute* (sauerkraut), sometimes flavored with juniper berries. Other beloved vegetables include the potato and, in season, asparagus. Both regions enjoy a variety of tasty freshwater fish such as trout, carp, and pike caught in the cool streams and lakes nearby. They can also boast of a rich supply of confectioneries selling excellent cakes, macaroons, pastries, and chocolates, all designed to satisfy the traditional sweet tooth of the local citizenry.

On the Lorraine regional border is Bar-le-Duc, the town that gives its name to currant preserves which some say are the finest in the world.

Unlike the wines produced in the other major wine-producing regions of France, Alsace's best wines are officially classified by grape type rather than by geographic location. Of Alsace's many wines, Riesling rates first, and the spicy Gewürztraminer second—but the other varieties such as Traminer, Sylvaner and Tokay d'Alsace make acceptable everyday drinking wines.

BORDEAUX

Food in Bordeaux is generally prepared in a straightforward manner without too many culinary embellishments. The local cooks prefer not to detract from the natural flavors of the region's fine ingredients.

Of all the local specialties, the most renowned is Sauce Bordelaise, made with red wine, marrow-based brown stock, shallots, and seasonings. It marries well with *entrecôte*, a grilled beefsteak cut that is much appreciated by the local cooks who love roasting or grilling meats, sometimes over the fragrant trimmings of the pruned vines.

Lamb is also a treat in Bordeaux, especially when the animal was reared along the seashore and riverbanks. Like a number of other dishes in Bordeaux, it is often prepared with a light touch of garlic.

The ultimate in seafood preparations is Lamproie à la Bordelaise, eel cooked in red wine. In addition to eels, the sizable Gironde estuary yields caviar of genuine sturgeon pedigree. Oysters, too, are standouts in the Bordeaux region, but when ordering, one should request the superior-tasting indigenous gravette as opposed to the more common, transplanted Portuguese variety.

Other regional food specialties include the Confit d'Oie (potted preserved duck) and, from the forests, wild berries such as strawberries, and *cèpes*, a large flat-top mushroom that is usually sautéed in butter, the preferred cooking medium in Bordeaux kitchens. From the town of St.-Émilion come some of the best macaroons ever baked.

Bordeaux wines, it goes nearly without saying, are

unsurpassed. The eight great reds are Châteaux Lafite-Rothschild, Mouton-Rothschild, Latour, and Margaux of Haut-Médoc district, Château Haut-Brion of Graves district, Châteaux Cheval Blanc and Ausone of St.-Émilion district, and Château Pétrus of Pomerol district, while Château d' Yquem of Sauternes district is the noble sweet white wine.

BRITTANY

The growing number of crêpe-specialty restaurants in Europe and America has done much to make us aware that Brittany is the crêpe capital of the world. Its oversized pancakelike crêpes can be made of wheat or buckwheat flour and filled with sweet or savory ingredients. Brittany should be equally famous for its bounty of succulent seafood, pré-salé lamb (reared on seaside salt marshes), and various pork products, including Morlais ham and sausages such as the Andouille made of pork intestines. The local vegetables, including the acclaimed onion and white haricot beans, are also excellent and, in keeping with the Breton culinary style, are usually simply cooked.

From Brittany also comes the invitingly dry white Muscadet wine that's perfect with fish and is usually a good value. It is not to be confused with the cloyingly sweet Muscatel-type wines produced elsewhere. The other major alcoholic beverage is hard cider, though beer is rapidly gaining a loyal following.

BURGUNDY AND THE LYONS ENVIRONS

Between the cities of Dijon in the north and Lyons in the south lies France's finest culinary area. Its cuisine is—like most other French regional cuisines—relatively uncomplicated, relying principally on the high quality of the local cooking ingredients for which the Burgundy and Lyons countrysides are famous.

Among these outstanding ingredients are the flavorful chickens reared in the Bresse subregion, the beef from the white Charollais cattle, the wild game from nearby forests and streams—the list goes on and on.

From Dijon come three celebrated products: the wine-based mustard, the spiced gingerbread honeycake called Pain d'Épices, and Cassis, the black-currant liqueur that transforms white wine into that jet-set aperitif named Kir. Farther south, we find these noted specialties:

Boeuf Bourguignonne   Beef braised with onions, mushrooms, and other vegetables in red wine.

Escargots à la Bourguignonne   Snails served in their shells with garlic-infused parsley butter.

Oeufs à la Bourguignonne   Eggs poached in red wine.

Pommes Lyonnaises   Potatoes cooked with onions.

Poulet à la Demi-Deuil   Literally, "chicken in half-mourning," referring to the shroudlike appearance of the breast when black truffle slices are inserted underneath the skin.

Quenelles de Brochet   Light and delicious pike dumplings.

Excellent goat and cow's milk cheeses come from the nearby foothills and mountains, the best ones being farmhouse produced.

Some Burgundy wines rank at the pinnacle of winedom. The very best come from the fabled Cote d'Or district that produces celestial red wines like Romanée-Conti, La Tâche, Richebourg, Grands-Échézeaux, Clos de Vougeot, Musigny, Bonnes Mares, Clos de Tart, Clos-de-Bèze, Chambertin, and Corton. This last is also a great white wine, as is the illustrious Montrachet, which has been labeled by most authorities as the finest dry white wine in the world. Still other Burgundian wines—Chablis, Beaujolais, and Pouilly-Fuissé—have lesser credentials but have become even greater household words and "musts" for restaurant wine lists both in France and abroad. Besides its reds and whites, Burgundy also produces

Marc de Bourgogne, a brandy distilled from the residue of grapes used to make wine.

Within Burgundy are two wine-related institutions of considerable reputation: the Hospices de Beaune and the Chevaliers du Tastevin. The first is a charitable hospital, which derives its income from an annual wine auction, while the second is a brotherhood of wine connoisseurs.

NORMANDY

Rich butter and cream sauces are but one of this region's hallmarks. Normandy is also renowned for its apples, cider, and Calvados, an apple brandy much used in local cooking. Still another mark of excellence is Normandy's coolwater fish and shellfish.

Normandy, a land of hearty eaters, has a number of well-known specialties, including:

Madame Poulard's Omelette   An omelet made fluffy by beating the egg whites and yolks separately.

Sole Dieppoise   Poached sole served with a white wine sauce and garnished with mussels and shrimp.

Sole Normande   Poached sole served with a thickened butter-egg-and-cream sauce.

Tripes à la Mode de Caen   A flavorful stew made by braising tripe up to twelve hours with ingredients such as calves' feet, cider, and various vegetables.

Cheeses excel in Normandy and include the famous Camembert and Pont l'Évêque, both surface-ripened. Among other well-known cheeses are the Neufchâtel, Livarot, and Petit Suisse (a brand name).

PROVENCE

Garlic—the "truffle of Provence"—olive oil, tomatoes, and fresh aromatic herbs such as rosemary, basil, and fennel are the characteristic flavoring ingredients of this sun-drenched land. As a general rule, the dishes are well seasoned.

Seafood is abundant and popular. The two most notable fish are the rascasse of Bouillabaisse fame (described later) and the sea-basslike loup de mer. Other important edibles from the sea include the octopus, squid, cuttlefish, mussel, langouste, langoustine, crab, and eel. River fish as well as preserved fish like sardines, anchovies, and salt cod often end up in the workingman's belly.

Much to the delight of both cooks and diners, marketplace stalls glow with a profusion of photogenically displayed fruits and vegetables including these locally grown staples: apricots, artichokes, asparagus, cardoons, eggplants, figs, haricot beans, lemons and other citrus fruits, melons, nuts, olives, peaches, potatoes, salad greens in general, scallions and other onion family members, summer squashes such as courgettes, table grapes, and, of course, tomatoes, oozing with juicy, succulent goodness.

Meat is not one of Provence's fortes, because the generally poor pasturage precludes rearing cows, sheep, and goats with tender meat. To overcome this culinary handicap, the people slaughter the animals while the flesh is still in the veal, baby lamb, or young kid stage. This meat is usually sautéed indoors or grilled outdoors over a bed of white-hot charcoal infused with rosemary or other herbs. Should the animal be allowed to mature, the resulting tough meat may be tenderized by such slow-cooking processes as braising or stewing. Young rabbits and wild hares also find their way into stewpots and onto grills.

Poultry is of good quality, but it is the delicate, local small game birds such as thrushes that most excite the gourmet's palate.

Any list of the famous dishes of the Provence region would have to contain:

Bouillabaisse This soup-stew—which is often served in two courses: soup and seafood separate—is the French Riviera's most famous contribution to world cookery. Yet, according to purists, it can't be duplicated by any cook whose pot is situated more than fifty kilometers from the quays of Marseilles. They argue that beyond that arbitrary border you won't have the one essential ingredient: absolutely fresh-from-the-sea rascasse, a local trash fish that has no counterpart anywhere else in the world. The other basic ingredients include saffron, herbs from the nearby hills, garlic, tomatoes, olive oil, and whatever fish (there should be several varieties) are available and desirable to the cook. Eel is often tossed into the simmering liquid, but shellfish is generally avoided except in recipes written for or by foreigners. But even the bona-fide Bouillabaisse recipe is a subject of heated debate within sight of the Marseilles harbor, as no two cooks agree exactly as to what should and should not go into the dish (except, quite obviously, the rascasse).

Pan Bagna   A French bread or roll topped with ingredients such as anchovies, tomatoes, olives, green peppers, and capers, then liberally doused with olive oil.

Pissaladière   Pizza, Provençal-style (there is a historical connection between these French and Italian flat breads, but the Provençal version usually has no tomatoes).

Ratatouille   A slow-cooked medley of eggplant, tomatoes, courgettes (think of zucchini), onions, garlic, and herbs.

Salade Niçoise   The ingredients, tossed in a garlic-permeated oil dressing, could include lettuce, tuna chunks, tomatoes, hard-boiled eggs, olives, anchovy strips, potatoes, green beans, green peppers, capers, and what have you.

Soupe au Pistou   Similar to a northern Italian Minestrone soup (made with a sometimes yes-sometimes no combination of vegetables, beans, pasta, onions, tomatoes, and stock) that has been impregnated with a Pestolike paste (basil, garlic, olive oil, cheese, and pine nuts; also of Italian inspiration).

Of the many sauces in Provence, two have earned worldwide recognition. The first is Aïoli, a garlic-mayonnaiselike concoction that has a special affinity for shellfish and vegetables. Next in popularity is Rouille, a garlic-and-chili, olive oil-based mixture that is a required addition to Bouillabaisse, but is equally beloved when stirred into other stews or soups, especially those of the seafood persuasion (collectively known as *soupe aux poissons*).

Bread is still the starch staple here, as in the rest of France, though potatoes, cornmeal, and rice are increasing in popularity.

Though Provençal wines seldom stir serious talk from wine cognoscenti, some varieties like Bandol and Cassis (not to be confused with the Dijonnais liqueur of the same name) are refreshing and likable, particularly with everyday local fare.

PARIS AND ENVIRONS

This is France's culinary melting pot and, consequently, it has lost much of its distinct regional character. Nevertheless, some specialties can be traced to within 100 kilometers of Paris. They include Sauce Bercy (white wine, stock, shallots, butter, and seasonings magically blended), Crème Chantilly (sweetened whipped cream sometimes flavored with vanilla or rum), Boeuf à la Mode (beef and vegetables braised in red wine), Potage Crècy (carrot soup), and Brie cheese.

Paris, of course, is a city of great restaurants, chefs, and gourmets—all made for each other. Paris is a food shopper's dream where fresh, quality cooking ingredients are rushed into the metropolitan markets via a nationwide food transportation system that has no equal. A chicken from Bresse, for instance, rumbles into Paris in a truck within hours after it has been killed, and tomatoes from faraway Provence are sped into the city via computer-directed railway freight cars. The food quality is exceptionally high because there are few city dwellers more demanding of fine ingredients than the Parisian.

SPECIALTIES OF OTHER AREAS

Every subregion and town, bar none, has its own specialties, much loved and touted by local citizens and visiting gastronomes alike. The complete list is too long to give here, but among the better-known favorites is the flavorful Cassoulet of Languedoc, made of slow-cooked white beans, sausages, and pork (the particular meat ingredients vary by town; for instance, the people of Toulouse add goose, while those from Castelnaudary use mutton). Languedoc is also famed for its Roquefort cheese.

From Périgord comes the expensive black truffle, from the old provinces of Dauphiné and Savoie, the multifarious gratin dishes, from Bayonne, splendid hams, and from the Loire valley, the Beurre Blanc Sauce that has a special affinity for the freshly caught river fish of that region. If there is one pan-French specialty, it is probably steak and French fries (or Pommes Frites, as they are called in France).

CLASSIC FRENCH CUISINE

The world-acclaimed *haute cuisine* of France is essentially a system of cooking that has transformed regional dishes into elaborate ones fit for the most discriminating epicure. Keep in mind that while the dishes thus evolved are generally more complex, they are not necessarily better. According to its rules, nothing but the finest cooking ingredients, equipment, and talent should be employed; recipes are exact and should be followed faithfully. Contrary to widespread opinion, being a *haute-cuisine* chef is not a truly creative profession. Because the preparation of many of the sauces requires an economy of scale and much time (measured in days), *haute cuisine* is better suited for well-staffed restaurants than to homes.

To give you an example of the types of dishes that fall under the *haute-cuisine* umbrella, a few of the better-known preparations are defined:

Homard à la Parisienne Made by poaching lobsters, removing the cooked flesh, then stuffing the empty shells with a mayonnaise-dressed vegetable mixture which is topped with lobster meat. The lobsters are artfully arranged on a platter, and elaborately garnished with such items as truffles and artichoke bottoms.

Poularde Derby Chicken stuffed with rice, goose liver, and truffles, then roasted and lavishly garnished with more truffles and *foie gras*.

Selle de Veau à la Prince Orloff The slices of a roasted saddle of veal are coated with Sauce Soubise, rice, and mushroom purée, and then reassembled on the saddle in their original position. The roast is then covered with Sauce Mornay and browned. This preparation exemplifies the ridiculous aspect of *haute cuisine* when taken to excess. The dish was created in the nineteenth century for the veal-hating Prince Orloff. To disguise the veal flavor, the delicate meat was literally bathed with two relatively overpowering sauces. If one detests veal, why have it in the first place—and if one likes it, why mask its flavor?

Tournedos Rossini A sautéed beef filet steak served on a circular crouton, then garnished with a *foie gras* slice, a truffle slice, and, finally, a Madeira sauce.

Sauces are generally rich (lots of butter, eggs, cream, etc.) and the presentation of each dish is meant to impress the eye.
The traditional birthyear of classic French *haute cuisine* is 1533, when Catherine de Médicis moved from Florence to Paris to become the child-bride of the future King Henri II. She was so appalled by the qualities and manners of the French table that, as part of her marriage agreement, she was allowed to bring an entourage of chefs from her homeland, where fine cooking was an art form. In due course, the imported talent introduced the Parisian courtiers to the glories that would soon develop into classic French cuisine.
In fairness to the French pride, it must be pointed out that

good local cooking existed long before Catherine's arrival, as is partially substantiated by Taillevent's fourteenth-century cookbook. Furthermore, Catherine merely precipitated and did not—as some food writers are fond of telling us—create classic French cuisine. If she had not done so, someone else would have performed the mission, because the time was right for the development of the latent French palate, farming skill, and kitchen expertise.

The other most potent influences on classic French cuisine include the eighteenth-century chef La Varenne, who wrote *Le Cuisinier François* ; the gourmet Brillat-Savarin (1755–1826), author of *The Physiology of Taste* ;the architecture-oriented chef Carême (1784–1833), who is probably the leading candidate for the title of "the father of classic French cooking"; the chef Dubois (1818–1901) who is best noted for creating the previously described Selle de Veau à la Prince Orloff, and for helping to establish in France the Russian-style table service, where the diner receives the food already served on his plate, as opposed to serving himself from a selection of dishes; and the chef Escoffier (1847–1935), who helped simplify and put the final touches on the codification of *haute cuisine* in his cookbook, *Le Guide Culinaire*.

Today classic French cuisine is slowly disappearing because of the increasingly prohibitive costs of the required ingredients and the growing reluctance of talented youths to undergo lengthy, slavelike, and financially unrewarding apprenticeships. Its critics say, "Good riddance"—who needs so many calories, such a high cholesterol count, and so much money spent on a meal while people around the world are starving? They would be right, of course, if such cuisine were our steady diet.

THE NEW FRENCH CUISINES

No matter how much Escoffier wanted to simplify the classic French cuisine, he didn't go far enough. The next great "make-it-simple" reformer to come on the horizon was chef

Fernand Point (1897–1955), owner of La Pyramide restaurant. In his wake came chef Paul Bocuse, who recently popularized the *nouvelle cuisine* (it is not really new in concept) that strives for a lighter style of cooking with great emphasis on bringing out the natural flavors of seasoned foods rather than masking them under superfluous sauces. The next major reformer on the culinary scene was chef Michel Guérard who created the low-calorie, low-fat *cuisine minceur* (slimming cuisine). He advocates the elimination whenever possible of eggs, cream, starches, butter, oils, sugar, and *foie gras*; he maintains you don't need those ingredients if you take certain steps such as building flavor with vegetable purées, using nonfrying cooking methods like steaming, and allowing foods to cook slowly in their own juices. But despite these new directions (and there will surely be more), the classic cuisine of France will continue to exist, though with less glamour and public awe.

But alas, the cuisine's quality is slipping in both the *haute* and regional kitchens throughout France because the nation's agricultural system is irrevocably changing from small-scale to industrialized, and hence large-scale, production. The food buying and cooking expertise of each succeeding generation of the French is also slipping—and without demanding customers, you don't get quality ingredients. Still another contributing factor is the trend away from eating a leisurely two-hour midday dinner.

LA CUISINE BOURGEOISE

Another way to classify French cuisine is to divide it into three categories: classic, bourgeois, and regional. *La cuisine bourgeoise* is actually not a cuisine per se. Rather, it is the general cooking style of many middle-class French homes that has borrowed culinary ideas from both classic and various regional cuisines (particularly, the regional cuisine where the bourgeois cook grew up and/or lives).

BEVERAGES

France is one of the world's greatest wine-producing and -consuming countries—even some school children are given their daily ration in the thermos bottle with their lunch. Besides the wine districts previously mentioned, France has other world-famous districts including those of Champagne, the Loire (principally known for its Pouilly-Fumé, Sancerre, Vouvray, and Muscadet white wines and its Anjou rosé), and the Rhone (best known for its assertive, full-bodied reds, such as Hermitage, Côte Rôtie, and Châteauneuf-du-Pape, as well as for its Tavel rosé).

Contrary to beliefs held by many foreigners, the average Frenchperson is not a wine connoisseur. They drink their wine with gusto and don't take it any more seriously than do Americans their Coca-Cola or Britons their beer.

Speaking of beer, that beverage is rapidly growing in popularity at the expense of wine consumption. The finest of French beers come from the north near the Benelux and German borders where beer has always been the favorite alcoholic drink. Fittingly, Kronenbourg—France's best-selling beer—is brewed in Alsace.

Mineral waters are popular in France for two principal reasons. First, many French people became accustomed to drinking mineral water because the ordinary tap, well, or stream water posed a health risk. Second, the flavor of most French tap water had, and continues to have, an off taste. Among the leading brands of French mineral water are the still Évian, and the lightly sparkling Perrier, the latter often served with a slice of lemon or lime.

⌐∽ GERMANY, WEST AND EAST

THERE IS NO BETTER testimonial to the Germans' devotion to *gutes Essen* (good eating) than their traditional five-meals-a-day eating pattern.

This routine usually begins with *Frühstück* (breakfast), which consists of coffee, white rolls and/or dark bread, butter, jam, and—in many homes—a soft-boiled egg.

The second meal, *zweites Frühstück* (second breakfast) at eleven is a more serious affair. Something like sausage and potato salad is usually washed down by beer, although deskbound students or office workers may have to settle for a mere sandwich and fruit.

Mittagessen (midday meal) is the biggest meal of the day. The diner can start with *Vorspeisen* (appetizers), proceed to soup (which Germans love), then continue with a *Braten* (roast), a *Schnitzel* (cutlet) or an *Eintopf* (one-pot meal of meat and vegetables), perhaps, accompanied by potatoes, noodles and/or dumplings, vegetables, and salad. The concluding course is often a cooked dessert. *Mehlspeisen* (flour desserts) such as Dampfnudeln (yeast dumplings served with vanilla sauce) or Schmarrn (eggy pancakes served torn into shreds) are considered appropriate. Cakes and pastries are not, as those are saved for *Kaffee* at five or a late evening indulgence.

Kaffee, the fourth meal of the day, taken at home or at the local *Konditorei* (pastry shop), is an opportunity for relaxation, gossip, and carbohydrate loading. Elaborate creations such as Schwarzwälder Kirschtorte, a chocolate layer cake stuffed with sour cherries and whipped cream, are favorites of the *Kaffee* break.

The final formal meal of the day (and there are always opportunities for snacks) is the *Abendbrot*. This "evening bread" is a simple supper of cold cuts, sausage, salads, and beer, affording the housewife a chance to relax. The food comes from the local *Feinkostgeschäfte*, a delicatessen store, rather than being cooked at home. Given this diet, the fame of Germany's *Baden* (spas) is understandable. The overfeasted burgher could relax, take the waters, then go from Bad to Wurst.

Today the five-meal regimen for most Germans is on its way to extinction, principally because of the limitation imposed by the modern one-hour employee lunch period, the concern for slimness, and the trend toward the internationalization of eating habits. An increasing number of Germans eat a light American-style meal at midday, saving the more filling dinner for the evening.

This movement toward lighter eating has probably had the least effect on German sausages, cheese, and bread, as these basic foodstuffs are too beloved to be tampered with. Of Germany's countless sausages, the best known include Bratwurst (the "roasting sausage" made with pork, sometimes mixed with veal), Mettwurst (mildly smoked pork-and-liver "spreading sausage"), Weisswurst (a mild Bavarian "white sausage" made with veal and pork), Leberwurst (liver sausage), Blutwurst (blood sausage), Knackwurst (a smoked, garlicky pork-and-veal sausage), Bauernwurst (smoked "farmer's sausage" made with pork), and finally Frankfurter Würstchen (the lightly smoked pork-and-beef sausage of Frankfurt, the ancestor of the all-American hotdog). Sausages keep for a long time, meld with potatoes, onions, rye bread, and other hearty foods, and help develop a thirst for beer, establishing them as a foundation of German cuisine.

Käse (cheese) has a similar status in German cuisine. Perhaps the five most famous varieties are these pungent-when-aged cheese: Limburger (originally made in Belgium, but currently produced in quantity in Germany), Münster (originally created in the Vosges Mountains in France, but now very much a German staple), Handkäse (the "hand-molded" cheese), Tilsiter (somewhat similar to the pale yellow French Trappist cheeses when young), and Bierkäse (also known as Weisslackerkäse). Other German cheese products include the mild Quark (cottage cheese) and the fungus-ripened Edelpilz. Germans have a host of ways to serve their cheeses. Handkäse mit Musik is a sour-milk cheese served with oil, vinegar, and chopped onions, while Halbe Huhn (half a hen) is a thick slice of cheese served on a mustard-spread roll and, customarily, eaten as a snack with a stein of beer.

The third basic food, bread, is the most natural accompaniment to the Germans' beloved *Wurst* and *Käse*. Full-flavored and -textured pumpernickel as well as lighter rye breads are popular, as are wheat breads. The latter are often artistically sculptured into "picture breads" depicting animals, objects, or symbols. Whatever the bread, it is usually excellent, for Germany is considered to have some of the best bakers in the world. This skill also extends to the preparation of elaborate cakes and pastries (tempting items served during the five o'clock *Kaffee*) as well as Lebkuchen (spiced honey cakes) and colorful Marzipan (sculptures made of almond paste, sugar, and egg whites). Even the mundane Pretzel is made with pride.

Potatoes also contribute to Germany's carbohydrate count, appearing either boiled, or shredded for pancakes or dumplings. But these tubers are a fairly recent addition to the German diet. The peasants distrusted new foods, but Frederick the Great, the mid-eighteenth-century King of Prussia, insisted that potatoes be planted. Soon it was possible to withdraw the troops from the fields because the new food became well liked throughout what is now Germany.

The characteristic German flavors come from combinations of many ingredients, not from heavy spicing. Herbs such as dill, chervil, basil, and thyme are used; so are caraway seeds, juniper berries, and prepared mustard. A sweet-sour flavor, obtained with vinegar and fresh or dried fruit, is highly prized.

Hearty vegetables such as red and green cabbage (fresh or fermented into sauerkraut), carrots, radishes, and turnips are popular, as is the delicate white asparagus for which Germany is famous.

Among meats, pork is the favorite, though beef and rabbit

(particularly when made into the famed peppery rabbit stew Hasenpfeffer) frequently appear on household tables. Fowl, including chicken and duck, is popular, but it is the goose (traditionally cooked and served with apples and prunes) that captures the fancy of most German diners.

The country abounds with forests and, consequently, game like venison, wild boar, hare, pheasant, river trout, and salmon contribute to the national fine-dining tradition.

Eating out is a major avocation among the Germans, who enjoy breaking bread with friends and fellow countrymen in a spirit of *Gemütlichkeit*, a soul-warming spirit of camaraderie. A variety of eating and drinking establishments is available, each affording a distinctive adventure in dining. The hungry German may choose the *Gasthof* (an informal inn), the *Ratskeller* (traditionally located in the city-hall cellar), the *Biergarten* (outdoor beer garden), the *Bierhalle* (indoor beer hall), or the *Weinstube* (a restaurant featuring wines).

Sometimes the merry-making takes on proportions which exceed those of the restaurant and overflows into the streets, as is the case during Germany's many feasts. The most famous of all is the *Oktoberfest* in Munich, where millions of local people and visitors revel for sixteen days every fall. In the late winter or early spring, the pre-Lenten feast *Fasching* reigns in many cities, including, once again, Munich. A constant atmosphere of festivity prevails year-round, thanks to the Germans' knack for finding continuous causes to celebrate.

REGIONAL GERMAN CUISINES

Both West and East German territories lie within the well-traveled crossroads of Europe and, as a result, the German cuisine has been greatly influenced by its neighbors. For instance, in the East German Prussian area in the northeast, one detects the widespread use of sour cream, characteristic of the cooking of adjacent Poland. Other influences have come from other directions, including Scandinavian, Dutch, French, Austrian, and Czechoslovakian.

Yet this in no way implies that the regions of Germany have not developed distinctive cooking styles. And because Germany was not unified as a nation until 1871, the regional cuisines are especially significant and well entrenched.

The regional cooking of Bavaria (southeastern West Germany) is the cuisine most foreigners recognize as typically German. Bavarians are known for their love of beer and sausage. "Meat is the best vegetable" is a local saying and, fittingly, Weisswurst, Gansebraten (roast goose), Schweinesbraten (roast pork), and Kalbshaxe (veal shank) are favorites of Bavarian "vegetarians." Of all the Bavarian meat dishes, however, the *Schnitzel* category is the favorite.

Essentially, a *Schnitzel* is a cutlet, usually veal, prepared in a variety of styles. A Naturschnitzel is sautéed without breading; a Wiener Schnitzel has breading but no sauce. Rahmschnitzel is covered with a cream sauce, while the sauce characteristic of Jägerschnitzel contains sour cream and mushrooms. Schnitzel à la Holstein is topped with fried eggs, anchovies, and capers and is surrounded by a garnish of luxury foods such as smoked salmon, caviar, and crayfish tails. On the evidence of these *Schnitzel* specialities, Bavarian cuisine has influenced and been influenced by Austrian cooking.

The other "southern" German cuisine center has its unofficial headquarters in Baden-Baden and is undoubtedly the most delicate of all, having been influenced by neighboring French kitchens. The area has a rich reserve of game from the Black Forest. This region also supplies delicious plums from Bühl and cherries that are transformed into the cherry brandy Kirschwässer and into the Schwarzwälder Kirschtorte (Black Forest cherry cake). From the Württemberg region (a Swabian land situated between the Baden and Bavarian regions) come two of Germany's most popular dumplings: tiny Spätzle, bits of dough dropped into boiling water, drained, and sautéed; and large Maultaschen, a Spätzle dough stuffed with chopped cooked meat and spinach. This green vegetable reappears in Kalbsvögel, rolled veal with a hard-boiled egg, spinach, and bacon stuffing.

Traveling northward, we come to central Germany. On the

western boundary is the first-rate wine-growing region, Rhineland, known for potato-based dishes such as Himmel und Erde (Heaven and Earth—sliced or puréed apples and potatoes topped with slices of blood sausage), Kartoffelsuppe (potato soup), and Reibekuchen (potato pancakes served with apple sauce). But most famous of all is Rhineland's Sauerbraten, which has become one of Germany's national dishes. It is basically a long-marinated, sweet-and-sour beef pot roast—and how the Germans love pot roasts! Potato dumplings, red cabbage, and stewed fruit are traditional accompaniments.

The Westphalian region lies just north of the Rhine region and is famous for its ham. You will also find a great appreciation for Pannhas, the progenitor of the American Pennsylvania Dutch Scrapple, though this original version is made with buckwheat rather than cornmeal. Bean dishes such as Blindhuhn (blind hen—a bacon-potato-onion-apple casserole) and Bean Soup with savory, are also typical Westphalian fare, as is Pfefferpotthast (a peppery stew of short ribs of beef and root vegetables). Kale is a popular vegetable.

To the west is the Hesse region, with Frankfurt its principal city. Popular dishes include Kasseler Rippchen, roasted smoked pork loin, which the Berliners also claim as their own. The area's most famous sauce is the green Grüne Sosse, made with a variety of herbs.

Farther east in central Germany is Saxony, now part of East Germany. This region is the home of the sweet yeast cakes Streuselkuchen, Bienenstich, and Dresdner Stollen—the latter, a nationwide Christmas favorite. Plinsen are yeast-raised pancakes of mixed wheat and buckwheat flours, flavored with lemon. Leber in Grünen Bett, wine-sauced sautéed liver with green herbs, is only one of the many Saxon liver dishes. Perhaps the most famous dish from this area is Leipziger Allerlei, a mixture of individually cooked young vegetables bathed in a rich sauce.

Lower Saxony is located in the northwest corner of Germany. As with most areas of northern Germany, seafood is a dietary mainstay because of the proximity to the North and Baltic seas. Particularly well liked are Rollmöpse, rolled, pickled herring filets. Eel is another well-loved gift of the water and is often served smoked or as the principal ingredient of an eel stew called Aalsuppe.

Schleswig-Holstein is West Germany's most northerly region. Its diet bears some resemblance to those of neighboring Scandinavia, and like Denmark, it is a dairy-loving land. Lübeck, one of its cities, is famous for its Marzipan.

The area in and around Berlin, which includes parts of old Prussia, is especially noted for its ground-meat dishes. Schabefleisch is Beef Tartare, as opposed to the tartare made with pork. Falscher Hase (mock hare) is a meatloaf; while Deutscher Beefsteak is the meat patty Americans call a Hamburger, named after the city of Hamburg, situated farther west. The most prestigious of all ground-meat dishes is Königsberger Klopse, poached mixed-meat balls (pork is usually included) served in a thickened sauce flavored with lemon and capers.

Berliners also enjoy Rinderbrust mit Bouillonkartoffel und Roten Rüben, boiled brisket of beef accompanied by beet salad and potatoes cooked in bouillon; Hoppelpoppel mit Salat, hash rolled omelet-style and served with lettuce dressed with sour cream; and Berliner Pfannkuchen, jelly doughnuts. Smoked bacon and sour cream are flavor keynotes in the rest of Prussia. Still another Berlin and Prussian favorite is Spickgans, pickled and smoked goose breast.

BEVERAGES

Germany has many beers and beer categories. One popular way to classify the so-called normal-brewed beers is into the two categories dunkels (dark-colored) and helles (light-colored); however, beers cover the full spectrum between these two extremes. In most instances, dunkels beers are on the sweet, full side and have a low hop content. One prime example is Bock beer, customarily consumed in the spring. The helles beers (Pilsner beers) have a higher hop content and, therefore, are slightly more bitter in flavor.

The non-normal-brewed beers include the dark, sweet,

low-alcoholic Malzbier (malt beers), the overfermented beers such as Berliner Weisse (traditionally spiked with raspberry syrup), and the underfermented beers. German beers may also be classified by their origin, their alcoholic strength, whether they are top or bottom fermented, and their method and duration of storage (*lager* means "stored"). Whatever your taste in beer, Germany probably brews one to quench your specific thirst. One has only to remember that the proper serving temperature is warmer than American, colder than English.

As if the Germans were in need of an alternative to their beer production and consumption, a flourishing wine industry exists, offering the same refreshing variety to thirsty Germans. Most of the wine is produced in the southwestern part of West Germany, and it is predominantly white, as the red grapes tend not to fare well in this northern climate. This white wine, some of the best in the world, is usually on the sweet side, and consequently is more suited for sipping between, rather than during, meals—and that is exactly how most wine is consumed in Germany.

Another major characteristic of German white wine is its pleasing flowery bouquet. Liebfraumilch, Moselblümchen, and Zeller Schwarze Katz are the German white wines known and consumed in great quantities around the world. Yet, with rare exception, these wines are ordinary. To taste those that have given Germany its wine-growing reputation, one must seek out top-rated Rheingau vineyards such as Schloss Johannisberg, Schloss Vollrads (in Winkel), and Steinberg (in Hattenheim); or the equally superb Mosel vineyards such as Bernkastler Doktor, Wehlener Sonnenuhr, and Piesporter Goldtröpfchen. If the wine is to be in its full glory, it must be of good vintage because year-to-year quality variations in German wines are significant.

In addition to vintage, the West German quality indicators must be grasped, too. Above the low-rated *Tafelwein* (literally, table wine) comes *Qualitätswein*, but it is on the next plateau—*Qualitätswein mit Pradikat* (quality wine with "special attributes")—that one's discriminating taste buds and olfactory receptors start to send harmonic signals to the brain. *Qualitätswein mit Pradikat* in turn is divided into five designations. In ascending order of quality and (except for those with the plain word "trocken" on the label) sweetness scale, the select five are *Kabinett, Spätlese, Auslese, Beerenauslese,* and, finally, *Trockenbeerenauslese,* the noblest and most expensive wine of all. West Germans also produce a sparkling wine called Sekt, and hard and soft cider from apples, which grow well in the central part of the country.

Coffee is a major liquid refreshment in Germany. Collectively, the Germans are among the most knowledgeable and demanding coffee drinkers in the world.

Germany is also the home of a variety of strong drinks, many of which, like Korn, fall into the clear grain-spirit Schnapps category. There are many fruit alcohols: Kirschwasser (cherry), Mirabellengeist (yellow plum), and Himbeergeist (raspberry). Allasch is flavored with caraway and other spices, Enzian with gentian root.

HUNGARY

PAPRIKA, A NEW WORLD spice introduced by the Turks in the course of their mid-sixteenth-to-late-eighteenth-century occupation in Hungary, has been a great influence there ever since. The Hungarians prescribe paprika, taken internally or applied externally, for virtually all human ills. Modern science is less enthusiastic, but it has proved that paprika is high in vitamins A and C and has objective benefits in stimulating appetite and promoting digestion.

The Hungarians, however, are more interested in the subjective effects. Six basic varieties of paprika are now produced in Hungary, each possessing a subtly distinctive taste. The spice may be used to enhance a stew, or found in a mélange of sautéed onions, tomatoes, and green peppers called Lecsó. Caraway and poppy seeds, dill, bay leaf, black pepper, and summer savory are other herbs and spices favored by Hungarians.

The Hungarians seldom serve plain vegetables; they prefer such triumphs of artifice over nature as pickled beets, knob celery salad, or mixed vegetables in cream sauce. Green peppers, cabbage, kohlrabi, or cucumbers are likely to be stuffed (töltött) with a meat mixture. Cabbage, fresh or fermented into sauerkraut, is a beloved vegetable in Hungary, as are kohlrabi, cauliflower, cucumbers, spinach, peas, carrots, beets, potatoes, and sorrel. Onions fried slowly in lard exude a typical Hungarian aroma.

Pork ranks as the favorite meat, as evidenced by the Hungarians' fondness for thick, meaty bacon and sausages. Chicken and goose (goose liver especially) also find favor, as does beef. However, use of beef is somewhat curtailed because of its limited supply.

The fogas, a white-fleshed fish from Lake Balaton, lives by eating other fish and pays for its sins by being eaten by Hungarians and Austrians. Fogas is traditionally served belly-down on a platter, head and tail curving to meet each other, looking particularly uncomfortable. Sturgeon, carp, lake trout, perch, catfish, and pike are also popular freshwater fish, which landlocked Hungarians prefer to imported ocean varieties.

Fish, poultry, and meat dishes are usually complemented by potatoes or a type of dumpling or noodle. Plain egg dough, pinched by hand into tiny grains, is called Csipetke, and usually accompanies soup or stew. Tarhonya, a centuries-old nomadic invention, are dried pellets of flour and egg which keep indefinitely. Gombóc are dumplings.

Other Hungarian flour creations include Palacsinták, small, thin pancakes served with sweet or savory fillings; Rigó Jancsi, made of chocolate cake with chocolate mousse filling and chocolate icing; and Doboschtorte, seven thin cake layers filled with chocolate cream and glazed on top with caramel.

Hungarians are likely to start their day with a light breakfast, followed by a sandwich or small Gulyás at 10 a.m., dinner at midday, afternoon coffee and pastry, and a light supper at 8 or 9 p.m. At least this appears to be the typical eating pattern of the middle-aged and older Hungarians. The younger generation tends to favor a lighter, less frequent style of eating.

Despite this trend toward lighter eating, paprika-spiked soup-stews will never disappear from the Hungarian diet. The most famous is Gulyás, which means "herdsman's dish." It can come in the form of a thick stew (Gulyáshús) or a soup (Gulyásleves) of diced meat flavored with paprika, onions, and green peppers. It is usually served with potatoes, noodles, or dumplings, or a combination of these—but seldom is sour cream used, as is typical with Anglo-American-style goulashes. One classic exception to the no-sweet-or-sour-cream rule is Székelygulyás, made of pork or mixed meats with sauerkraut.

Other stews which are generously seasoned with paprika include Paprikás (this usually does contain sweet or sour cream) and Pörkölt (made of diced meat and onions braised in their own juices). From Transylvania comes another stew, called Tokány, made of strips of meat (generally beef or lamb) braised in their own juices, seasoned with black pepper and paprika or another spice, depending on the cook's intention.

Rétes is the popular pastry well known in Austria and many other parts of the Western world as Strudel. To make good Rétes, one must have high-gluten flour and much dexterity. The ball of dough is hand-stretched until it is paper thin and large enough to cover a table. The filling is then placed inside, and the dough is rolled the short way, producing a cylinder several feet long. The Hungarians also make nonsweetened Rétes with meat and cabbage fillings. Most Rétes, though, is sweet: filled with apples, poppy seeds, sweetened cottage cheese, and the like.

BEVERAGES

The Hungarians differ from most of their Central European neighbors in their strong preference for wine over beer. Hungary's most famous wines are the hearty, crimson Egri Bikaver (Bull's Blood from Eger) and Tokaji.

Tokaji (or Tokay, as it is often called outside Hungary) is named after the town of Tokaj in eastern Hungary. The best of this wine is labeled Tokaji Aszú and is made from grapes that are left on the vine past the normal harvest period. This late picking allows the Botrytis cinerea mold (nicknamed the "noble rot") to form on the grape's outer skin. The "roots" of this fungus sink into the grape's interior, sucking out part of the water, shriveling the grape, and concentrating its nectar. The finished wine is rated from one to five puttonyos, depending on how many baskets (puttonyos) of the late-picked grapes go into each cask of wine. The more puttonyos, the sweeter and more costly the wine. Prior to World War II, Tokaj also produced Tokaji Eszencia (essence), made exclusively from the juice that naturally exudes from the stored late-picked grapes prior to their pressing. Unopened bottles of this sinfully sweet, rare, and dear wine can still be found in private wine cellars.

Barackpálinka is a brandy distilled from apricots, perhaps the favorite Hungarian fruit.

IRELAND ⌒

THE WHITE ("IRISH") POTATO is as much a part of Ireland's image as clover, Catholics, and cable-knit sweaters. This New World tuber immigrated (via the Continent) to Ireland in the eighteenth century and became such an important source of food that mid-nineteenth-century potato-crop failures were able to cause famine. An outgrowth of this drastic food shortage was mass emigration to America and other lands. Today the potato still reigns as Ireland's chief starch staple, but in a less dominant way.

Irish cooks have managed to develop an extensive potato repertoire. In their simplest form, potatoes may be served boiled. For the sake of diversity, the Irish cook may prepare Colcannon, a purée of potatoes and kale (or cabbage) or Champ, a mound of mashed potatoes and spring onions, flooded with butter. Grated raw potatoes are mixed with mashed potatoes and flour to make bread or pancakes called Boxty.

A natural complement to the potato is meat, and in Ireland, the pig provides bacon and ham for the Irish table and for export. Crubeens are pigs' trotters. Drisheen, blood pudding shaped like thick sausage, is made with sheep's blood when prepared in the city of Limerick. Lamb or mutton cooked gently with potatoes, onions, herbs, and water results in hearty Irish Stew, the country's most famous dish.

Fish is also a dietary mainstay in Ireland, which seems appropriate when one considers the extent of surrounding shorelines, internal rivers, and lakes. Catholicism, the dominant religion of this country, is also responsible for incorporating fish into the menu. Irish salmon is eaten fresh or smoked. The smoking process uses a peat fire to produce a firm dry fish with a heavy taste of smoke as opposed to the Scottish oak-cured salmon, which has a lighter taste. Dublin Bay prawns are the treasures from the waters of the same name. Another product of the sea is Carageen (Irish moss), a gelatinous seaweed used as a thickener (for example: setting custard desserts).

Large, round loaves of Irish Soda Bread, etched with a cross on top, are common sights on the dinner table. Caraway seeds and raisins are generously dispersed throughout the dough, which is raised with baking soda and sour milk or buttermilk. Barm Brack is predominantly a fruit bread, historically raised with *barm* (hops and malt); today yeast is commonly used.

A good deal of Poteen, home-brewed whiskey, is still being made from barley or anything else that happens to be handy. However, the legal Irish Whiskey always has a barley base, which is kiln-dried and run through the pot stills. Compared to Scotch Whisky, the Irish product has a less-pronounced smoky flavor because the Irish kiln is not as exposed to peat smoke as is the Scottish counterpart.

The famous Irish Coffee (made of Irish whiskey, hot coffee, sugar, and whipped cream), does not have very deep emerald roots. It was invented a few decades ago, supposedly to boost the sale of Irish whiskey. If that is true, it has succeeded.

ITALY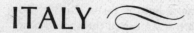

ITALY'S CUISINE IS THE result of a broad array of ancient culinary forces. In chronological order these influences include: the Etruscans, whose sovereignty over central Italy preceded that of the Romans; the seafaring Phoenicians and Greeks; the many peoples of the Roman Empire; the plundering Vandals; the Carolingians, who ruled the north; and the Arabs, who conquered Sicily.

During the time of Marco Polo, when Venice was the spice-trade center of Europe, many Middle Eastern influences flowed into that port. Rice was one of these immigrants, but pasta was not.

For the record, Marco Polo did not introduce pasta to Italy, as some cookbooks would have us believe. Neither did he introduce pasta to China, another common misconception. There is written evidence of the existence of macaroni in Italy as early as 1279, some thirteen years before Marco Polo's journeys. There is also evidence that noodles predated Marco Polo in China by over a thousand years.

REGIONAL CUISINES—AN OVERVIEW

Regional Italian cooking as we know it today didn't take form until as late as the sixteenth and seventeenth centuries. This evolution coincided with, and was abetted by, the introduction of the tomato, one of the many staple fruits and vegetables that were unknown until Columbus discovered the New World.

We will now explore the major regional cuisines, beginning in Naples, proceeding south to Sicily then moving northward to the Alps.

NAPLES AND THE CAMPANIA REGION

To most Americans "Italian cuisine" is basically Neapolitan cooking because most of the Italian immigrants to America came from Naples and its environs. When this ethnic group opened restaurants in the United States, it naturally served the style of food it loved and knew best: Neapolitan-Campanian cooking.

The Campanian countryside produces superb fruits and vegetables, particularly tomatoes and eggplants. The bland Mozzarella cheese that is made from water buffalo milk is also a food staple, as are spaghetti and other pasta—often covered with seafood and Marinara (meatless tomato) Sauce. Other basic regional ingredients include garlic, onions, oregano and other heady herbs, olive oil, and bread. The principal protein source is seafood including scungilli (a conch), clams, mussels, octopus, squid, shrimp, and a wide variety of locally caught fish. Although Italian restaurants in America serve a lot of meatballs, red meat is infrequently eaten by the average Campanian because it tends to be expensive owing to poor pasturage conditions. Poultry, in terms of use and popularity, falls between seafood and red meat.

Some of the world-famous Neopolitan specialties include:

Bistecca alla Pizzaiola   A thin, usually tough beefsteak masked with a garlicky, oregano-flavored tomato sauce.

Calzone alla Napoletana   Deep-fried, crescent-shaped dough stuffed (usually) with ham-flecked Mozzarella cheese.

Lasagna   A baked dish comprising alternating layers of wide noodles, seasoned meat sauce, and cheese. (This dish is equally popular in several other Italian regions.)

Mozzarella in Carrozza   Literally, Mozzarella in a Carraige. The cheese is inserted between slices of bread, then dipped in an egg batter and cooked in hot oil—it resembles a deep-fried cheese sandwich.

Parmigiana di Melanzane   Sliced eggplant baked with cheese and a garlic- and oregano-laced tomato sauce.

Pizza   Disc-shaped bread dough topped with various garnitures such as Mozzarella cheese, green peppers, onions, sliced sausage, anchovies, and tomato sauce, then baked.

SICILY

Though several Mediterranean powers of old controlled all or parts of Sicily, it was the conquering Arabs who made the most enduring culinary imprint on this mountainous island anchored off the tip of the Italian peninsula. During the Middle Ages, the Arabs introduced the now famous Sicilian art of making sweets: sugary ices and rich pastries studded with candied fruits and almond paste.

Palermo, located in the western section of the island, is the most interesting culinary region in Sicily for the majority of traveling gourmets. Flavorful pasta and breads reign as the staple starches, as they do throughout all of Sicily. However, in contrast to most Sicilians, the Palermo cooks prefer butter to olive oil as a cooking medium.

Popular fruits and vegetables include the tomato, eggplant, and artichoke (all of which are frequently stuffed), citrus fruits, almonds, and olives. Ricotta cheese is the island favorite. Seafood—including tuna, swordfish, and sardines—is the leading protein source because of its abundance, while meat is usually tough and expensive, owing to a lack of suitable pasturage. Some of the best-known Sicilian specialties include:

Cannole   A confection consisting of a hard, tubular pastry shell stuffed with Ricotta cheese enriched with cream, candied fruit, and sometimes chocolate.

Caponata Chopped vegetables such as eggplant (the most essential ingredient), tomatoes, onions, green peppers, olives, and celery individually cooked in olive oil, then combined. Caponata is similar in concept to the French Ratatouille.

Cassata alla Siciliana A sponge cake sliced into several layers and spread with a Ricotta cheese, cream, candied fruit, chocolate, and liqueur mixture, and then reassembled and covered with chocolate icing. Cassata alla Siciliana may also refer to an Italian ice studded with candied fruits.

Pasta con le Sarde Macaroni cooked with sardines along with various flavorful seasonings. This dish is particularly popular in Palermo.

Sicily's best-known wine is Marsala, a fortified wine similar to Sherry and Madeira. It can be dry or sweet and is widely used by chefs as a cooking wine. The best-known table wine is the dry white Mt. Etna.

ROME AND THE LATIUM REGION

Because of the cosmopolitan nature of Rome, you will find hundreds if not thousands of restaurants that either offer nationalized Italian cuisines with French overtones (mainly for the benefit of the foreign visitors) or specialize in the cooking from Italian regions (principally for the sake of noninsular local gourmets). Nonetheless, Rome and its surrounding regions, have an ample share of well-known local specialties that include:

Abbacchio al Forno Rosemary-scented roast suckling lamb that is particularly popular at Easter.

Cannelloni A flat sheet of cooked pasta spread with meat, cheese, or another filling, then rolled into a tube, topped with a sauce, and baked. It is served as an appetizer or entrée—and is also very popular elsewhere in Italy.

Carciofi alla Guidea Literally, Artichokes Jewish Style, which are deep-fried and flattened out to resemble flowers.

Fettuccini al Burro Also known as Fettuccine Alfredo or alla Romana. Flat ribbon-shaped pasta is tossed, generally, with cream, butter, and cheese—and given a good sprinkling of freshly ground peppercorns.

Gnocchi alla Romana Poached-and-baked cork-shaped dumplings made with semolina and/or potato flour and topped with a tomato meat sauce and grated cheese.

Pinzimonio A simple but popular appetizer consisting of an olive oil-dipped celery stick sprinkled with salt and pepper.

Porchetta alla Romana Suckling pig pieces sautéed in olive oil and seasoned with white wine, garlic, and herbs. (Romans and their surrounding neighbors also love spit-roasting the baby pig whole.)

Saltimbocca Literally, Jumps into the Mouth. Consists of thin Prosciutto and veal slices (the first laid upon the second) sauteed in butter and accented with sage and white wine.

Spaghetti alla Carbonara One standard recipe calls for the pasta being tossed simply with a sauce comprising pancetta (a salted but unsmoked form of bacon, which may be described as a meaty, rolled version of salt pork) and raw egg yolks; while other equally popular versions suggest additional ingredients such as cream, butter, and cheese. This dish was partially catapulted to international fame by World War II American GIs, who—being homesick—took to it because of its "bacon and egg" ingredients.

Spaghetti all' Amatriciana Pasta topped with a sauce incorporating bacon, pepper, onions, and sometimes tomatoes, among other ingredients.

Stracciatella Rome's egg-drop soup, consisting of a beaten egg stirred into a rich, hot chicken or beef broth and sprinkled with grated cheese; sometimes it is thickened with semolina.

Supplì al Telefono   Rice croquettes stuffed with Mozzarella cheese (and, perhaps, other ingredients), then deep-fried. When the balls are opened and pulled apart, the cheese stretches out like telephone wires, hence the specialty's graphic name.

Stufatino alla Romano   A well-seasoned veal stew.

Zuppa Inglese   Literally, English Soup, but really a rich, rum-soaked, custard-layered sponge cake covered with rum-spiked whipped cream and candied fruit. It is definitely Italian in origin.

The native cooking style in the average home is direct and unpretentious. Most of the available fruits and vegetables are generally outstanding, particularly the artichokes, strawberries, watermelons, celery, peas, beans, and lettuce. Rosemary, mint, and cloves are among the most widely used herbs and spices. Important cheeses from the cook's point of view include Pecorino Romano (a ewe's milk grated cheese somewhat like the cow's milk Parmigiano-Reggiano from the north) and the local versions of Càcio a Cavallo, Ricotta, and Mozzarella.

Wines are refreshing, but undistinguished and include the white Castelli Romani and the slightly better Frascati. The Est! Est! Est! wine is amusing to discuss but not to drink. Espresso houses abound in Rome and are enjoyed for their casual ambience.

FLORENCE AND THE TUSCANY REGION

Beautiful Florence—situated within the homeland of the ancient Etruscans—offers simple, straightforward food without embellishments. Among its culinary masterpieces are:

Bistecca alla Fiorentina   A thick, choice steak cut from the local Chianina cattle, charcoal-broiled and flavored with olive oil, salt, and pepper.

Cenci   A crisp, deep-fried sweet pastry lightly dusted with sugar.

Fagioli al Fiasco   Beans charcoal-simmered in an empty Chianti wine flask with water, olive oil, and garlic.

Trippa alla Fiorentina   Simmered tripe cut into strips and cooked in a casserole with tomato sauce, sprinkled with grated Parmesan cheese.

Olive oil rather than butter is widely used in cooking. The Tuscan town of Lucca is considered one of the best if not the finest producer of that pale gold liquid. Another characteristic cooking ingredient is the bean, which goes into many soups and stews, "Alla Toscana" on a menu usually suggests a side order of beans. Although it is not true in the rest of Italy, beef is very popular in Tuscany. But don't look for a spinach-dominated cuisine in Florence despite the fact that "à la Florentine" implies "with spinach" on menus beyond the Florence city limits.

Along the Tuscan coast one finds seafood specialties: the well-seasoned soup-stew Cacciucco as well as dishes made with baby eel.

Tuscany is the home of the world-famous, ruby-red Chianti wine which can be mediocre or very good. For the latter, you will be on a right course if you look for Chianti Classico, identified by the black rooster insignia on the neck of a bottle without a straw covering.

BOLOGNA AND THE EMILIA-ROMAGNA REGION

Bologna, by authoritative consensus, is the culinary capital of Italy. With good reason, the region has been nicknamed "La Grassa," literally translated "the fat" and referring to the rich diet that the local citizenry has been enjoying for centuries.

One characteristic of the Bolognese cuisine is the extensive use of pork. It is the base ingredient of Bologna's famous sausages (hence our "baloney") including Mortadella, seasoned pork mixed with pork fat chunks, and the somewhat spicy Cotechino. Pork is also used to produce Prosciutto, Parma's classic mountain-air-cured ham and Modena's Zampone, a boned pig's foot stuffed with spiced pork.

Moreover, pork is the chief meat ingredient in Bologna's famed *ragù*, a thick, rich, and complex tomato sauce ideally suited for pasta. Finally, pork fat rather than butter or olive oil is the principal cooking oil of the region (though the city of Bologna, like Rome, proves itself egalitarian by using all three).

Bologna's pasta creations are well known: Tortellini (small, stuffed ring-shaped pasta), Tagliatelle (ribbon-shaped pasta, the favorite base for a *ragu*), and the spinach-dyed *pasta verde*. Two noted *pasta verde* dishes are Lasagna Verde and Paglia e Fieno, literally Straw and Hay, referring to the look when green and yellow noodles are combined.

The fat dairy cattle give rich milk and cream, frequently used in local dishes and in producing Parmigiano-Reggiano, that universally cherished grating cheese Americans call Parmesan.

Along the region's Adriatic coast, fish become the mainstay. The *brodetti* (stews) are especially good.

Emilia-Romagna's famous wine is Lambrusco, a slightly sweet, slightly effervescent red wine—nothing very special, but a fair foil for the region's rich, well-seasoned food.

GENOA AND THE LIGURIA REGION

Genoa is the birthplace of Columbus and Pesto, that fragrant, thick, green sauce which Genoese liberally dollop on their Trenette (egg noodles), as well as their versions of Minestrone (soup) and potato flour Gnocchi dumplings. Pesto is made by pounding together with a pestle (hence, the name) in a mortar basil, garlic, Parmesan and Sardinian ewe's milk cheeses, along with pine nuts and olive oil. This last ingredient, olive oil, is Liguria's chief cooking oil and creates one of the several exceptions to the "butter in the north" rule.

Ligurian cuisine is very dependent on the sea as its lands are mostly mountainous, not ideally suited for farming and cattle grazing. The best-known local seafood specialty is the Burrida stew.

Other popular Ligurian favorites include the Nice-influenced Pizza all' Andrea (easily distinguished from the Neapolitan variety by the generous topping of olives) and Torta Pasqualina (a flaky spinach-and-cheese Easter pie). Throughout Liguria, herbs are generally used with a free hand, spices with a stingy one.

Although wines are only fair, Cinqueterre is a curiosity because some of its vineyards are reachable only by boat along the steep, rugged coastline.

VENICE AND THE VENETO REGION

Rice, not pasta, is the principal starch staple of Venice and is typically served combined with other ingredients. Its most splendid application is in the vegetable dish Risi e Bisi, literally Rice and Peas. Outside Venice, in the Veneto region, the firm cornmeal-mush specialty, Polenta, rivals and in some places supplants rice as the primary starch staple. Pasta, though in the third place in the starch popularity poll, has over the last century been steadily increasing its share of the market.

The principal source of animal protein comes from the seafood caught in the cool waters of the northern Adriatic, which exclusively yields one of the world's greatest culinary delights, the scampo. (When seen on American menus, "scampi" almost invariably means oversized shrimp, lacking the delicate, sweet flavor of true scampi.) Other excellent local seafood worth sampling includes shrimp, crayfish, cuttlefish, mussels, eel, sole, and mullet.

Though meat dishes are a minority in Venice, one is world famous: Fegato alla Veneziana, tissue-thin calves'-liver slices sautéed with onions.

From southwestern Veneto near the "Romeo and Juliet" city of Verona come three reasonably good wines: the dry white Soave, the light-bodied red Bardolino, and its sibling, the slightly fuller-bodied and better Valpolicella.

MILAN AND THE LOMBARDY REGION

Generous use of butter is a hallmark of Milanese/Lombard cooking. So is the preference for rice or polenta (as in neighboring Veneto) over pasta. Rice is in its fullest glory when used to prepare Risotto alla Milanese, a saffron-colored and -flavored side dish that is the classic accompaniment to the area's most famous specialty, Osso Buco. This internationally renowned dish is veal shank braised with tomato, onion, stock, and wine, then topped with Gremolata, a parsley-garlic-lemon-rind garnish. The choicest morsel in Osso Buco is the cooked marrow clinging to the hollow of the bone, and it is best scooped out with an especially designed marrow fork or spoon (an oyster fork makes a good substitute).

Another popular meat dish of this landlocked (and, in places, heavily industrialized) region is Costoletta alla Milanese, a breaded veal chop that is somewhat like its more famous offspring, the Wiener Schnitzel of Austria and Germany. Frito Misto, a "mixed fry" of various meats is also well loved in Lombardy, as it is in some other northern Italian regions, where it can also be a "mixed fry" of seafood.

Soups are much appreciated in the relatively cool Lombard climate. Two of the best known are Minestrone (Liguria also claims credit for creating this soup, thick with rice and/or pasta and vegetables) and Zuppa Pavese (consommé with a poached egg).

For a treat with coffee at breakfast try Milan's splendid Panettone, a dried- and candied-fruit-studded, light yeast cake enriched with eggs and butter that is now popular throughout Italy, especially at Christmas time.

Regional Lombard cheeses include the blue-veined Gorgonzola, the creamy and mild Bel Paese, and the surface-ripened Taleggio.

Wines are of little note from a serious wine drinker's perspective, but Lombardy does manufacture Campari, a bitter-sweet aperitif sipped in chic bars around the globe.

TURIN AND THE PIEDMONT REGION

Turin is Italy's most modern and industrialized metropolis, but the approach to food remains reasonably loyal to yesteryear's principles of bringing out rather than masking the natural flavors of the cooking ingredients yielded by Piedmont's remarkable culinary cornucopia.

Perhaps the regional specialty that best epitomizes this concept is Piedmont's pride and joy: Bagna Cauda, which translates as "hot sauce." Its ingredients are olive oil, chopped garlic and anchovies, butter, and sometimes sliced *tartufo bianco* (white truffles, another Piedmontese edible ecstasy). Into this heated sauce the diner dips a wide choice of cold raw vegetables. Red wine is the traditional accompaniment.

Fonduta is another Piedmontese culinary triumph, easily but not inexpensively made by melting the superb Fontina cheese from the neighboring Val d'Aosta region with milk, butter, and eggs, then topping the resulting "fondue" with sliced white truffles.

Another cool-weather favorite is the Piedmontese version of Bollito Misto, mixed boiled meats. Soups and Agnolotti (Piedmont-style Ravioli) are also popular, as are Grissini, those thin, crisp breadsticks that originated in Turin.

Chicken (or Veal) Marengo, a dish that appears on restaurant menus throughout the Western world, was born in Piedmont: to help Napoleon celebrate his victory at Marengo. While still other influences from neighboring France can be seen in the regional cuisine, Piedmontese cookery is nonetheless distinct unto itself.

Piedmont is without question Italy's finest red-wine-growing district, Tuscany and its Chianti Classico notwithstanding. Using the noble Nebbiolo grape, Piedmont produces the great full-bodied Barolo and Gattinara reds and the near-great Barbaresco red, none of which should be drunk younger than five to ten years. There is also a varietal Nebbiolo red, as well as Barbera and Grignolino reds (of lesser breed). Regional white wines are few and uninteresting. On the sparkling side there is Asti Spumante, more famous than great, and often a bit sweet. Greater Turin is Italy's Vermouth capital, with several giant producers, including Martini & Rossi and Cinzano.

OTHER REGIONS

Italian cuisine, of course, is much broader in variety than we have just outlined. In the Tyrolean northeastern corner of Italy, one's palate detects an obvious Austro-German accent, while in the upper northeastern corner, Valle d'Aosta, a slight Swiss-French influence creeps into the kitchens.

The Umbrian regional cooking shares certain characteristics with Tuscan cuisine such as a predilection for beef, though in Umbria one is more likely to come across more pork and game dishes. In the realm of wine, Umbria is noted for its white Orvieto that can range from dry to sweet.

A neighboring region to Umbria is The Marches, which prides itself on dishes prepared from seafood caught along its Adriatic Sea coastline. The locally produced, crisp, white Verdicchio wine makes a harmonious accompaniment for this fare.

A little farther south is the Abruzzi region that is known for its fine cooks, many of whom have migrated throughout Italy to work in restaurants.

While the southern regions of Apulia, Basilicata, and Calabria have not been blessed with an abundance of prime farmland and pasturage, the local people make do with a rich harvest of seafood and rely quite heavily on staples such as pasta, eggplants, tomatoes, garlic, onions, olive oil, and fragrant herbs.

And finally, across the Tyrrhenian Sea, we find the unpretentious cuisine of mountainous Sardinia, the home of numerous shepherds who particularly enjoy roasting whole animals outdoors, such as wild boar and baby lamb. Sardinia is also very well known for its ewe's milk Pecorino Sardo cheese and its flat "music sheet" bread.

NATIONAL CHARACTERISTICS

Today regional differences are slowly becoming blurred as a result of effective transportation systems and advertising programs in this land of some 60 million people. The food quality, too, is gradually slipping as old-fashioned small-scale farming methods are giving way to mass-production agri-technology. All this is particularly true in the more industrialized north.

Also, despite the striking regional cuisine differences, certain nationwide culinary characteristics exist. These include the heavy reliance on seafood as a source of protein, especially in the port cities that line Italy's lengthy coastline. Pork and its products such as ham and sausages as well as veal (seldom beef) are also protein mainstays; although in the poorer households, the proportion of meat in the daily diet is minimal.

Both the northerners and southerners share a fondness and respect for fresh fruits and vegetables. Well-received processed foods include cheese, ice cream (which can be incredibly good), and, of course, pasta of infinite shapes and sizes. While the quantity of flavoring agents that are used varies by region and cook, some, such as basil, bay leaf, celery, cloves, coriander, fennel, garlic (and other members of the onion family), green pepper, lemon juice, marjoram, mint, olives, oregano, parsley, peppercorns, rosemary, sage, salt, tarragon, thyme, tomato, vinegar, and wine are apt to be found in kitchen pots up and down the Italian peninsula.

In the average home, lunch is the main meal of the day and usually begins with soup or pasta—or sometimes a combination of both, in a Minestrone-type preparation. The entrée is served next, with vegetables, followed by the concluding course, fresh fruits and often cheese. The rich and sweet desserts for which Italy is famous are usually reserved for between-meal treats at restaurants or at home when entertaining friends.

BEVERAGES

Italians vie with the French for the title of "the world's foremost wine drinkers." The major table wines have been mentioned in their appropriate regional sections. Italy is also celebrated for its aperitifs: Vermouth, Campari, and the artichoke-based Cynar being three of the best known. On the after-dinner side are the almondy Amaretto, the anise-flavored Sambuca, and the cardamom-infused Strega liqueurs. Grappa is Italy's leading brandy—its taste is slightly harsh, partially the result of having been made from the grape skins, pips, and stems left over from the wine-making process.

Coffee drinking is firmly entrenched—Espresso bars permeate the Italian peninsula, particularly in large cities like Rome and Venice.

Beer is well liked and growing in popularity. Though each region has its own brands, the most famous of the nationally sold labels is Peroni from Milan. Another countrywide favorite is the more robust Messina beer from Sicily.

As in France, bottled mineral water is consumed in great quantities, especially in the northern two-thirds of Italy.

THE NETHERLANDS

DUTCH CHEESE CONFRONTS THE tourist early in the day. The traditional Dutch breakfast includes cheese, hot tea, bread, soft-boiled eggs, and perhaps a portion of ham. The most popular cheeses are Edam, Gouda, and cumin-flavored Leyden. Edam is a spherical semiskim cheese; Gouda is a whole-milk cheese prepared in wheels—both are semisoft and mild. When encountered in the Netherlands, both have yellow rinds (Edams for export are swathed in red wax). Not every Dutch person can face a large meal in the morning; some prefer a light Continental breakfast. But everything stops at 10:30 a.m. when the Dutch, en masse, drink café au lait and eat *koekjes* (sweet cakes or biscuits).

Lunch is usually a cold meal—perhaps a *broodje* (sandwich) or *Hollandse koffietafel* (a buffet of sandwich fixings and a hot dish). Cheese, Tartare Biefstuk (Steak Tartare), and Uitsmijter (roast beef or ham crowned with fried eggs) are popular sandwich fillings.

After work comes the cocktail hour. Many of the Dutch enjoy a predinner drink: Sherry or Jenever. This latter spirit is somewhat similar to its English offspring Gin—both are strong and juniper-berry flavored (in fact, both "gin" and "jenever" are derivatives from the Latin word *juniperus*). The major difference between the Dutch and Anglo-American products is that the former is thicker ("old" Jenever is thicker and stronger than "young" Jenever) and is not suited for use in mixed drinks.

Dinner in a restaurant is likely to be an occasion, with elegance expected and provided. *Rijsttafel* (Rice Table), developed in the former colony of Indonesia, is a favorite restaurant meal. This bit of culinary theater is an array of Indonesian-style foods served with rice. There will be several main dishes, several *sambals* (condiments), several fruits and other desserts, all selected to emphasize one another by flavor, color, and texture contrast. For more information, see Indonesia.

But dinner at home is unlikely to be disappointing. A country almost half of which is below sea level, the Netherlands is literally *constructed*: fine farmland has been built by pumping out sea water and holding it back with embankments. Dutch farms are productive; the dairy industry, based on Holstein and Friesian cattle, is exceptional. Brown beans, cabbage, carrots, and other vegetables grow in this rather damp, chilly climate and provide hearty dishes to keep out the damp and chill.

There are a number of famous dishes in the Netherlands. Thick Erwtensoep, dried split peas with sausage and hearty vegetables, is a favorite soup that can be a full meal. The classic simple Hutspot met Klapstuk is boiled beef with carrots, onions, and potatoes. Hutspot is cognate with the English "hodgepodge," which shows what creative cooks can do with (or to) this dish. Lamstongen met Rozijnensaus is lamb's tongue in a spicy, raisiny white wine sauce. This very popular dish is atypical in the Dutch cuisine; beer is more popular than wine, Heineken's more popular than other beers. Well-loved brown beans, baked with pork products, onions, carrots, and apples appear in Vijfshaft. Other popular vegetables include asparagus, cabbage, spinach, potatoes, and sorrel.

Dessert might be Speculaas, the hard, spicy cookies (also popular in Belgium) traditionally baked in elaborately carved molds to produce edible sculptures; Oliebollen, yeast-raised doughnuts without holes; or Flensjes, thin pancakes often eaten with fruit or jam.

However, the favorite Dutch snack is neither the cookie, the doughnut, nor the pancake, but the herring. Young ("green") herring are eaten in the spring, raw and lightly brined. Each May the nation waits impatiently for the first herring. The fishing boats race, knowing that the crew that catches the very first herring will be famous and will be honored by being allowed to present the first barrel of herring to the royal family. Then the common people have their chance with the herring. The purist's technique is to sprinkle the herring with a bit of raw onion, grasp the tail, and down the fish in two or three bites. Bottoms up!

 # POLAND

UNTIL SEVERAL DECADES AGO, Poland had been a country of shifting borders. This helps explain the detectable culinary influences from Germany in the west, from Russia in the east, and from Czechoslovakia, Austria, and Hungary in the south. The other three major influences have been French, Jewish, and Italian, for historical reasons.

While sour cream and dill are the two cooking ingredients most commonly associated with Polish cuisine, there are a couple of dozen equally important staples that, if eliminated, would markedly alter the table of the hearty-eating Poles. One of these is the pig (the country's favorite source of meat), which is transformed into Poland's famous hams and equally renowned garlic-laden sausages called Kiełbasi. Other food staples include beef and forest game; seafood (especially herring) from Poland's Baltic seacoast, freshwater fish from the nation's many rivers and lakes; honey; cereal grains such as rye (the leader), buckwheat, and barley; and last but not least, the hearty vegetables and fruits such as cabbage (eaten fresh or as sauerkraut), beets, turnips, potatoes, cucumbers, horseradish, plums, and apples.

Poland endures long, hard winters and consequently, the Poles preserve a lot of food by salting, pickling, drying, or smoking. The last method frequently uses juniper wood, which gives the meats a distinctive flavor. Another characteristic flavor comes from the sweet-and-sour Polish Sauce, served over any meat or fish.

The Poles are fond of soups, ranging from "nothing" soup (Zupa Nic), a thin custard topped with small meringues, and

75

duck soup (Czarnina), to dainty cold fruit soups, to substantial hot meals such as the famous Krupnik (a barley, potato, and sour cream soup) and Chlodnik (a cold soup of sour cream and beet stock, garnished with dill, cucumbers, hard-boiled eggs, and crayfish). Another Polish classic is Barszcz, a clear soup based on fermented beet juice or beef stock, with beets and other vegetables and sour cream; sometimes it contains pieces of meat. Uszki (small dumplings) filled with soaked dried mushrooms are a traditional accompaniment to Barszcz, though dark rye bread is the countrywide favorite for soups in general.

Bigos, Poland's national dish, originated on hunting parties. This "hunter's stew" is based on sauerkraut and/or cabbage laced with chunks of fresh pork, sausages, ham, beef, game, poultry, or whatever meat comes to hand. It is not unlike the Alsatian Choucroute Garnie or the Swiss Berneplatte. Some versions add onions and mushrooms, or even fruit. The traditional version limits the meat additions to leftover game.

Other popular main dishes include the various stuffed cabbage rolls such as Zrazy. Another Polish specialty is Karp po Żydowsku, made with carp (very popular in Poland), prepared "Jewish style" by steaming slices of carp on a bed of aromatic root vegetables. It is served hot, or cold in its own aspic. Sometimes this dish, a Christmas Eve tradition, is served with Polish Sauce.

Plain and filled noodles and dumplings are much enjoyed. Meat, potato, and sauerkraut fillings are used for main courses; fruit for desserts; cheese for either, depending on the spicing. Pierogi, made with noodle or yeast dough, are shaped like a half moon; Uszki are tiny packages with twisted corners. Kolduny are stuffed circles of dough; Kulebiak are small cylinders.

Sweet dumplings are only one class of desserts enjoyed in Poland. Babka is a well-worked yeast dough, with plenty of butter and eggs, nuts and raisins. Chrust-faworki are sugar-sprinkled bowknots of fried dough; Mazurek is an almond bar served with a variety of toppings.

Polish working hours begin and end earlier than those of

other East European countries, so meals are earlier: breakfast at about 5:30 or 6 a.m., lunch at about 11, dinner at about 4 p.m., supper at 7:30 or 8.

Wódka is the widely-acclaimed Polish Vodka, distilled from rye rather than from potatoes (as was once the custom). Add a blade of buffalo grass to steep inside the bottle, and you have Wódka Żubrówka, one of Poland's leading exports. Goldwasser, another globally sold spirit, is a liqueur made of spiced Wódka. The gold in the name is not metaphorical; there really are flakes of metal in the drink. Poland's other major beverage of note is the fermented honey drink Mead, which is of ancient origin.

PORTUGAL ⌒

PORTUGAL AND SPAIN SHARE the Iberian Peninsula, cooking philosophies, and certain food resources. These include the use of the fruit and oil of the olive tree, almonds as a popular garnish, and, most especially, a penchant for fish. Yet despite this close geographical and cultural association, Portugal's cuisine has managed to establish its own individual flavor.

There are lots of good fish in the sea, which forms the southern and western boundaries of Portugal; and native cooks have improvised tasty ways of utilizing this resource. Salt cod (Bacalhau) is one such example. Cooked with potatoes, onions, olives, and hard-boiled eggs, it is Bacalhau à Gomes de Sá. Spiked with fresh coriander, mixed with breadcrumbs and shaped into cakes, it becomes Bolinhos de Bacalhau. The patties are fried and crowned with poached eggs. The seafood supply is augmented by Peixe em Vinha de Alhos, sautéed fish filets previously marinated in wine and vinegar; and Caldeirada à Fregateira, a soup of fresh fish, potatoes, and herbs.

Contrasting with this wealth of products from the sea, is the lack of high-quality meat. Beef is practically absent from the Portugese diet, upstaged by chicken, pork, and sausage, common ingredients in soups and stews. Caldo Verde is a very popular soup of shreds of kale, mashed potatoes, and slices of Linguiça or Chouriço sausages. Sausage reappears in Grãos de Bico com Linguiça, chickpeas slow-cooked with sausage and onion.

Air-cured mountain ham (Presunto) and fresh pork also

supplement the limited selection of meat dishes. Soupa à Alentejana is a soup of pork and eggs, thickened with bread and flavored with garlic. Porco con Amêijoas à Alentejana calls for pork made ready in a highly spiced marinade and sauced with clams, tomatoes, onions, and pimientos. The finished dish is sprinkled with lemon juice and coriander. This same herb flavors Açorda, another bread-based dish made with meat, poultry, or seafood. Meat, poultry, sausage, and sturdy vegetables also comprise Cozida à Portugesa, a soup-stew similar to the Spanish Cocido.

These dishes are often washed down with wines such as the popular Portuguese rosés or the white versions of the Vinho Verde (made from young or "green" grapes). However, Porto, a fortified wine, is Portugal's most celebrated alcoholic beverage. Porto is spiked with brandy and aged in wood vats. Often Portos of different years are blended; but in exceptional years, the product of a single year will be used to make Vintage Porto.

SCANDINAVIA ⁓

THROUGHOUT DENMARK, NORWAY, SWEDEN, and Finland, even as you read this, thousands of defenseless slices of thin rye bread and flatbread are being seized, thickly buttered, and covered with fish, meat, eggs, and garnishes. The open sandwiches the Danes call *smørrebrød* are the ubiquitous Danish lunch and a common Finnish breakfast. (The Finns take their oatmeal or other porridge at 11 a.m.). The herring, roast beef, ham, meat patties, and other bread toppings are features of the buffet the Danes call *kolde bord*, the Norwegians call *koldt bord*, the Swedes *smørgåsbord*, and the Finns *voileipäpöytä*. Scandinavians are great fanciers of herring; cod and salmon are also popular fish. Late-summer crayfish eating is a pan-Scandinavian obsession; dried and salted fish a regional love object. Pork is a popular and festive meat. Roast goose is another holiday tradition.

Long, cold winters inhibit the growth of green vegetables. The few that succeed are especially intense in flavor (as a result of long hours of summer daylight) and especially well loved. The rest of the year, imports and long-keeping carrots, cabbages, onions, turnips, and rutabagas must be used. The strawberries, blueberries, raspberries, lingonberries, cloudberries, and rose hips that grow wild in summer are coveted for their vitamin content and their sweet-tart flavor.

Scandinavian breads have a hearty taste. They range from firm loaves to hard, wafer-thin flatbreads. Many Scandinavian breads (the anise-flavored, candied-fruit-studded, Swedish Limpa, for example) have a tang of rye, a grain that grows well in Scandinavia's short, cool summers. Because rye is low in gluten, these breads don't rise very high. Cakes and cookies sometimes contain rye flour, which stays fresh longer than wheat flour.

Traditional Scandinavian brick ovens are hard to fire up, so the housewives prefer to bake large batches infrequently. Hartshorn (ammonium carbonate), which gives a crisp, long-lasting product, is a traditional substitute for baking powder. Sometimes baked goods are sophisticated concoctions of fine wheat flour, plenty of butter and eggs, vanilla, sugar, and almond paste.

Other characteristic Scandinavian flavors are cardamom (frequently used in desserts), dill, and caraway (typically used in savory dishes). Cream and mayonnaise are used everywhere.

Scandinavia depends heavily on its waters and, particularly in the south, its pastures. Fishing and dairying are significant industries. Danish butter is a major export; Scandinavian cheeses are well known at home and abroad. The Scandinavians down glasses of milk, boilermakers, and cups of coffee on different occasions, but with equal aplomb.

DENMARK

The low-lying Danish pasture lands yield plenty of milk, cream, butter, and cheese. The cow is valued primarily as a milk producer, not a meat producer. Therefore, meat extenders are used in such dishes as Hakkebøf, patties of minced beef smothered in onions and thick brown gravy.

Frikadeller, butter-sauced cakes of mixed meats (pork and veal is the favorite combination) extended with onions, egg, milk, and breadcrumbs, and lightened with carbonated water, are also used to make a big meal out of a bit of meat. Pickled beets or Asier (cucumber salad), both Scandinavian favorites, are traditionally served with Frikadeller.

Pork is the favorite meat, loin of pork a cause for celebration. The loin may be stuffed with a cylinder of apples and prunes, or accompanied by cabbage with caraway seeds or red cabbage with apples. Brunede Kartofler, caramelized new potatoes, are a special treat, especially after a winter of spongy stored potatoes.

One of the favorite desserts is Rødgrød med Fløde, a sweet, creamy, fruity mixture of raspberry and currant juices, thickened and dolloped with sweet cream. Appelkaka is apple "cake," a mixture of applesauce, sweetened breadcrumbs, and lots of whipped cream.

Interestingly, the pastries called "Danish" in America are called Wienerbröd (Vienna Bread) in Denmark. Their puff paste encloses pastry cream, preserves, currants, nuts, or almond paste.

SWEDEN

Smörgåsbord means Bread and Butter Table, a deceptively modest name for a buffet that can include everything a cook can manage to provide. Smörgåsbord can be sampled as an appetizer, or as a full meal in a restaurant or on festive occasions at home. Its component dishes appear many times on Swedish tables.

Smörgåsbord etiquette demands that you begin with a plate of herring, which will be presented in many guises. Inlagd Sill (pickled herring) and Glasmästarsill (herring vinegar-marinated in glass jars with carrots, onions, and sugar) are very popular. Strömming are small Baltic herring. Surströmming are fermented Baltic herring, adored by some Swedes but few non-Swedes. After the herring, you get a clean plate and sample the other fish dishes. Gravad Lax (or Gravlax), heavily dilled salmon dry-cured with sugar and salt and served with mustard sauce, is a classic. Take another plate and munch cold meats and salads (more likely to be "composed" salads than green salads). The next clean plate is for the småvarmt, "small warm," another example of Swedish understatement. These are the hot meat dishes. Jansson's Frestelse (Jansson's Temptation) is a creamy casserole of anchovies and potatoes: very salty, like much Scandinavian food. Biff à la Lindström (also popular in Finland) is a hamburger enlivened by onions, capers, and bits of cooked beet. Färsrulåder are small rolls of minced veal with slivers of leek inside; Köttbullar are meatballs, usually served gravyless.

The Swedes are also fond of homely food. Ärter med Fläsk, the ginger-and-marjoram-flavored soup of whole dried yellow peas, appears on every traditional Swedish table each Thursday night in winter. The time-honored complement is a dish of Plättar, small, thin pancakes with lingonberry preserves. Kalops is a stew of beef chunks flavored with allspice and bay leaves, perhaps served with Rårakor, thin, crisp potato pancakes, on the side. Pickled beets are prescribed as the accompaniment to Pytt i Panna, a hash of Sunday's leftover roast, potatoes, and onions, all cut in neat, tiny mosaic shapes and topped with raw egg yolks or fried eggs. Lutfisk, lye-treated dried cod, is soaked, boiled, then served with cream sauce, peas, and boiled potatoes. This combination is traditional for Christmas and other festive dinners.

Spettekaka is a spectacular dessert reserved for festive occasions. A thin, eggy batter is poured onto a paper cone turning on a spit in front of a fire. The finished cake is an uneven cylinder with fantastic branchings and a tracery of white icing.

FINLAND

There are two major heritages in Finnish cooking: that of western Finland and the Karelian. Karelia, once an eastern province of Finland, now belongs to the Soviet Union, but many of its former inhabitants are scattered throughout Finland. Therefore, Karelian dishes can be found in all parts of Finland.

The custom in the west of Finland is to bake flat, hard rounds of bread with a hole in the center. This hole allows the Finn to store the bread (for as long as half a year) on horizontal poles suspended from the ceiling. The Karelians prefer to bake a lighter, softer loaf twice a week. Both breads use the same sour-rye dough.

The Karelians use this dough to make Kalakukko, a round

loaf stuffed with a small fish called *muikku* (vendace) and fat pork. The loaf is baked, producing rich, soft fish and a bread crust. Piirakkaa are small shells of rye dough conventionally filled with rice or potatoes, then baked.

The Finnish diet depends heavily on fish. Mixed-meat dishes are popular: Vorsmack is a garlicky dish blending beef, mutton, and salt herring; Karjalan Paisti, a slow-baked casserole of pork, beef, and lamb. Merimiespihvi is the Finnish version of "sailor's beef" (beef chunks baked with onions, potatoes, and beer), a dish that is popular throughout Scandinavia, regardless of occupation.

Unusual Finnish delicacies include reindeer (favorite meat of the Lapps; the tongue is an especially choice morsel) and the caviar of the burbot, a freshwater fish.

The Finns enjoy porridge (rice, rye, or oats especially); Christmas wouldn't be the same without Mämmi, baked rye porridge flavored with malt and orange peel. With their porridge (and almost everything else) the Finns drink milk—straight, buttermilk, or Piimä, a cultured-milk drink. Viili is a solid cultured milk something like rubbery yogurt.

When not drinking glasses of milk (or Vodka), Finns are likely to sip coffee. The "coffee table" is the focus of informal Finnish hospitality: Pulla, a braided yeast cake, and several other kinds of cake and cookies will be featured.

NORWAY

The Norwegian table is characterized by plainly cooked fish that is flavorful because it is *blodfersk*, or blood-fresh. Norwegian cooks won't accept frozen fish; many won't even buy fish that are not alive and vigorous. Fiskepudding or Fiskefarse is a light, spongy pure-white baked pudding of fresh fish (preferably cod or haddock), milk, and cream. Old-fashioned households still dish up Fiskepudding not less than once a week. Trout and salmon are also very popular, whether eaten fresh or preserved for later use. Klippfisk is salted dried cod; Lutefisk, sald cod treated with lye. Rakørret is fermented trout. These preparations do not pretend to be fresh fish; they have their own forthright flavor.

Mutton is a favorite meat. Får i Kål is a simple stew of mutton and cabbage. Adding carrots and potatoes yields Puss Pass. Fenelår is well-preserved mutton: the meat is both cured and air-dried.

Lefser, a holiday bread, is made of potato dough usually grilled in thin layers. The flexible bread is eaten folded, with butter and sugar. Festivities (especially country weddings) may include Rømmegrøt, porridge made by boiling sour cream and serving the curds with butter and sugar. Citified celebrations may end with Kransekage, a pyramid of almond-paste rings also popular in Denmark.

ICELAND

Since Iceland was settled by Continental Scandinavians, its cuisine is understandably similar to that of its Scandinavian neighbors, though fish plays a dominant role in this island nation whose economy is dependent upon the fishing industry. Lamb, too, is more of a staple in Iceland than in mainland Scandinavia. Some of the favorite specialties of Icelanders include: Hákarl (pickled shark), Hreindýrasteik í Potti (reindeer pot roast), Humar Á Búttudeigsbotni (lobster pie), Raekjupönnukökur (shrimp-filled pancakes), Reyktur Lax (smoked salmon), Sunnudagssteikin (Sunday's roast leg of lamb), and Skyr (a thick creamlike dessert), which is perhaps Iceland's national dish.

SCANDINAVIAN CHEESE

Where milk is important to the diet, cheese can be expected to follow; so it does in Scandinavia.

Denmark makes and exports many cheeses. A cheese name ending in "-bo" (Danbo, Elbo, Tybo, Fynbo, Maribo) usually signals a Danish cheese. All of these are related to Samsoe, itself a second cousin to Emmentaler. King Christian IX is a Samsoe with caraway seeds. Havarti is a mild, slighly sour cheese. Danablu and Mycella are blue-mold cheeses. Crema Danica is a modern cheese with a Brielike texture and a flavor reminiscent of both Camembert and Brie. Esrom is a version of Port-Salut.

Norway's Jarlsberg looks very much like Emmentaler, but tastes sweeter. Norwegian blue cheese is very creamy. Gammelost is a sharp mold cheese made from sour milk. Taffelost is a long-keeping cheese with an Edamlike texture. (The suffix "-ost" indicates a Norwegian or Swedish cheese). Tilsit is a mild cheese. Nokkelost is sprinkled with cloves and/or caraway seed and cumin. Gjetost, a sweet brown cheese made from whey, is the subject of a great deal of invective, some of it quite imaginative.

Sveciaost and Herrgard are mild cheeses which are very popular in their native Sweden.

BEVERAGES

The classic Scandinavian drink is Akvavit, a colorless liquor usually distilled from grain or potatoes and slightly flavored with caraway seeds. The Finns, though, prefer Vodka. A shot of Akvavit is called a *snaps* in Sweden, Denmark, and Finland; a *dram* in Norway. A *skål* or *skol* is a toast (the Finns say, *"Tervevdeksenne"*); you lift the glass chest-high, look deep into the eyes of the person you toast, say the secret word, and knock back your Akvavit in a single gulp. You look once again at your partner, put down your tiny Akvavit glass, and address yourself to the traditional beer chaser or the food on your plate. (Custom demands that you *skål* only while eating drinks are seldom served without food). The Akvavit bottle is traditionally presented inside a block of ice; the liquor has a much lower freezing point than water, and is chilled, not solidified, by the treatment.

The Scandinavians often restrict themselves to beer with

meals; it allows them to drive without facing stiff penalties for drunken driving, and it is much cheaper than heavily taxed liquor. Considering the quality of the best Scandinavian beers, the hardship is not too great.

SCOTLAND

DR. JOHNSON'S *DICTIONARY* DEFINES oats as "a grain which in England is generally given to horses, but in Scotland, supports the people." The Scots respond, "That is why England has such fine horses and Scotland such fine men."

The Scottish day is likely to start with a steaming helping of oatmeal porridge. Some type of bread is served, usually topped with butter or marmalade, a preserve of citrus-fruit peel. Like their English neighbors, the Scots also enjoy smoked fish for breakfast. Kippers, gutted herring, may be rolled in oatmeal and fried.

Haggis is one of Scotland's most celebrated dishes. The procedure involves stuffing a sheep's stomach with oatmeal or barley, sheep offal, and beef suet and boiling this self-contained package in a caldron. Haggis is properly eaten with Nips and Neps—whisky and turnips. Finnan Haddie, smoked haddock, is another popular native dish.

The Scots have a number of well-known baked goods to their credit. Scones can be made with oatmeal, though today they are usually made with wheat or barley flour. The dough consists of flour, baking powder, and buttermilk or sour milk, which is baked on a griddle or in an oven. Bannocks are flat oatcakes (or cakes of rye or barley meal), also baked on a griddle or in an oven. Dundee Cake is a fruitcake studded with almonds; Black Bun is a mixture of dried fruits and nuts baked in a rectangular pastry crust. Petticoat Tails are triangles of shortbread.

Barley is another essential grain in the Scot's diet. Scotch Broth combines barley with mutton, carrots, and turnips—all mainstays of the cuisine—to make a thick soup. Cullen Skink is another soup-stew made with smoked haddock, potatoes, and onions. Cockaleekie soup derives its name from its two basic ingredients, chicken and leeks.

Orange Marmalade is closely associated with Scotland—some culinary historians say this breakfast-table condiment was invented in Bonnie Scotland. Whatever the true story may be, this bittersweet preserve has made the town of Dundee and the Keiller name well known in fancy-food shops around the world.

Scotch Whisky, the most famous commercial product of Scotland, falls into three basic categories: single malt, blended (or straight) malt, and blended. Most Scots drink the first two while virtually all non-Scots consume the last one. A single malt is the product of a single distillery and is made entirely of barley that has been malted (allowed to sprout) before distillation. A blended (or straight) malt is also a 100 percent barley malt whisky; but, as the name partially implies, it is a mixture of the product of several or even scores of different distilleries from different parts of Scotland. A classic mixture is approximately equal parts of the malt whiskies from the Scottish Lowlands and Highlands (the whiskies from the latter area are generally considered superior and have a more assertive peat-smoke flavor) plus a small amount of the even stronger peat-smoke-flavored malt whiskies from Islay and Cambeltown. The third category, blended Scotch Whisky, is principally made to suit the milder taste preferences of the English, Americans, and other foreigners. To create this product, blended malt whiskies are mixed with an equal or large proportion of blander whiskies made from unmalted barley and other grains.

Scotch Whisky is customarily sipped abroad on the rocks, diluted with soda or water, or made into a cocktail such as the Rob Roy. The red-blooded Scot, however, likes his national beverage neat, minus the ice and other flavor modifiers.

SOVIET UNION ⁓

IT IS MEANINGLESS TO generalize about Soviet cuisine because the USSR encompasses many distinct cooking styles, not to mention dozens of different languages, ethnic groups, climates, and soils. Of the culinary regions within the federation, by far the most significant to foreigners is Russia, a republic containing half the Soviet Union's quarter-billion population and the cuisine that most Western Europeans identify as Soviet cooking.

RUSSIA

The Russian Republic stretches over two continents, from the Baltic to the Bering seas. It is in the western portion, where the people are predominantly of Slavic blood, that almost all the Russians reside.

Russians, who are noted for their hearty appetites, eat quite a lot of starch. This is consumed in the form of dark, crusty, slightly sour bread, predominantly made from rye flour; yet as one travels south into the warmer growing regions, wheat bread becomes increasingly popular. Another popular starch is Kasha, cereal grain cooked and served porridge-style—more often than not, it is buckwheat. Potatoes, rice, millet, oats, and barley also contribute to the high starch intake of the Russian people.

Leading nonfarinaceous vegetables include cabbage, beets, mushrooms, cucumbers, sorrel, turnips, eggplant, squash, sweet peppers, tomatoes, carrots, and onions. While meat from domestic animals such as cattle, hogs, sheep, chicken, geese, and ducks is entrenched in the daily fare, game from Russia's vast forest and inland waters plays a major dietary role. Flavoring agents often used by the Russian cook include dill, bay leaves, parsley, sour cream, yogurt, garlic (a touch), honey, and sugar (Russians have a sweet tooth).

Russia's long, cold winters have led to the abundant preservation of produce (especially cabbage and cucumbers) by such means as pickling. The bone-chilling weather has also made soup-making and -sipping a national pastime. Of the innumerable soups, four are particularly famous:

Borsch A beet-based soup-stew that can be red or not, cold or hot. It may or may not contain meats, vegetables, and a dollop of sour cream. Pirozhki sometimes accompany this specialty.

Ouha A delicate fish-in-a-clear-broth soup-stew. Russian food connoisseurs believe that it reaches its peak when made with freshly killed sterlet sturgeon (from the river or the storage tank).

Shchi Undoubtedly this—and not borsch, as some believe—is Russia's most popular soup. Shchi is based on fresh cabbage in the summer and sauerkraut in the winter, though some cooks combine both ingredients when available. The cook can also add a meat ingredient and/or sour cream.

Solianka A thick, flavorful fish (or meat) soup typically flavored with salted cucumber or other saline agents.

When summer arrives, cold soups find their way on to the Russian table. Those made with fruits are appreciated the most.

Well known-Russian main dishes include:

Beef Stroganoff There are endless variations to this recipe, but basically it is sliced beef steak sautéed and served with a mushroom, onion, and sour-cream sauce.

Chicken Pojarsky A seasoned and breaded ground chicken patty that is sometimes fashioned to resemble a cutlet. It can also be made with the addition of veal, pork, or other meats.

Golubtsy Stuffed cabbage rolls (the old Central European standby).

Kulebiaka Salmon mousse, baked with a flaky pastry dough. This creation is one of Russia's greatest contributions to the world.

Throughout the less populated central and eastern regions of Russia, such as Siberia, Pelmeni are everyday fare. These half-moon-shaped dumplings are stuffed with a filling such as a savory minced meat mixture, thus similar to (and perhaps derived from) the Chinese Dim Sum.

Zakuski is the great Russian custom of loading a table with various predinner hors d'oeuvres such as caviar, salted herring, smoked salmon, sliced hard sausages, pickled mushrooms and onions, liver pâté, and salted cucumber. Sometimes you will also be offered Pirozhki, miniature turnovers stuffed with minced meat, vegetables, and fruits. Vodka, drunk neat, icy cold, and in one gulp from a tiny glass, is the almost mandatory liquid accompaniment because it helps cut through the oiliness of some of the zakuski offerings.

The Easter season affords the Russian people the opportunity to observe several deeply entrenched traditions. Just before the forty-day Lenten fast begins, Russians (believers and atheists alike) stage eating orgies featuring the Blini, a small yeast-raised pancake that is traditionally smeared with butter or sour cream, then topped with delectables such as caviar, fruit preserves, or cheese. Finally, after nearly six weeks of fasting ends, rich and abundant food reappears. Easter Sunday brings a large, joyous dinner that ends with the pyramid-shaped Pashka (a molded creamy cottage-cheeselike substance, stuffed with candied fruit and nuts marked with the Cyrillic letters XB, initials standing for the Russian translation of "Christ is risen"). The cylindrical Kulich raisin-and-nut yeast cake is another component of this holiday feast.

Two famous year-round desserts are the French-inspired Charlotte Russe (a mold lined with sponge-cake lady fingers, filled with a cream mixture) and the jellylike Kissel (a concoction made from puréed fruits or their juices). Russians also have a love affair with ice cream, a quality product that they make in quantity.

French chefs, such as the illustrious Carême, have noticeably influenced Russian cuisine since the turn of the eighteenth century, when Czar Peter the Great encouraged the importation of Western European culture, including prominent Parisian cooks. These Frenchmen created new dishes or modified old ones: Beef Stroganoff and Charlotte Russe being two famous examples.

Russians are by reputation big drinkers. This cultural characteristic goes back at least a thousand years when the Russian ruler Vladimir chose Christianity over Islam for his subjects because, as he observed, "Russians cannot live without the enjoyment of drinking." Of the many alcoholic beverages favored in Russia today, Vodka is the best liked, though homemade drinks such as Kvass (made from fermented black bread) and Mead (from fermented honey) have their adherents. Wine from areas such as the sister republics of Georgia and Moldavia is increasing in popularity, as is locally brewed Western-style beer.

Tea is the most widely sipped nonalcoholic drink and is customarily prepared in the samovar, a metal urn that is usually ornate—some are priceless art treasures. If tradition is observed, the men drink from glasses and the women from cups, with both sexes sipping milkless black tea through a sugar lump held between the teeth.

OTHER CUISINES

The specialties of the Ukraine somewhat overlap those from Russia. Ukrainians, like their Slavic brethren in Russia, are fond of culinary basics such as crusty breads, Pirozhki, Kasha, Zakuski, Vodka, and soups. However, the Ukrainians have imprinted their own regional stamp on these dishes. Borsch, for example, is generally more flavorful and contains a greater number and variety of ingredients than its Russian counterpart. This is partially due to the fact that the Ukrainian farmland is—on the average—more fertile than that belonging to the western Russians. Specialties that are very much Ukrainian as opposed to Russian include Chicken Kiev (the famous breaded and fried butter-stuffed chicken breast that was created by an imported French chef) and Vareniki. The latter is a dumpling stuffed with a savory or sweet filling such as fruit, cheese, potatoes, or meat.

The three Baltic republics of the Soviet Union are from north to south—Estonia, Latvia, and Lithuania, three lands with deep-rooted ethnic pride and traditions. Nevertheless, there are long-standing culinary influences from neighboring lands. In Estonia, the Scandinavian persuasion is apparent in the craving for cold, open-faced sandwiches. In the Lithuanian cuisine, the German and Polish accent is noticeable, as evidenced by Sult, a version of the German Sülze, a cold aspic with bits of meat and perhaps pickles and vegetables.

Historically, and to some degree today, Baltic cooking has been a feast-or-famine affair. During the spring, summer, and fall seasons, the rich lands and long daylight hours yield some of the world's tastiest vegetables, fruits, and dairy products— but come winter, the average person's diet is transformed into one of monotonous preserved foods, or even worse, no food. Even the usually bountiful supply of fish from the Baltic Sea becomes scarce when winter storms and icy-cold winds keep most skilled fishermen close to their home ports.

The Soviet Caucasus region consists of Armenia (its cuisine is discussed more appropriately in the Middle Eastern part of this book), Georgia, and Azerbaijan. These people, by and large, are known for their wines as well as for their cattle, goat, and sheep husbandry and dairy products. Outdoor barbecue specialties such as the skewered lamb Shashlik are well entrenched in the cooking repertoire of the entire region. Yet each land has its individual dishes and culinary philosophy. In Georgia, for instance, we find the unique Tabaka, a pressed and fried whole chicken that is often served with one of the local walnut-based sauces. This dish is virtually unknown in nearby Armenia and, if it were, pine nuts rather than walnuts would probably be used. Moreover, the accompanying starch staple would more likely be bulgur wheat than corn, the Georgian favorite.

The south-central zone of the Soviet Union contains Kazakhstan, Turkmenia, Kirgizia, Tadzhikistan, and Uzbekistan, lands of the ancient caravan trade routes linking Europe with the Orient. Their cuisines are not unlike those of neighboring nations—thus, depending on proximity, one can easily sample Persian-style fruits, breads made in the tandoor-type clay ovens used in Afghanistan, Pakistan, and northern India, and yak butter, reminiscent of China's Tibet and Sinkiang Provinces. One interesting beverage is Koumiss, fermented mare's milk.

SPAIN

SPANISH FOOD SUFFERS A slight identity crisis. Besides being closely linked to its Iberian neighbor, Portugal, Spanish cuisine is also confused with Mexican food, red-hot and highly seasoned. Spanish food is colorful, but involves few hot spices or assertive seasonings, with the exception of garlic and the favorite, parsley.

The people are not great beef consumers. Lean, rangy hogs yielding lean meat and sausage are more popular than beef cattle, which are more expensive to raise. The most prized dish is likely to be a tender milk-fed kid, piglet, or veal calf, not a steak from a mature animal. Between roasts, bits of meat, sausage, and chicken will be combined with vegetables in soup-stews. However, this limited selection of meat is partially offset by the country's abundant fresh seafood, which in turn is supplemented by dried cod.

The olive is one of the most prominent contributors to the country's eating and economy. Cooks benefit from the oil of the olive tree, preferring it to butter or other fats; diners benefit from the fruit of the olive tree as an appetizer or a salad ingredient; and everyone benefits from the fragrance of the olive groves. Almonds, another specialty, are used as a flavor and texture ingredient in a variety of dishes—from the almond-and-olive mixture munched with predinner drinks to the Marzipan eaten for dessert.

The roster of regional dishes contributes to the cuisine's identity crisis. In Spain there are more than fifty recognized ways of serving potatoes and at least thirty recipes for making cold soups and stews. Paella is a good illustration of this diversity. This famous specialty of Spain's southeast has endless variations, changing from town to town. To compound the confusion, a dish of saffron rice, chicken, sausage, seafood, peas, and peppers, cooked in a large round pan with a flat bottom and two handles, is called Paella à la Valenciana outside Spain. The real Paella of Valencia is more austere: the yellow rice may be mixed with chicken, snails, and green peas—no meat, pimientos, or onions. But Barcelona delights in rich combinations of varied ingredients, so its Paella adds Chorizo sausages and mixed seafood to the basic Arroz con Pollo (stewed chicken pieces with rice, usually colored with saffron).

From the Andalusian region comes Gazpacho, a soup-stew. The simplest Gazpacho is Córdoba's Gazpacho Blanco: just olive oil, vinegar, garlic, and almonds diluted with cold water. Other Andalusian cities add items like bread, green peppers, tomatoes, cucumbers, onions, raw eggs, and croutons to the basic garlic broth. An interesting variety is Málaga's Ajo Blanco con Uvas, a garlic broth in which peeled white grapes float.

Not every garlic soup is Gazpacho. To prepare Sopa de Ajo the cook starts with browned bread and garlic cloves, simmers them in water and adds an egg topping, either by poaching the egg in the soup or by baking the soup and egg in the oven.

Galicia, in the northwest of Spain, is known for its fish and shellfish, such as the centolla (giant crab), viera (scallop), and percebe (rock barnacle). Empanada Gallega is a two-crust pie filled with an oniony fish or meat mixture. (Empanadas and Empanadillas, pies and turnovers made with savory fillings, are popular throughout Spain.) Caldo Gallego is a rich soup of meat and vegetables, flavored with ham.

The same smoky tang is found in Fabada Asturiana, the mélange of white beans and pork products that is the specialty of Asturias, just east of Galicia. The Galicians and Asturians often eat cornbread; most Spaniards prefer long, tough-crusted loaves of white bread.

The Basques, in north-central Spain, are sheepherders, so they enjoy roast baby lamb. They are also fishermen; they eat the small squid they call *chipirones* (and other Spaniards call *calamares*) in the squid's own ink. Kokoxtas, the most delicate cut of hake head, is cooked with green peas, garlic, and parsley. Salt cod from past catches is eaten as Bacalao Pil-Pil, simmered slowly in olive oil. Minestra de Legumbres is a dish of the tiniest spring vegetables, individually cooked and combined with ham and sometimes poached eggs.

Spain's northwest corner, Catalonia, is rich in game. Xato is a salad that starts with endive and builds with sausage, meat, and/or eggs. Tallinas are small clams. They, and any other fresh seafood and fish—cigalas (small lobsterlike crustaceans with big claws), langostas (big spiny lobsters without claws), shrimp, and squid—are fair game for Zarzuela de Mariscos. A *zarzuela* is literally an operetta, figuratively a big deal or a mess; a Zarzuela de Mariscos is a "mess of shellfish" in a white wine sauce.

Meats à *la chilindrón*, stewed with tomatoes and red peppers, and trout stewed in red wine and herbs, or stuffed with air-cured *serrano* ham, are specialties of the inland northern provinces of Aragon and Navarre.

Castile, in central Spain, is renowned for its roast meats such as Cochinillo (suckling pig) and Ternera (milk-fed lamb).

Madrid's pride is the Cocido Madrileño, a soup-stew of chickpeas, hearty vegetables, and mixed meats. The broth is served as a first course, then the vegetables, and finally the meat. Similar dishes, whose flavor comes from long boiling of pork products and vegetables, include the Asturian Pote, the Puchero of La Mancha, the Caldo Gallego, and the Catalonian Olla Podrida. Pisto Manchego is a stew of vegetables, sometimes enriched with egg and ham; it comes from La Mancha, south of Madrid.

The eastern area of Spain, called the Levante, shows its Moorish heritage in its use of rice and citrus fruits, both imported by the Arabs. Turrón, a very sweet confection of almonds, honey, egg white, and flavorings, is another Middle Eastern touch.

Andalusia, in the extreme south of Spain, is a center of olive oil production. The ostión (similar to an oyster) and the chanquete (a small anchovy) are Andalusian gustatory delights that come from the sea. Seville's Huevos à la Flamenca is a baked dish of eggs broken over a bed of stewed vegetables such as tomatoes, peppers, green peas, and asparagus tips.

The Spanish commonly break their fast with an early-morning cup of coffee or chocolate, perhaps with some bread or Churros (crullers). *Almuerzo* around noon might be a sandwich, a hot dish, or a flat pancake-style omelet (Tortilla). *Comida*, in midafternoon, is the main meal. A salad, arranged on the plate rather than tossed, is a popular first course, with fish, meat, or poultry to follow. Dessert is likely to be a piece of fruit—perhaps a Seville or Valencia orange—but it may be Flan (baked custard) or pastry. *Merienda* is an evening snack; *cena* a light late-night supper. Either meal can expand and become elaborate if guests are invited or if the family goes out to a restaurant.

Any time of day (especially in Madrid) is appropriate for *tapas* and a glass of Sherry. *Tapas* are hors d'oeuvres, ranging from the simple combination of olives and almonds to an elaborate spread of hot and cold dishes. Seafood *tapas* are especially popular.

Sherry is a fortified wine made from grapes grown in Cadiz. Wines of various years are blended in the *solera* method; a balance of old and young wines of varying characteristics ensures reasonable uniformity of sherries bottled from year to year. The wines that develop *flor*, a blanket of white yeast cells on the surface of the wine, become pale, very dry *fino* sherries. *Amontillado* sherries have more alcohol and a hint of nuts in their bouquet. Some of the *oloroso* sherries are even stronger, with a dark gold or red color and a full body. "Cream sherries" are blends of *oloroso* and very sweet Pedro Ximenes sherries. Spain's Rioja wines, especially the reds, are renowned for table use. Sangria is a punch that, at its simplest, mixes red wine and citrus juice and, at its most complex, is a *zarzuela* of mixed fruit, carbonated water, sugar, liquor, liqueurs, brandy, and wine.

SWITZERLAND ⌒

NO OTHER COUNTRY OF comparable size in the world can begin to match Switzerland for conjuring up such a variety of stereotyped—albeit delightful—images: isolated verdant valleys echoing with the sounds of calling horns, yodeling hikers, and cowbell-necklaced cattle; magnificent snow-capped mountains with St. Bernard dogs rescuing lost skiers and climbers; gingerbread-decorated chalets with alpine-hatted occupants making precision watches and huge wheels of hole-filled cheeses; tradition-bound banks with secret accounts; tourism and the hotel industry.

Yet there are three Switzerlands, not one; as each section of the country speaks (with a few exceptions) the language and cooks in the style of its influential neighboring nation. Thus the area called the Suisse-Romande, which lies near France, is French-speaking and -cooking. Likewise, the Deutsch-Schweiz region bordering Germany and Austria converses and eats in the southern German manner. If you visit the Ticino region adjacent to Italy, you will hear the Italian tongue and taste Italian specialties such as Pasta, Gnocchi, Osso Buco, and Polenta. Both the adopted "foreign" languages and the cuisines of these regions do have a detectable Swiss accent.

Thanks to the splendid pasturage coupled with fresh mountain air and streams, the Swiss cow produces excellent milk, which eventually becomes some of the world's greatest cheeses. Swiss Emmentaler—the type that most of mankind calls "Swiss cheese"—is the most famous. However, the majority of cheese connoisseurs consider the best one to be Gruyère, a similar cheese with fewer holes and a somewhat more complex, nuttier flavor. Other outstanding examples of Swiss-made semihard to hard cow's-milk cheeses include Appenzeller, Bagnes, Raclette, and Sbrinz. Also worth getting to know are the soft Vacherin Mont d'Or and the hard Sap Sago, the latter a grating cheese perfumed with alpine clover.

Cured meats such as sausages, hams, and Bündnerfleisch are particularly good in Switzerland, especially those coming from the eastern sector around Graubünden (the Grisons, in French). Bakery goods are also outstanding.

Freshwater fish is a treat, the choicest being the *omble chevalier*, a salmonlike char caught in Lake Geneva and other nearby still waters. It is often poached and served plain or with a rich cream sauce.

Fruits and vegetables are good, but tend to be comparatively expensive because of the severe shortage of flat, arable land. (It was once stated that if you flattened Switzerland, it would be the largest country on earth.)

The food served in peasant homes differs quite unmistakably in origin from that which one finds in the large hotels for which Switzerland is famous. While home cooking tends to be hearty, simple food of local inspiration, the hotels usually offer what has come to be known as international or Continental cuisine. Basically this cuisine is a bastardized cooking style with mostly French and northern Italian roots, designed to offend no one. Its cliché menu items are generally overcooked and covered with predictable cream sauces and bland seasonings. Moreover, the hotel menus usually neglect indigenous Swiss dishes, such as these:

Berneplatte A substantial dish of the German-speaking city of Berne, featuring all or most of the following items served on top of a bed of sauerkraut: smoked pork chops, any of several varieties of sausages, pig's feet, simmered beef, bacon, tongue, and boiled potatoes. Beer makes the best liquid accompaniment.

Birnbrot A flat, elongated pastry-loaf filled with dried pears and other preserved fruits. (A specialty from the Deutsch-Schweiz region.)

Bündnerfleisch   A slightly salted slab of beef that has been hung to dry for months in the cool alpine air of eastern Switzerland. This rather expensive, semihardened product is sliced paper-thin and served as an appetizer with a sprinkling of pepper.

Émincé de Veau   Thinly sliced veal sautéed and served with a creamy white-wine sauce. In the Deutsch-Schweiz region, this popular dish is called Geschnetzeltes Kalbfleisch.

Fondue   To prepare this world-famous do-it-yourself dish, a semihard cheese is cut up, lightly floured, and slowly melted in simmering white wine inside a special earthenware chafing dish called a *caquelon*. The mixture is then spiked with Kirsch, cayenne, and white pepper. The diners dip into the sauce (kept warm over a gentle flame) pieces of crusty, day-old bread that they have impaled on the tips of long-handled forks. If the piece of bread falls off the fork into the sauce, tradition dictates that the unlucky person pay a predetermined penalty, which can be the purchase of the next bottle of wine, or a round of drinks—or, if the loser has appeal, a kiss. When the Fondue is nearly finished, the diners remove and share the thickened residue clinging to the bottom of the *caquelon*; to many Fondue fanciers, this is the most desirable portion of the entire Fondue. Most cantons have their own recipe, which may vary according to cheese type and whether certain ingredients such as garlic and mushrooms are used. The best-known version is Fondue Neuchâteloise, which calls for Gruyère and/or Emmentaler cheese and Neuchâtel wine, though Fendant or most other dry white Swiss wines would be equally suitable. Some say hot tea or Kirsch is the ideal beverage accompaniment, with digestive properties to help counteract the heaviness of the Fondue. However, other Swiss enjoy drinking the same type of wine (if not overchilled) that went into the Fondue. Beer, except in a few German-speaking households, is considered too bloating for such a filling dish. You will also find two other dishes cooked at the table that are called Fondue in Switzerland, but in fact they are neither traditional nor indigenous. The first is Fondue Bourguignonne, in which small cubes or strips of beef filet are fork-fried in hot oil, then dipped in a choice of sauces. The second is the dessert dish called Chocolate Fondue: marshmallows and a variety of fresh fruits such as strawberries are dipped and coated in a creamy chocolate sauce.

Leberspiessli   Skewer-broiled calves' liver and bacon that is a specialty of German-speaking Zurich.

Raclette   A section of semihard cheese, such as Bagnes or Raclette, is placed in front of a roaring fireplace—or, less traditionally, in a modern tabletop raclette oven. As the cheese softens, it is scraped with a knife onto a warm platter or directly on to a boiled potato and given a grinding of pepper. Other accompaniments include pickled pearl onions and *cornichons*, a type of sour gherkin. Serve Kirsch or a light dry Swiss white wine, like a Fendant or Neuchâtel.

Rösti   Switzerland's potato pancake prepared by grating, then pan-frying parboiled potatoes.

Veal Cordon Bleu   A breaded and sautéed combination of slices of veal, ham, and cheese, preferably Gruyère.

Wähen   Any of various open-face pastry tarts filled with fruits, vegetables, cheese, onions, or whatever.

BEVERAGES

The Swiss are insatiable wine drinkers. Despite their own extensive vineyards, this tiny mountain nation is one of the world's leading wine importers. While native wines are never great, they are seldom bad, and often slightly effervescent, giving them a refreshing quality. Most of the best wines are white and come from the French-speaking region: Neuchâtel, Fendant, and Dézaley are the three leading labels. The number-one red wine is Dole, from the Suisse-Romande region, though a lot of reds are produced by the Italian-influenced Ticinese. Perhaps the most interesting Swiss wine of them all, from a conversational point of view, is the Vin du Glassier (ice wine). It is aged up to fifteen years in high-altitude cellars, acquiring a strong, hard, and bitter flavor, not to every wine imbiber's liking. What happens to some of Switzerland's least desirable wine? Much of it disappears into *Glühwein*, a hot spiced punch popular with the après-ski set.

If you want a different kind of punch in your après-ski life, try the crystal-clear, national firewater Kirsch, or Kirschwasser, a brandy distilled from fermented cherry juice and pits. (There is also a popular Kirsch on the market that is no more than a cherry-flavored grape brandy, but don't bother your taste buds with this impostor.) Kirsch is also a rewarding cooking ingredient if splashed into Fondues, fruit salads, Cherries Jubilee, and other dishes.

Other Swiss-produced kickers include the herbaceous, aptly named Appenzellerbitter liqueur, and Marc, a brandy distilled from wine-grape residues.

Beer is quaffed with gusto in the German-speaking region, though its popularity and quality fall short elsewhere.

Moscht is one of the frequently consumed apple-cider variants. You will also discover a Swiss preference for hot beverages like coffee and chocolate, the latter made from the universally known "Swiss chocolate."

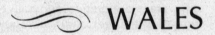 # WALES

WALES, A PRINCIPALITY WITHIN the United Kingdom of Great Britain and Northern Ireland, nowadays has assimilated so much of the English culinary style that most peripatetic palates would not know for certain when they crossed the border from England into Wales. Still, the Welsh imprint survives in some discernible ways.

Of all the Welsh foods, it is the leek that is most closely associated with Wales. Not only does it go into the making of a host of dishes such as Leek and Bacon Pastry and Leek Porridge, it is the national emblem of Wales because, so the story goes, a victorious sixth-century Welsh army attached leeks to its helmets to help distinguish its troops from those of the enemy.

The rearing of the small-sized Welsh sheep is a principal industry, giving the local farmers, fishermen, and miners the needed wool to ward off the wet, bone-chilling wintry climate, as well as the mutton and lamb that are the favorite red meats of these Celtic people.

Also well-loved are Welsh Cawl (mutton-based soup), Snowdon Pudding (flavored with raisins and lemon marmalade), Bara Brith (currant-and-raisin-speckled bread), Bara Ceirch (oatcakes), Crempog (buttermilk pancakes), and griddle cakes in general.

The famous Welsh cheese is the dry, white, mildly acid Caerphilly (pronounced more or less the way porcupines make love). Today, most of this cheese is made across the Bristol Channel in England.

Foods from the wild abound and include game from the

highlands and mountainous inland regions and shellfish and fish from the rugged and beautiful coastline. Welsh Cockle Pie and Cockle Cakes are seashore classics.

Beverage preferences generally resemble those of England, with tea, lager beer, stout, ale, and whisky among the staples.

✑ OTHER EUROPEAN CUISINES

CZECHOSLOVAKIA

Czech cuisine can be distinguished by two major zones: the west has Germanic overtones, while the east has Slavic underpinnings. Yet this country's cooking, as a whole, can be characterized by roast meat and poultry redolent of caraway seeds, chewy sausages, dumplings, and sweet desserts.

Roast goose (Pečeně Husa) and roast pork (Vepřová Pečeně) are traditional favorites often served with sauerkraut and dumplings, to counterpoint and complement the richness of the meat. Roast duck, Svíčková na Smetané (beef filet sauced with sour cream), and Dušené Telecí na Kmíně (veal stew with caraway seeds and mushrooms) are other popular examples of hearty meat entrées.

Houskové Knedlíky are bread dumplings, a particular favorite. Leftover bread is crumbled or cubed, combined with milk and eggs, and steamed in a napkin. The long cylinder of steamed dumpling is then customarily cut with a thread—never a knife—for distribution around the table.

Sausages are common, convenient snack food for any time of day. Párky (Pairs) are long, thin sausages eaten two at a time. The steamed sausages are served on a plate with a roll alongside. Vuřty are shorter, thicker sausages in a tougher casing, but the garlicky Klobasy have the thickest, toughest skin. Taliány are speckled with bits of bacon; while Jaternice are liver-and-lung sausages. Jelita are made with liver, blood, and rice.

Czech desserts include Koláč, yeast rolls stuffed with jam

(apricot and plum are especially popular), poppy seeds, nuts, or cottage cheese; Palachinky, thin pancakes topped with cheese, chocolate, or jam; and the Pišingruv Dort. The last, known outside Czechoslovakia as Pischinger Torte, is a stack of eight-inch circles of *oblaten* wafers (descendants of communion wafers) filled with chocolate meringue and covered with chocolate icing.

Czech beers, especially the light Pilsner, are world famous. Today the best of these beers, like the equally famous Prague ham, are more likely to be exported for foreign exchange than to be enjoyed at home.

YUGOSLAVIA, ROMANIA, AND BULGARIA

The Balkan lands of Yugoslavia, Romania, and Bulgaria combine European and Middle Eastern influences in their foods. Sausages are popular, as they are in Central Europe. Yet the skinless, thumb-shaped minced-meat patties like the garlicky beef Mititei of Romania, the varied meat Ćevapčići of Yugoslavia, and the mixed meat Kebabcha of Bulgaria are all skewer-grilled, like the Middle Eastern *kebabs*, indicative of their origin.

The Middle Eastern Baklava is echoed in the Yugoslavian Dul-Pita, strudel dough filled with walnuts. Yugoslav Slatko (a preserve of whole plums or other fruit, nuts, or flowers cooked in heavy sugar syrup) is a child of both cultures. While the fruit is European, the serving glasses of water as Slatko's traditional accompaniment is Middle Eastern in origin. The Ratluk of Yugoslavia, a rose- and almond-flavored candy, is similar to the Levantine Rahat Lokum.

The Bulgarian Shopska Salata of tomatoes, cucumbers, and Fetalike, brined goat cheese, Sirene (Brynza in Romania) is very much like the Greek Salata Horiatiki. Tarator, a cold yogurt-and-cucumber soup sprinkled with chopped walnuts and dill, also has many Middle Eastern cousins.

Djuveč (Yugoslav), Ghiveciu (Romanian), and Ghivetch (Bulgarian) are medleys of stewed vegetables, sometimes with meat included. The Bulgarian version is topped off with a puff of baked yogurt and eggs, a presentation similar to the Middle Eastern Moussaka. Central European stuffed cabbage gets a Balkan twist in Sarma (Yugoslav), the Romanian Sarmale, and Bulgarian Sarmi—the meat mixture stuffed into cabbage leaves that have been pickled in brine. Ciorba is like the thick and hearty Central European meat or fish and vegetable soup, but in this Balkan version, it assumes a sour taste. Local river and lake fish also add a distinctive note to the Balkan cuisine.

Lacking the Moslem prohibition against alcohol, the Balkan lands produce their world-renowned plum brandy (Slivovitz, Slivova, Sljivovica, or Tuica). Good everyday wines are also produced, especially in Yugoslavia and Romania. Coffee is the most popular nonalcoholic beverage.

Bulgarians are distinguished by their love of yogurt and other dairy products. The salami-type sausage Loukanka is another Bulgarian favorite. Ciubritsa may also be sampled in this area; it is a mixture of powdered herbs and spices made mostly of the herb named *ciubritsa*, which resembles tarragon.

Romanian specialties include Pastramă, meat preserved by heavy salting and smoking, and Pui Românese, chicken stew with white beans. Never order Pui de Baltă unless you're prepared to get "chicken of the marsh"—frog. A popular side dish for any dinner is marinated roasted peppers.

Yugoslavia's famous Dalmatian ham is called Pršut, similar to Italian Prosciutto gastronomically as well as linguistically. Romanian Mamaliga, solidified cornmeal mush, is similar to Italy's Polenta, while the chief starch staple for most other Eastern European people is that good old Central European standby, dark well-textured farmer-style bread. Lonac (meaning "pot"), a specialty of Bosnia, is a stew of mixed meats, root vegetables, and wine, thickened by calves' feet and long cooking.

Of course, each of these three Eastern European countries—Bulgaria, Romania, and Yugoslavia—has distinct regional culinary styles. In Yugoslavia, for instance, the cooking of Slovenia in the northwest is obviously Slavic (and

Germanic), borrowing heavily from Hungary (and Austria). In contrast, the Croatian-Dalmatian cooking is more closely allied to that of Italy. In Yugoslavia's southern regions, such as Macedonia and parts of Serbia, the cooking bears a strong imprint of the Middle East.

PART II
The Middle East
and Africa

 # THE MIDDLE EAST

GENERAL CHARACTERISTICS

Most Middle Eastern cuisines have certain similarities: the chief starch staple is wheat (including bulgur), followed by rice, lentils, chickpeas, and fava beans; the leading vegetable is eggplant; spices and herbs are used lavishly, as are the various members of the onion family (including garlic); the principal cooking oil is olive oil, with sesame oil a distant second. Yogurt is widely used, as the hot climate and the general lack of refrigeration hampers the storage of milk and butter. Sweets are much appreciated but are eaten as between-meal treats. Fresh fruits are the preferred desserts.

Eggplant is roasted, stuffed, or puréed with the sesame-seed-based Tahini sauce for Baba Ghanooj. Tahini added to chickpeas makes Hummis bi Tahini, another popular appetizer. Any vegetable large enough to be stuffed gets a lining of meat and/or vegetables and rice somewhere in the Middle East. Tough meat often ends up in Dolmas, stuffed dishes, or Kufte, meatballs.

Rice, whole wheat, and cracked wheat are served boiled, steamed, or made into Pilaf by sautéeing the grains, adding vegetables, fruit, or nuts, and gently cooking the mixture in a broth. Whole, ground, or crushed nuts are common ingredients, as are tomatoes, lemons, peppers, and olives. Cardamom and cinnamon find their way into most pots.

Classic Middle Eastern sweets include the sugar-frosted, jellylike Rahat Lokum (Turkish Delight), the flaky honey-and-nut Baklava, the shredded-wheat-looking Kadaif, and the various kinds of Halvah, sweet pastes of fruits or nuts.

Coffee and, to a lesser extent, tea are essential to Middle Eastern socializing. Cold drinks made of very sweet fruit syrups, diluted with water, are popular. Yogurt, used by itself, as a sauce, a soup, and thickened into cheese, may also be served as a beverage with the addition of water and a little lemon juice. When an alcoholic beverage is drunk in the Middle East, it is usually the anise-flavored white spirit called Arak, Raki, or Ouzo, depending on where you happen to get thirsty. Beer is also popular.

Arabs traditionally eat with their fingers, with or without an assisting piece of bread. This eating method requires more skill and practice to master than most Westerners realize.

Dishes tend to cross international borders with only slight changes in ingredients or spellings, so it is often difficult to pinpoint which country deserves the titular claim to a particular dish.

GREECE

The cuisine of Greece has been considerably influenced by Turkish cuisine, since Greece was part of the Ottoman Empire from the 1400s until the last century. Though most of the Western world identifies such dishes as Moussaka (baked eggplant casserole), Dolmas (stuffed grape leaves), and Baklava (flaky honey-and-nut pastry) with Greece, they are actually more Turkish in origin.

Because most Greeks are Christians, the cuisine has certain idiosyncrasies vis-à-vis Middle Eastern norms. Pork eating is a good illustration: most Greeks can enjoy it. This is not true in the other Middle Eastern nations (with the exception of Lebanon and Cyprus) because the great majority of their citizens are forbidden to eat pork by the Islamic or the Jewish faith. And because the Greeks as a whole are Christians rather than Moslems and are not forbidden alcohol, they produce and drink a good deal of wine. Much of it is resinous, a flavor that seems to go well with the hearty local fare, particularly when consumed in a *taverna* filled with the pulsating rhythms of the *bouzouki*, the national musical instrument. Ouzo, the licorice-tasting aperitif, is also a popular *taverna* refreshment.

The Greeks are acknowledged masters of spit-roasting whole suckling lamb, a countrywide Easter Sunday tradition. Lamb is also a prime ingredient in countless other Greek dishes, including Souvlakia, skewered broiled lamb chunks wrapped in Pita bread; Gyro, molded minced lamb served in Pita bread; Pastitsio, minced lamb baked with macaroni in a cheese sauce; Kapama, lamb braised with tomatoes; and Arni Kokkinisto, lamb stew. Even Moussaka often contains minced lamb.

Seafood is also popular, especially in the many fishing villages that dot the lengthy coastline. Fish is most frequently used in stews or else simply fried or broiled with olive oil and lemon juice. Octopus and squid are favorites, as is Taramasa-lata, fish roe whipped into a fluffy paste with olive oil, lemon juice, and breadcrumbs. Garides are shrimp, served broiled or prepared with tomatoes and Feta cheese.

Greeks love the lemon-and-egg Avgolemono soup or sauce, the goat's milk Feta cheese, and the flaky spinach-and-cheese Spanakopita. Greek honey is among the world's finest. Coffee is brewed thick, black, and sweet.

LEBANON

Many gastronomes consider this agriculturally rich, half-Moslem, half-Christian nation to have the most refined cuisine in the Middle East, owing partially to the colonizing French influence prior to World War II. The Lebanese citizenry enjoy an abundance of fresh Mediterranean seafood, caught along the country's 100-mile coastline. These and other foods are flavored with cayenne pepper, paprika, and cinnamon, favored spices in the Lebanese kitchen. The leading hard liquor is Arak, a colorless anise-flavored spirit. Some of the Lebanese culinary highlights include:

Kibbe Ground meat—usually lamb—pounded with

cracked wheat and shaped into balls, cakes, or cylinders; served raw, baked, or fried.

Mazza   One of the world's most visually striking feasts: the host places on the serving table anywhere from a dozen to 100 plates, each containing a different type of appetizer or snack: olives, raw vegetables, thickened yogurt, salads like Baba Ghanooj, Hummis bi Tahini, stuffed vegetables, stuffed grape leaves, ad infinitum. (Other spellings of this feast include Mezze and Meze.)

Tabbouleh   A warm-weather salad of cold cracked wheat, mint, parsley, onions, and sometimes tomatoes.

ISRAEL

It is difficult to define Israeli cuisine at this time, since the cooking style of the nation is still evolving. But it is safe to say that it is not the heavy chicken-fat-based cooking style brought to Israel and the United States by Jews who emigrated from cool Middle European countries. Such food is inappropriate to the hot Middle East. Moreover, the general unavailability and/or perishability of certain European cooking staples such as beef has led Israelis—whether they are kosher or nonkosher cooks—to develop cooking styles more like the Arab than the European. The popular sandwich consisting of Arab Pita bread stuffed with meat or Falafel, a deep-fried ground chickpea mixture, is one of many examples. So is the growing practice of cooking meats with fresh fruits.

The orchards and farms of Israel's coastal plains produce some of the world's finest fruits and vegetables, including creamy avocados, dates, and magnificent Jaffa oranges. Many of these products appear on the breakfast table. It is the Israeli custom, perhaps borrowed from the *kibbutz*, to eat a large buffet-style breakfast, often including cheese, bread, fruit, vegetables, yogurt, and hard-boiled eggs.

What determines if foods are kosher? Four rules stand out.

First, dairy foods cannot be eaten with meats. Separate sets of cooking and eating utensils must be maintained for both categories, and two additional sets kept for Passover use. Second, meat may be eaten if it comes from a cud-chewing animal with a divided hoof (consequently, beef can be kosher but pork cannot); if the animal has been ritually slaughtered; if the meat is soaked before cooking to remove the blood; and if the meat is a permitted cut (the hindquarter of the meat is generally forbidden). Third, only fish with fins and scales may be eaten; thus water creatures such as lobster, shrimp, crab, oysters, clams, eels, snails, and frogs are not permissible. Finally, a group of "neutral" foods known as *pareve* (such as eggs, vegetables, fruits, oils, and permitted fish) may be eaten with either meat or dairy foods.

EGYPT

The ancient Egyptians discovered the secret of leavening, and today their descendants are among the world's leading per-capita bread consumers. What is low is the consumption of animal protein. Meat is precious because of scarce pasturage, and fresh seafood can be prohibitively expensive, except along Egypt's Mediterranean and Red Sea coastlines (the Nile is not a fish-filled river). Grains, vegetables, and fruits are the regular diet of most peasants, with beans contributing much of the needed protein. Garlic and coriander are popular seasonings.

Leading specialties include:

Bamia   The Arabic word for "okra," also the name of this popular stew of okra, vegetables, and meat, in portions varying in quantity and quality according to the family budget.

Ferique   Chicken cooked with grains of whole wheat and, sometimes, hard-boiled eggs.

Ful Medammes   This preparation of small brown broad beans with garlic, oil, and hard-boiled eggs reigns as the national dish of Egypt.

Hamam Meshwi   The popular Egyptian grilled pigeon, for those who can afford it.

Melokhia   A soup made by Egyptian peasants for thousands of years with dark-green, gummy *melokhia* leaves, meat or vegetable stock, and a garnish of garlic sauce.

Ta'Amiyah   Spicy fritters of pounded fava beans similar to the Israeli and Arab Falafel.

IRAN

If Lebanon's cuisine is not the best in the Middle East, then perhaps Iran's is. Though basically Middle Eastern in character, the cuisine, especially in and around Teheran, runs counter to the regional norm. Garlic is seldom used, tea rather than coffee is the national drink, and rice rather than bread is the preferred starch staple.

Meat and fruit are frequently cooked together. Apricots are especially popular, as are melons, the legendary fruit of Persia. Lentils and yellow split peas are frequently used to thicken sauces.

Iran's most famous export is its Caspian Sea caviar, with the lightly salted, fresh *beluga malossol* most highly prized by Westerners. The less expensive *sevruga* is also extraordinary if bought fresh rather than in its salty state.

The best-known Iranian specialties include:

Abgusht   A soup-stew of lamb, potatoes, and chickpeas, served over chunks of stale bread.

Chelo   Iranian name for plain rice, often served with a stew—*khoresh*.

Chelo Kebab   Iran's national dish consisting of plain rice cooked with a crisp crust called the *tah dig*, then topped with skewer-barbecued lamb, a raw egg yolk, and a sprinkling of sumac (a slightly sour spice).

Fesenjon   A *khoresh* of duck or chicken with walnuts and pomegranate sauce.

Kuku   A thick, pancakelike omelet, prepared with vegetables and/or meat, that is usually baked and served in wedges.

Polo   Rice cooked with other ingredients such as fine chopped meats, vegetables, and/or fruits, similar to the Indian Biryani.

TURKEY

Turkey, once the nucleus of the Ottoman Empire, has had a great influence on the cuisines of many Middle Eastern countries. It has also borrowed much, making Turkish cookery the most typical example of Middle Eastern cuisine.

Some of the better known Turkish specialties include:

Börek   Cheese- or meat-filled *phyllo*-dough pastries.

Döner Kebab   A large vertical spit used to roast large pieces of lamb or mutton. The constant turning of the spit gives all sides of the meat a crisp crust, which is sliced off and served.

Imam Bayildi   A dish of eggplant stuffed with tomatoes and onions, then baked in olive oil. The name derives from the classic Turkish tale about a priest *(imam)* who fainted *(bayildi)* because his bride used up her entire multi-barrel-sized dowry of olive oil preparing a few eggplant dishes.

Midya Dolmasi   Steamed mussels stuffed with rice and pine nuts; served cold.

Shish Kebab   Marinated cubes of lamb grilled on a skewer; if vegetables such as onions or tomatoes are to complement the Shish Kebab, they are grilled separately.

Within Turkey the local cuisines absorb discreet hints of the cooking styles indigenous to the surrounding countries, be they Greek, Syrian, Iranian, Armenian, or Iraqi.

The world-famous Turkish coffee (some call it Greek

coffee) is made in a *jezve* (or *ibrik*) which looks rather like a long-handled metal cream pitcher. Fine-ground coffee and water are boiled three times in the *jezve* before being poured into tiny cups, grounds and all (the grounds settle to the bottom and are not consumed).

OTHER MIDDLE EASTERN CUISINES

Armenia, today, is a republic within the Soviet Union. Yet, as recently as a century ago, Armenia encompassed a large portion of modern-day Turkey, so little wonder that there is some similarity between Armenian and Turkish cuisines. One of the differentiating characteristics of Armenian cuisine is that its cooks frequently use sesame oil in place of olive oil. They also tend to season more mildly. But, like the Turks, Armenians love to stuff vegetables and eat a lot of rice, wheat grains (including bulgur), lamb (often as Shish Kebab), and yogurt. Meat and poultry are often cooked with fruit. Shusha Kololik and Harpoot Kufta are two of the many Armenian soups containing stuffed meatballs in broth. Lavash is a very thin, crisp, dark bread. Armenian "pizza," also enjoyed in other Middle Eastern lands, is called Lahma bi Ajeen, and is made of small circles of yeast bread topped with cooked ground lamb, sometimes in tomato sauce. Ekmek Kadayif is the famous Armenian bread pastry baked in honey and topped with Kaymak, a clotted cream. Overall, Armenian culinary standards rival the fine cuisines of Lebanon and Iran.

Bedouin nomads roam the deserts of several Middle Eastern nations, carrying with them their tents and traditional foods including lamb, camel, milk, dates, wheat, and rice. Hospitality is a major virtue and best manifests itself in the *mansaf*, a formal banquet. The guests sit around large communal platters piled with Shrak (flat unleavened bread), rice, and boiled lamb, sauced with butter and yogurt. Women customarily do not eat with men. Traditional courtesy demands silence at the *mansaf*; talkative joviality at meals is more common in other Middle Eastern cultures.

Cyprus, the island nation, has two major cuisines: Greek and Turkish. While Cypriots of Greek ancestry outnumber those of Turkish descent by four to one, both cooking styles remain relatively unmingled because both ethnic groups keep and savor their heritages, sometimes at gunpoint. Yet Cypriots are known for their generous dining room hospitality to foreigners. Of the many wines produced in Cyprus, the sweet dessert wine Commandaria is world famous.

Iraq is famous for its *masgoof*, an outdoor barbecue of skewered whole river fish. Pacha is a slow-cooked combination of sheep's head, stomach, feet, and other variety meats in broth. The usual accompaniment to Pacha, and to much other Middle Eastern food, is Turshi, a mixture of pickled vegetables.

Jordan is noted for its creative assortment of Kebabs: plain lamb, marinated lamb, bits of variety meats, or meatballs. *Maqlouba* is a meat-and-vegetable stew served over rice. In the *tabboun*, or clay oven, one bakes Musakahan: chicken parts nestled on circles of whole wheat bread with onions, sumac, pine nuts, and oil.

Saudi Arabia grows wheat, so its people eat bread, Khubz 'Arabi, which is like Pita, and dishes made with kernels of whole wheat, as well as rice dishes. To make Mufallaq, browned wheat grains are cooked with chunks of meat (usually lamb, goat, or camel), onions, and tomatoes. Qursan consists of layers of fresh-baked bread rounds, spicy braised lamb, and vegetables. Eggplants, tomatoes, beans, and green or yellow squash are likely candidates for Qursan. Saliq, a side dish served with meats, is rice cooked twice: once with broth, once with milk.

Syria's cuisine is similar to that of the Lebanese but—for geographical reasons—relies less on the sea. Kibbe, the lamb-and-bulgur (cracked wheat) paste, is very popular. It is often served in fried patties stuffed with meat, onions, and pine nuts. Sfeeha is a small tart shell filled with spiced ground lamb, pine nuts, and yogurt. Grape leaves stuffed with rice are called Waraf Ainab. Karabeej is a Syrian pastry made from semolina shells with often an almond and rosewater filling. The finished dish is bathed in syrup.

 NORTH AFRICA

THE THREE NATIONS OF Morocco, Algeria, and Tunisia, located in the northwestern corner of Africa, are collectively called the "Maghreb," Arabic for "West."

Couscous is the most famous dish of the Maghreb. It is made in a special two-part pot called a *couscousière*. The bottom section contains a stew of meats such as lamb, chicken, fish, beef, or camel—and various vegetables and fruits such as turnips, onions, chickpeas, and raisins. The colanderlike top section holds the grain—usually semolina or cracked wheat—which cooks in the rising steam produced by the stew. An Algerian Couscous is likely to include tomatoes; a Moroccan, to include saffron; a Tunisian, to be spicy. Any Couscous will probably be accompanied by a bowl of Hrisa (or Harissa), a hot pepper sauce. The finished product is heaped on to a large plate, grain below, meat and vegetables on top. All the diners eat from this one plate, scooping up the Couscous with chunks of bread.

Another classic Maghreb dish is the Tagine, a stew cooked in a low, covered earthenware casserole of the same name.

Since most of the inhabitants of this area are Moslems, pork and alcohol are traditionally avoided. The Maghreb, like other Moslem lands, enjoys sweet cakes and pastries, often made with nuts and honey. Thin, flaky rounds of *maslouqua* pastry, similar to the Greek *phyllo*, are used to make savory or sweet pastries. Pastries, dinners, and business transactions are often washed down with very sweet tea brewed with mint leaves.

123

MOROCCO

Moroccan cooking is characterized by the subtle use of multispice blends, and by the frequent combination of meat and fruit. Some famous Moroccan dishes are:

Bisteeya   Sheets of *warka (maslouqua)* pastry layered with cooked pigeon, chopped almonds, egg sauce, cinnamon, and sugar, shaped into a disc, and pan-fried.

Harira   A soup of lamb chunks in an egg-thickened broth. Harira is the traditional food for breaking the Moslem Ramadan fast each night.

ALGERIA

If it were placed over the United States, Algeria would stretch from New York to Florida. But much of Algeria's territory is occupied by the Sahara Desert. The Bedouin nomads of the Sahara contributed Mechoui, whole baby lamb, rubbed with spices and roasted on a spit. The Bedouins also eat one-pot stews of sheep, goat, or camel meat and vegetables; such Tagines are also enjoyed by more settled Algerians. Sferia, a non-Bedouin Tagine of chicken, served with cheese or mutton croquettes, is also popular.

Kesra, the round Arab bread called Pita in other countries, dominates the countryside. Some urbanites prefer the French Baguette, considering it more sophisticated.

TUNISIA

Here are some specialties from this small nation of spicy-food lovers:

Brik   Fried *maslouqua* pastry turnovers containing a whole egg and, often, a spicy filling.

Chakchouka   A spicy stew of tomatoes, peppers, and poached eggs.

Merguez   A very hot sausage.

WEST AFRICA 〜

WEST AFRICA COMPRISES SOME twenty disparate countries stretching for several thousand miles along sub-Saharan Africa's Atlantic coast. From north to south, these largely tropical, densely populated, independent nations include Senegal, Gambia, Guinea, Sierra Leone, Liberia, Ivory Coast, Ghana, Togo, Benin, Nigeria, Cameroon, Gabon, Congo, and Zaire. (The latter three countries are also classified by some people as part of Central Africa.)

While all these countries except Liberia fell under the lengthy colonial rules of Britain, France, or Belgium, the cooking styles of the West Africans (especially those living outside the large cities) were only minimally influenced by the foreign overlords. Yet West Africa did significantly influence the cuisines of the New World. The culinary "roots" of the soul food of America's South as well as the underlying cooking philosophies of the Caribbean and the Bahían region of Brazil can be traced directly back to the slaves' homeland. This demonstrates the strong character of West African cuisine.

Many West African nations have typical national stews. The Congolese version is called Mwamba; it is made with browned beef, lamb, chicken, or fish. Wuolo Sutulu is the Ghanaian chicken stew; Yassa is a Senegalese *ragout* that may be made with chicken, lamb, or fish. Senegal is especially rich in these one-pot meals; it also serves up Mafé, stew with peanuts, and Thiebou-Dien, fish served over tomato-blushed rice and vegetables.

Another famous dish is Jollof Rice, a well-seasoned concoction of meat (red meat, chicken, and/or seafood), tomatoes, and vegetables with rice in the Spanish Paella fashion.

Palavar Sauce is also a well-known culinary creation. Really more of a stew than a sauce, this rich and thick specialty is made with one or more types of dark green leaves (taro, yam, etc.) and various meats such as salt pork, tripe, and/or smoked fish. It is served with or over a starchy preparation like Fufu (see below).

Obviously, between and within each of these many nations, striking cuisine differences exist. The names for nearly identical dishes change within one day's foot journey, which is not surprising when one considers that well over 100 languages and dialects are spoken within West Africa's boundaries. All we can attempt to do in limited space is to provide a perspective on the most significant patterns—and give you the most popular name for any given dish.

One of the most salient characteristics of West African cuisine is the serving of a small portion of hot stew accompanied by a generous helping of a cooked starch staple. Usually the stew is highly seasoned with three recurring flavoring agents: hot chilis (the cuisine tends to be fiery), tomatoes and onions, and, quite often, shallots. In keeping with regional preferences, the stews tend to be glutinously thick and on the oily side. When red meat or chicken is used in the stew, the cook uses only a small portion because of its cost—the poorer the household, the smaller this becomes. Sometimes the stew will contain no meat at all.

Depending on the region, the principal starch staples are yams, cassava, corn, and rice, none of which is indigenous to any particular African country. Neither is millet, which is the leading starch food in the nontropical areas such as northern Ghana and Nigeria. Whatever the starch, it is typically cooked into a porridge or molded into a loaf, mound, or balls. Eating with the fingers, the diner scoops up the savory stew with a small piece of the bland starch staple, deftly placing the combined mass into his mouth.

The principal starch-based specialty is Fufu. More often than not, it appears in the form of small, individual balls of cooked yam, cassava, rice, or plantain paste—though some Fufu is molded into leaves. Still other West African starch classics are Liberia's Dumboy (similar to Fufu) as well as Kenkey and Banku, both usually made from fermented corn dough. You will also find that inexpensive, yet nutritionally sound, mixture of beans and rice on many a household menu.

In addition to the mandatory starch preparation, you will sometimes see a side dish consisting of fresh or cooked fruits or vegetables, on the table or mat. Seldom, however, do you find a fruit or vegetable prepared and served by itself, as is the custom in Europe.

While the various native cuisines may seem unsophisticated by Western definition, the individual dishes can be delicious because most cooks have access to an extensive choice of prime-condition fruits and vegetables. What the home cook doesn't grow in her kitchen garden or can't gather in the wild can be purchased quite readily in open-air markets bustling with colorfully attired buyers and hawkers. In time, you will encounter almost every type of produce found on your own supermarket shelves—cherries, oranges, eggplant, rice, spinach, tomatoes, and onions—not to mention the hundreds of exotic foods. The African shopper finds ackee, breadfruit, cassava, corn, millet, taro root, yams and *garri* (toasted cassava flour) to prepare the meal's starchy foundation. Peanuts, cashews, kola nuts, melon and sesame seeds, and a variety of beans add protein. The market offers beef, goat, lamb, chicken, and other meats; snails, shellfish, and other sea creatures. Okra (called *gumbo* in Swahili), lettuce, spinach, taro, and other green leaves are on display. Fruit is especially tempting: coconuts, fresh and prepared, custard apples, guavas, mangoes, papayas, sour- and sweet-sop, and star apple may all be available. Ginger, herbs, and many kinds of chili peppers are featured to flavor the food. Any good foreign cook is sure to look upon these markets with envy.

The ocean and coastal rivers teem with fish, molluscs, and crustaceans including prawns and shrimp, West Africa's culinary pride. These seafoods are readily available to the shopper in fresh, dried, and smoked states, and, unlike meat, are within most budgets. On a hot tropical day one of the best ways to serve shrimp or prawns is in a cold salad: marinate them in combination with fish, tomatoes, onions, chili peppers, and lime or lemon juice—delicious and cooling.

Mutton and beef are used more sparingly than seafood, and are usually expensive and tough, tenderized by being marinated in lime or lemon juice, a flavor that at times is too pronounced for some Western tastes in West African cooking. Chicken is a traditional favorite, but tends to be too tough, needing marination. Other meats such as pork, lamb, goat, and the indigenous Guinea hen, are used even less. In the northern portion of West Africa, pork eating is not prevalent because a large percentage of the population is restricted by the Moslem faith.

Milk, curd-cheese, and other dairy products are major foods, especially in the less humid interior.

Throughout West Africa the peanut plays a key role as a cooking ingredient and a flavoring agent, rich in protein. Its most celebrated use is in the omnipresent Peanut Stew, also called Groundnut Chop, a combination of whatever is available on a given day—say, chicken and okra—plus the nearly omnipresent tomatoes, onions, and hot peppers. Peanut Soup and peanut sauces are also mainstays.

Palm nut oil is the principal cooking oil and lends a distinctive taste, scent, and mustard-yellow color to the dishes. Next in line come the oils of the peanut, corn, coconut, and sesame seed.

The principal cooking method is slow-stewing—deep-frying comes in second. Broiling, pan-frying, and baking/roasting are also employed, but less often. The beer bottle and the cigarette tin are common measuring devices.

Most of the potent beverages are home-made, in the form of palm wine or beer, brewed from grains like corn or fruits like the banana. Popular nonalcoholic drinks include various tropical fruit beverages, commercially bottled or freshly made by street vendors. Carbonated cola and factory-produced beer are increasing in popularity as are cups of steaming hot (seldom cold) tea and coffee.

Hunger is an ever-present specter that the marginal West African farmer must contend with, a condition largely caused by overpopulation. Nigeria, for example, is merely the size of Texas, yet has to feed a population of 60 million with only a limited number of arable acres.

 # EAST AFRICA

ETHIOPIA

The most characteristic feature of Ethiopian cooking is the use of the tongue-scorching Berberé, a red paste of hot chili peppers, garlic, ginger, fenugreek, cardamom, cloves, allspice, turmeric, and nutmeg, among other spices. Berberé is found in every Ethiopian kitchen and in many dishes, including these well-known specialties:

Injera This large pancake, traditionally made from a fermented batter of teff (a form of millet that grows in the highlands of Ethiopia), is both Ethiopia's daily bread and its tablecloth and silverware. Meals are often served by piling the food onto the Injera; the diners tear off strips of bread and roll the food inside.

Kitfo This dish of raw beef, chopped and seasoned with Berberé and other spices, is also served as a stuffing for peppers. Teré Sega is a similar dish of raw beef cubes dipped into clarified butter and Berberé.

Wat A highly spiced stew of chicken (Doro Wat), meat (Sik Sik Wat), fish, or vegetables cooked in clarified butter with Berberé and plenty of other spices. Metin Shuro is a *wat* of mixed dried legumes, popular with Ethiopian Christians on religious fast days.

Yeshimbra Assa These "chickpea flour fish" are made of ground chickpeas, oil, onions, and Berberé; the mixture is formed into a paste, then molded into fish-shape and fried. Yeshimbra Assa is another traditional dish for meatless days.

Sweet and hot spices are even used in the common cooking medium, Niter Kebbeh, a clarified butter.

Ethiopia's celebrated beverage is Tej, a honey wine dating back to ancient times. Citizens who live in regions that do not produce honey brew Talla, a wheat-, barley-, or corn-based beer.

OTHER EAST AFRICAN COUNTRIES

The East African cuisine in general makes use of classic African ingredients such as peanuts, plantains, bananas, coconuts, spinach, rice, corn, and beans. The usual diet is heavy in starches and often supplemented with dairy products; meat consumption is very low by Western standards. And some East African pastoral tribes such as the Masai seldom if ever slaughter their herds for meat because the animals are more valuable alive as providers of milk and nourishing blood. If done correctly, the tapping of blood does not harm the animal. Arabic influences are noticeable in East African cooking; so are Indian influences such as the use of curry powder.

Kenya's main starch dishes are Ugali (cornmeal or millet porridge) and Irio (a purée of beans or peas and potatoes mixed with corn kernels). M'baazi, another basic dish, is made of boiled pea-beans simmered with onions, spices, and coconut milk. Being a former British colony, Kenya has some British influences, particularly in the introduction of agricultural products—for instance, tasty beef from cattle grazing in the rich grasslands. Kima is a stew of chopped beef and red pepper and/or curry powder (the name and the dish are similar to the Indian *keema*). Maziwa ya Kuganda is a non-alcoholic beverage made of soured skim milk.

Much of Sudan is desert, but central Sudan is a fertile region washed by the Nile. The language and much of the food heritage is Arabic. When meat can be afforded, it is used in such dishes as Bania-Bamia (a stew of lamb and okra) and Maschi (tomatoes or cucumbers stuffed with browned chopped meat). But for the most part, as in Egypt to the north, the average diet is based on starch. Abre, also called Tabrihana, is a sweet fruit-based soft drink.

Tanzania's food resources include bananas, plantains, cassava, coconut, corn, and Zanzibar cloves. Ugali mush, made here with semolina, is a dietary staple. Beef, goat, and chicken are eaten in stews, curries, or simply charcoal-broiled. Ndizi na Nyama is a stew of bananas, onions, tomatoes, and coconut milk—beef can be added if it can be afforded. Wali na Samaki is a peppery concoction made with fried fish chunks on a bed of rice and vegetables. Beer is brewed locally; for more horsepower, try Konyagi, the native gin.

SOUTHERN AFRICA

SOUTHERN AFRICA (AN UNOFFICIAL geographical term) comprises some one dozen countries snuggled together on the lower portion of the vast African continent. Of these, we have chosen three for discussion, the Republic of South Africa, Angola, and Zambia.

REPUBLIC OF SOUTH AFRICA

This nation has a remarkable blend of culinary heritages: the indigenous Africans who, for the most part, lived a primitive hunting-and-gathering existence before the first Europeans arrived; the Dutch settlers who began coming in the 1650s; the Protestant Huguenots who voluntarily emigrated in the 1680s to escape religious persecution in France; the Cape Malays who came as slaves from the Malay Peninsula and the East Indies; the Asian Indians who arrived in great numbers to work on the sugar-cane plantations; the British who settled and took over in the late eighteenth century. Of all these influences, the Dutch, Cape Malay, and Asian Indian had the most noticeable culinary impact.

While most of South Africa is not suitable for serious agricultural pursuits, the areas that are arable tend to be so productive that one could regard this nation as the biblical land of milk and honey. Fruits and vegetables of pleasing variety and quality, including the famous *naartje* (a tangerine), and luscious ripe tomatoes, are grown in home gardens and commercial farms. This bounty is often preserved by home-canning methods, a chore that, along with baking, is enjoyed by the middle-income homemaker.

Seafood is an important part of the South African diet. This is especially true around Cape Town, where the cold Atlantic waters meet the warmer Indian Ocean, yielding a wide selection from both habitats. Best known is the South African rock lobster tail, frozen and exported around the globe. (Technically, the exported crustacean is not a lobster in terms of ichthyological classification and taste.) Another noted product of the sea is periwinkles, those tiny sea snails that are locally eaten raw or cooked. Bivalves such as oysters, clams, and mussels can also be delightfully flavorful.

Chicken, followed by lamb/mutton and pork, is the best-selling meat, although beef is growing in popularity. The availability of that long-time favorite, game, is decreasing, the direct result of overhunting, diminishing wild acreage, and new environmental protection laws. Still, if you can sample a legally acquired springbok gazelle, your palate may never stop thanking you. This eating experience will be even more memorable if the springbok is cooked at a *braaivleis*, South Africa's great barbecuing tradition, where sausages, corn-on-the-cob, and other outdoor treats complement the grilled or roasted meat.

Other well-known specialties of the South African cuisine include:

Biltong   Air-dried beef, or—sometimes—game meat. This jerky-type product was a life-sustaining mainstay of the Boers during their historic, northward Great Trek into Africa's interior in the 1830s.

Bobotie   A baked, curry-seasoned, ground-meat pie, often with a frothy egg-and-milk custard topping.

Bredie   A heavily seasoned spiced stew, made of meat (usually lamb), onions, and vegetables, served with rice. Tomato Bredie is the best-known version of this specialty, introduced by the Cape Malays. Spinach and Pumpkin Bredies are also popular.

Ingelegde Vis The best-known example of South Africa's many types of pickled fish. The prepared fish, originally developed by the Cape Malays, can last for months without refrigeration.

Mealie Name for corn (maize), which is frequently served on-the-cob, or made into a beer. Mealie is also a popular ingredient in bread or porridge—the basic diet of the poor South African. The porridge is also frequently made with "Kaffir corn," the local name for millet.

Melktert Literally, Milk Tart, a milk-egg-and-sugar dessert custard prepared in a round pastry shell.

Sosaties The Cape Malay version of Shish Kebab: marinated, cubed meat grilled on a skewer, a very popular *braaivleis* dish.

Other popular South African dishes include Chicken Pie; Frikkadels (seasoned meat patties); Boerewors (literally, Farmer's Sausage, made of seasoned beef with pork); Cape Gooseberry Jam; Blatjang (a type of chutney); Scrambled Oyster Eggs; and numerous dishes adopted from India (curries) and the East Indies (*sambals*, etc.). Dessert items include Koesisters (braided crullers) and Soetkoekies (spice cookies).

South Africans are the world's greatest per-capita drinkers of brandy, practically all of which is Cape brandy. The country also manufactures the tangerine-flavored Van de Hum liqueur as well as Sherries that some connoisseurs consider to be almost the equal of the fine Spanish Sherries.

Table-wine-making is also a major industry—the best coming from the Paarl Stellenbosch area east of Cape Town. Much of it is bottled under the KWV cooperative label. Distinctive South African wines include white Steen and the red Pinotage, a cross between the Pinot Noir and the Hermitage groups.

Beer is rather popular. Rum has many adherents, especially in the sugar-cane region in the northwest section of the country.

ANGOLA

The stamp of Portuguese cuisine is indelible in Angola, the last of several dozen African countries to become independent of European suzerainty. A visitor is quick to spot Portuguese dishes (and even Brazilian specialties from Portugal's one-time colony directly across the Atlantic Ocean) in restaurants and in high-income homes.

Yet, for the average Angolan, the cuisine remains basically mid-African, reflecting what the nearby lands and waters can best yield—though some obviously Portuguese cooking methods and ingredients are apparent, like salt cod and goat meat.

Fresh seafood is a basic along the lengthy coastline; the crustaceans are superbly succulent. As we travel inland, the chicken and the goat gradually replace seafood as the chief protein source. Even farther inland on Angola's vast, thinly populated, pastoral highlands the inhabitants rely heavily upon milk and its derivatives, such as fresh cheese curd, to supply the body's protein requirements.

Starch, the backbone of practically all ethnic diets, comes in the form of porridges (usually cassava meal) and breads made from wheat and other flours.

If one dish deserves to be tagged "Angola's national dish," it may well be Galinha Muamba. Chicken pieces are fried in a palm nut oil with hot chilis, onions, and various vegetables.

Angolan coffee is a major international commodity and is much appreciated by the Angolans, especially those belonging to the middle and upper classes. Wine, too, has some devotees, though cheaper beverages—beer and fruit juices—are more popular with the average citizen.

ZAMBIA

This landlocked country, surrounded by seven nations, does not fit perfectly into either the Southern African or the East African cooking category. Instead, Zambia is a buffer zone between these two vast African regions. Because the cuisine does bear a slight resemblance to that of Southern Africa, it is placed within this section of the book.

The basic dish of this country is Nshima, a thick porridge consisting of cornmeal in the south or millet in the northeast. It is typically served with a vegetable or vegetable stew, all eaten with the fingers. If the family can afford meat (such as chicken) or dried fish, this luxury replaces or shares the spotlight with the vegetables. When fish is used, the bones are not wasted, they are eaten.

In addition to corn and millet, an assortment of fruits and vegetables is available, including groundnuts (peanuts), cassava (both the root and the more nutritious leaves), sweet potatoes, pumpkins, onions, rape, tomatoes, and pawpaw (papaya). The latter is eaten uncooked when ripe, or cooked when it is still green. The leaves of this fruit can also be used for tenderizing meat.

Salt is Zambia's characteristic seasoning, and for some Zambian cooks, the only seasoning. By European and American standards, the saline flavoring agent is used to excess.

Virtually every village in this country has its own recipe for corn or millet beer. The beverage is usually drunk by itself, not to enhance a meal; and in difficult economic times, it may substitute for a meal. It must be noted, however, that this brew is significantly more nutritious than Western-style beer, the type of refreshment that has become the most popular alcoholic beverage of the Zambian middle class.

A new food pattern is evolving in Zambia. Marketplace stalls are increasingly becoming laden with fresh fruits and vegetables traditionally associated with faraway lands. In the capital city of Lusaka, for instance, the shopper is apt to find luscious oversized strawberries in season. Even the more remote towns and villages feature items such as Chinese cabbage.

In the past, the dramatic seasonal change in Zambia's climate—wet to dry—usually resulted in an equally dramatic seasonal change in the people's diet. Today the contrast is fading, thanks to the major agricultural advancements, such as irrigation techniques, which help in the cultivation of fresh produce from otherwise parched land. But, as is the case everywhere, no one has discovered a way to keep prices from escalating during this rainless period.

PART III
Asia and the Pacific

 # AUSTRALIA

AUSTRALIANS BY AND LARGE enjoy their food simply cooked and in hearty portions. Most of the first European settlers (who arrived less than two centuries ago), were hard-working British commonfolk, seldom known for their devotion to sophisticated cooking techniques. Once rooted in Australia, they were too preoccupied with their pioneer duties to think of food preparation in terms other than appeasing hunger and nourishing the body.

This culinary attitude was firmly entrenched until just after World War II when new immigrants began to enter Australia from Europe. These "new Australians" or "newcomers," as they are called by the old-generation Aussies, came and continue to come from countries like Italy, France, Greece, Switzerland, Germany, and Holland, bringing with them the cooking methods and preferences of their homelands. Newcomers also migrated from Canada and the United States as well as from relatively nearby Asian lands such as China, Japan, and the Philippines. But the percentage of Asians who have gained entry is small, owing to Australia's restrictive immigration quotas.

While this multifaceted culinary impact has been moderate to date, the foreign influence is sure to blossom eventually. Australia's tropical, subtropical, and temperate regions yield an incredible variety of high-quality fruits, vegetables, dairy products, meats, and seafoods, the essential foundations of any great cuisine. It's merely a matter of time before Australia's culinary triumph will come.

Fruits are generally superb and include passion fruit,

mangoes, pineapples, avocados, oranges, bananas, soursop, papayas, tamarillos (tree tomatoes), grapes, apricots, loquats, apples, pears, and a wide assortment of berries. Vegetables also come in wide variety and are almost as outstanding as the fruits; many pumpkinlike squashes are particularly relished.

Meat is the principal source of protein. Leading the way is beef which, while seldom aged, is relatively inexpensive in Australia, since that is one of the world's biggest cattle-rearing countries. The favorite beef products are steak and roasts, prepared in a variety of ways. Breakfast is likely to consist of steak and eggs; lunch and dinner is likely to feature roast beef, Yorkshire Pudding, and meat pies, all obviously British in origin. Beef is fundamental to the classic Australian dish, Carpet Bag Steak, a roast or steak stuffed with fresh raw oysters, then grilled or sautéed.

This great island continent of meat-eaters also loves lamb, but to a lesser degree. In New Zealand, the reverse is true.

Kangaroo meat is not very popular in Australia. When this national animal is eaten, it is usually in the form of Kangaroo Tail Soup, though barbecued kangaroo roasts are enjoyed by some pioneers living on the open stretches of the country's vast Outback.

Australians enjoy fish and shellfish from their extensive coastline, though not as much as they enjoy beef. The bountiful ocean provides sweet and succulent rock lobsters, crayfish, prawns, shrimp, crabs, and other crustaceans. The most famous shellfish is the celebrated rock oyster. Rarer seafoods include the Moreton Bay bug and the Queensland mud crab, the latter in itself worth a trek to the "down under" continent. Fish, which come from warm tropical and cool temperate waters as well as from inland streams and lakes, include local varieties of snapper, whiting, and trout, and the barramundi, a much-appreciated ocean denizen. Some of the firmer-fleshed fish end up in the British-inspired Fish and Chips.

Baking is one of the mainstays of Australia's culinary tradition, a direct outgrowth of the days when every family produced almost everything it needed for sustenance—and some families still do. Today the ovens of professional bakeries and home kitchens produce items such as scones, biscuits, and cakes, often for teatime. Damper Bread, a simple flour-and-water dough wrapped around a stick and baked over a campfire, is a strictly indigenous creation. Pavlova Cake, also popular in New Zealand, was apparently named in honor of the renowned Russian ballerina who visited both these countries in the early twentieth century. Basically, it is a baked meringue shell filled with whipped cream and decorated with one or more types of fresh fruits. (Except for the fruit garnish, it resembles the Vacherin or the Viennese Spanische Windtorte).

Australian pioneers depended on home-preserved fruit, vegetables, and meat. Their descendants, despite access to a wider range of fresh food, continue the tradition. A contemporary offshoot of this traditional desire to preserve food is the propensity to freeze food, sometimes to the detriment of flavor and texture. Another characteristic of Australian cooks is their tendency to overcook.

Foreign food influences are most readily apparent in the fast-food sector. You will find the local population queuing for pizzas, hotdogs, hamburgers, french fries (sometimes called Tasmanian Fries) and Coca-Cola. In large cities such as Sydney, you will find an array of ethnic restaurants representing various cuisines. These restaurants are not particularly popular because of the Aussie's general preference for the familiar.

Aussies are not staunch advocates of eating out—except in the sense of picnicking or backyard barbecuing. Smörgåsbord-type meals are very popular. This self-service style is an outgrowth of Australia's long-standing (though decreasing) labor shortage.

The workday starts and ends early; consequently, the Australians eat their meals at an earlier hour than do Europeans.

BEVERAGES

Tea is the national drink of Australia. Of special interest is Billy Tea, traditionally made by tossing loose tea in a water-filled "billy" can, placing it on top of a campfire, and allowing the brew to steep until it is very strong.

Australian beer is among the world's finest, and it is strong in both alcohol and character. Beer brands tend to be regional. You'll find, for example, Toohey's in Sydney, Swan in Perth, Foster's and Victoria Bitters in Melbourne. The southern-brewed beers tend to be the strongest.

Wine is big business and the latest mass-production techniques from harvesting to bottling are employed. Variations in vintages are not as pronounced as in France.

Australian red wines are on the robust side without much subtlety, though some interesting examples come from small areas like the valleys of Hunter and Barosso as well as from Coonaware. Chateau Tahbilk is also worth sampling. Shiraz and Cabernet Sauvignon are two of the best red varietals, though most Australian red wine is generic, usually Claret or Burgundy. White wines almost always lack sufficient acid (including the generic Riesling and Chablis), though most have some fruit, a saving grace. The best white is probably the varietal Rhine Riesling. A great deal of cloyingly sweet fortified wine is also produced, as are sparkling wine and brandy.

THE ABORIGINES

The original Australians—the Aborigines—arrived in prehistoric times, some believe 30,000 years ago. Theirs was principally a primitive food-gathering society. Most of their cooking was done on a spit or in a fire pit. One favorite method was to encase a food like a lizard in clay, then let it slowly bake in the hot coals. After an hour or two, the hardened clay packet was removed from the heat and was cracked open. Today few Aborigines remain faithful to their ancestral culinary traditions.

Except for those dwindling Aborigine tribes who still live off the land in sparsely settled regions, most of the modern-day Aborigines have joined the white man's economic structure and have more or less adopted his twentieth-century cooking methods, equipment, and ingredients.

CHINA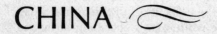

CHINESE COOKING IS KNOWN internationally for its excellence, but it should also be recognized for its remarkable economy of materials and fuel: a little meat or seafood is shredded into quick-cooking pieces; a whole fish is presented and enjoyed in full; several steamers full of dumplings are stacked in a hot wok. Even chicken and pork bones and trimmings are saved to make stock.

Chinese cooking stresses a harmonious blending of foods—a dynamic balance between sweet and sour, rich and lean, bright-colored and neutral, smooth and crunchy. Each food should be *hsien*—at the peak of flavor or quality. Some foods are eaten fresh; others are preferred smoked, dried (cloud-ear fungus, scallops, and oysters, for example), or fermented, because the flavor emerges best in that form.

MEAT, FOWL, AND FISH

Pork is the most popular meat, eaten fresh, barbecued, or in the small dried sausages called Lop Cheung. Beef is well liked, but less common because cattle are traditionally raised as work animals, not for milk or meat. When beef is eaten, the shin is a favorite cut; it is sinewy and cooks to a gelatinous texture much appreciated by the Chinese. Lamb is popular in the north, but seldom eaten in the rest of China. However, chicken and duck are favorites throughout most of the country. Fish (especially fresh fish such as carp and yellow pike), shrimp, prawns, lobster, fresh and dried oysters, and dried abalone are also significant in the traditional Chinese diet. To preserve all the flavor, fish are often cooked and served whole. Fish heads are a delicacy in China.

VEGETABLES AND FRUITS

Popular leafy vegetables include *bok choy* (a vegetable with white stems and dark green leaves), celery cabbage, head cabbage, spinach, mustard greens, and red-in-snow (a leafy green similar to mustard greens; often pickled). Melons, eaten in savory rather than sweet dishes, include bitter melon (a dark green squash containing quinine), hairy melon (a fuzzy cylindrical squash), and winter melon (a pale green squash with a hard rind coated in white). Snow peas (small sweet edible pods with tiny peas inside), small white eggplant, lacy lotus root, various fresh and dried fungi, bamboo shoots, and water chestnuts are other texture and flavor ingredients. Vegetables of the cabbage and turnip families are preserved for winter use, often by salting. The soybean, yielding soy sauce, bean sprouts, bean milk, and bean curd, is a mainstay of Chinese agriculture and diet. Bean milk, prepared by forcing water through mashed cooked soybeans, serves many of the functions milk serves in a dairy culture. Bean curd, which is bland, inexpensive, and high in protein, is used to absorb other flavors and add nutrition to many dishes. Fruits such as the lichi, kumquat, red date, longan (dragon's eye), and peach (a symbol of longevity) are popular at the end of meals or as snacks. Sweetened pastes of sesame seeds or red beans are used to fill sweet pastries.

STARCH STAPLES

Rice is the main food of south China, while other cereal grains, such as wheat, reign in the north. Boiled or steamed rice *(fan)* is the heart of every family meal. Congee or Jook is a thin rice gruel eaten for breakfast with bits of spicy relishes, or eaten plain, in times of illness, overindulgence, or stress—security food. In addition to wheat, the north grows millet, sorghum, and barley more easily than rice, so steamed breads, pancakes, cooked grains, and noodles are more common starch staples. White rice or bean-flour noodles (cellophane noodles) are popular throughout China for snacks and light meals. Lo Mein are wheat noodles that resemble vermicelli. Noodle dishes—with the noodles in long, uncut strands—are traditional at birthday parties because they symbolize long life. Wheat dough is used to make spring rolls, erroneously called egg rolls in the West; the true Chinese egg rolls are omelets rolled up jellyroll-style around a filling. Wheat dough is also the base for dumplings, buns, and "dot-hearts." A "dot-heart" (Tien Hsin in the north, Dim Sum in the south) is a morsel of dough wrapped around a savory filling to touch the heart with happiness. To *yum cha* is to eat a light meal or snack of "dot-hearts" and drink plenty of tea.

TEA

The Chinese divide their teas into "red" (the color of good omen and the color of the brewed tea, yet referred to as "black" in the West because the leaves are blackish) and "green" teas. Like the Japanese, the Chinese enjoy teas scented with flowers; jasmine is a favorite. Also like the Japanese, the Chinese steep the same tea leaves several times, esteeming the subtlety of second-brewed tea.

FLAVORING INGREDIENTS

Chinese cooking makes use of comparatively few herbs and spices. Garlic, coriander, Chinese chives, star anise, and five-spice powder are among the most important. Five-spice powder is a mixture of sweet and pungent spices such as anise seed, Szechuan pepper, fennel seed, cloves and cinnamon. Szechuan pepper, also called *hwa chiao* and *fagara*, resembles a reddish-brown peppercorn in appearance. The Chinese kitchen also relies on condiments such as dark and light Soy Sauce, Oyster Sauce (made from dried oysters), Sesame Paste, Black Bean Sauce, Plum Sauce (familiar to Westerners as Duck Sauce), and Hoisin Sauce. Hoisin Sauce is a thick, dark, spicy mixture with a soybean base. Lobster Sauce is not made of lobster; it is a blend of eggs, ground pork, ginger, and Black Bean Sauce served on lobster. Similarly, "fish flavor" (as in the Szechuan dish of Pork with Fish Flavor) indicates a blend of seasonings such as garlic, ginger, and rice wine used to cook fish.

COOKING METHODS

The accomplished Chinese cook must master many techniques, and must be able to choose the right method to bring out the full flavor of each foodstuff.

Stir-frying (chow) is a method of quick-cooking in oil the previously prepared slivers of food. The traditional utensil is the wok, a squat, bowl-shaped pan made of thin iron. The foods must be cut in small pieces with a maximum surface area so that the oil (usually peanut or soybean oil) can cook the food very quickly, preserving fresh flavor, color, and vitamins. The principal ingredient (meat, poultry, seafood, or the most important vegetable in a vegetarian dish) is cooked first, in the center of the wok. When that is cooked, it is pushed to the sides of, or temporarily removed from, the wok, and the complementary food (vegetable or vegetables) is cooked in the center. The principal ingredient and its complement are combined, perhaps with a sauce. The traditional cooking technique calls for "hot wok, cold oil": the pan is preheated, the oil added just before the principal ingredient is cooked. Often a splash of sesame oil is added at the end of cooking to perfume the stir-fried food. Wok hay ("wok aroma" or "presence"), the sign of a great cook, is a Chinese term for the smell and taste of food perfectly stir-fried in a well-seasoned wok.

Jing is deep-frying, also done in a wok. Deep-frying is used for dumplings, spring rolls, and sometimes for fish. *Cha shao*, barbecuing, is especially popular with the Cantonese. The food to be "lacquer-roasted" is marinated in a sweet soy-based sauce, then roasted with several bastings of the same sauce. *Shu*, or oven-roasting, is a method of suspending meat over a pan of water in an oven. The meat stays juicy in the steam; the pan catches the savory drippings. *Jow* is a method of cooking food by contact with live steam. Several cylindrical bamboo steamers can be stacked inside a wok, so that several foods are cooked at once with little expenditure of fuel. "Red cooking" is slow braising with dark soy sauce and sugar. The food is actually brown or black but is called "red-cooked" because the color red is associated with happiness in China.

Methods of cooking include the *lu*, fire-pot, and clear-simmering. A *lu* is a master sauce of broth and flavorings, in which partly cooked foods are simmered. When the food is done, it is removed, and the *lu*, richer than ever, is ready to go on. Some *lus* have ongoing lifespans measured in decades, some even in centuries. As long as the *lu* is periodically reheated to kill bacteria and is replenished with fresh liquid and flavoring ingredients, it can be immortal. The fire-pot is a northern Chinese chafing dish used for table-cooking or reheating fine-cut foods in broth. The cooked foods are dipped in a spicy sauce. There are many versions of the fire-pot, among them the Chrysanthemum Pot, using a large variety of meats and vegetables; the Mongolian Pot of lamb and vegetables; the Ten Varieties Pot, with at least ten kinds of precooked vegetables and meat. Clear-simmering is a slow-cooking method of immersing meat or vegetables in water. Clear-simmering produces a very rich broth, esteemed in China as a cooking ingredient or as a soup.

EATING METHODS

Eating is the Chinese diner's only task. The chefs consider it their responsibility to provide properly seasoned food appropriately portioned for eating with chopsticks. Sometimes whole fish or whole birds are served; the flesh is so tender it can be stripped off with chopsticks.

Soup is an important part of the Chinese meal. Slurping your soup is perfectly good manners at a Chinese dinner table; it shows you appreciate the soup and want to savor it steaming-hot.

A traditional Chinese family dinner includes soup and one dish per person. All the dishes are placed on the table at once and the diners help themselves, eating a few morsels at a time from their rice bowls. The boardinghouse reach is more polite than asking for dishes to be passed. Soup is sipped throughout the meal; tea comes at the end. Some Chinese from particular areas in the south drink tea with the meal, but they are in the minority. The custom of drinking tea with dinner was spread outside China by restaurateurs seeking to gain customers.

THE BANQUET

A Chinese banquet—a *chiu hsi*, or "wine spread"—is a very different matter. The foods are served in courses, and very elaborate or expensive dishes such as Shark's Fin Soup, Bird's Nest Soup, Sea Cucumber, and Braised Bear Paw are served. The banquet begins with nibbles of dried fruits and nuts, goes on to cold plates and stir-fries, then pauses for a midmeal dessert, such as Eight Precious Pudding (steamed rice colorfully accented with dried fruit), its purpose being to clear the palate for the *daah tsai*, or "big affairs." Pork is considered too commonplace for a banquet; the host will present the most exotic dishes he can almost afford. Two or more soups are served at various stages of the banquet, again, to clear the palate and add variety. The guests will enjoy the food and endless toasts in Shaosing, warmed yellow rice "wine" (really a non-brewed beer), Mur Guri Low, potent rose-flavored wine, or Mao Tai, the centuries-old liqueur (*not* named after Chairman Mao) or other wines or spirits. A whole fish may be presented at the end of the banquet with the head pointed in the direction of the guest of honor. Rice, which has been conspicuously absent from the meal thus far, is sometimes served as the final course, but no one is expected to eat it. The bowl of rice illustrates that the host has served more food than the guests could consume. Outside the banquet, it is a social sin not to finish every grain of rice served; leaving even a bit is an insult to the labor needed to grow the grain. Chinese children are taught that every wasted grain of rice means a pockmark on the future spouse's face.

The fillings of "dot-hearts," the stir-fries, and red-cooked dishes on the family table, the *daah tsai* at banquets, vary from place to place within China; so we shall examine the major regions of the Chinese cuisine.

CANTONESE CUISINE

Cantonese cooking is the most diversified and subtly seasoned and least oily of China's major cuisines. Because the region produces China's finest raw ingredients, Cantonese chefs strive to bring out natural flavors rather than obscuring them with extra seasoning. Flavoring agents much employed in Cantonese cooking include oyster sauce, salted fermented black beans, light soy sauce, rice wine vinegar or beer, ginger, and chicken stock. Color harmony is deemed especially important.

Canton cooks stir-fry many of their dishes, the meat until *just* done; steaming and "lacquer-roasting" are other popular cooking techniques. Seafood, pork, and chicken—in small portions—are the chief sources of animal protein. Some famous dishes include:

Buddha's Delight   A meatless dish of many fresh and dried vegetables combined in a stir-fry. China's Buddhist monks, forbidden to eat meat, evolved a rich and diversified vegetarian cuisine. They developed recipes for bean curd and wheat gluten (developed from wheat flour) that mimic meat or simply provide variety.

Lemon Chicken   Batter-dipped chicken pieces are fried, then stir-fried with lemon and cornstarch until they are glazed.

Lobster Cantonese Lobsters are little known in China outside of Canton. In this treatment, stir-fried lobster chunks in the shell are sauced with ground pork, eggs, and garlic. One of the major differences between this dish cooked in the Cantonese style and the style used for foreigners is that the non-Cantonese sauce is thickened too heavily.

Steamed Fish with Black Bean Sauce, Barbecued/ Lacquered Pork or Duck, and Sliced Pork in Oyster Sauce are also Cantonese specialties.

The terms on Chinese restaurant menus are usually transliterations of Chinese words pronounced with a Cantonese accent. This is so because most Chinese restaurant owners in the West are of Cantonese extraction. Because few Westerners who enter these restaurants are equipped with a working knowledge of Cantonese or any other Chinese dialect, we believe this glossary of common food and menu terms will be helpful.

Bao Filled bun

Bok Choy A Chinese vegetable with white steams and dark green leaves

Bor Choy Spinach

Bow Yu Abalone

Cha Tea

Chow Stir-fried

Chaing Yu Soy sauce

Char Shu Roast pork

Chow Fun Stir-fried broad wheat noodles

Chow Mai Fun Stir-fried rice noodles

Chow Mein Wheat noodles stir-fried to crispness

Chow Yua Dark soy sauce

Choy Vegetables

Chu Boiled

Dim Sum Small filled pastries and dumplings

Ding Diced

Don Egg

Dow Foo Bean curd

Dow Nga Bean sprouts

Faa Tsai Chopsticks

Fan Cooked rice or a meal

Gai Chicken

Gee Yuk Pork

Geong Ginger root

Gow Yuk Beef

Gum Wah Ham

Guy Choi Mustard greens

Har Shrimp

Hing Yoke Clams
Hon Lon Dow Snow peas
Ho See Oysters
Ho Yu Oyster Sauce
Hong Shew Braised
Hy Crab
Jing Steamed
Jook Sun Bamboo shoots
Jow Deep-fried
Jup Gravy
Lo Mein Long wheat noodles
Loong Har "Dragon shrimp"—lobster
Lop Cheung Sausage
Lou Gravy
Mai Fun Rice Noodles
Mein Noodles
Mi Yee Carp
Moo Goo Mushrooms
Opp Duck
Pai Spareribs
Pien Sliced

Shen Ch'ou Light soy sauce
Shi Shredded
Shu Roasted
Soong Minced
Subgum Mixed
Sun Sour
Tim Sweet
Wonton Stuffed noodles
Wor Casserole
Wor Ba Sizzling rice cakes
Wor Hip Har Butterfly Shrimp
Wor Shew Pressed
Wun Yee Cloud-ear fungus
Yeung Yuk Lamb
Yo Yu Squid
Yu Fish
Yu Chee Shark's fin
Yu Cho Scallops
Yu To Fish maw
Yuk Meat

NORTHERN AND "MANDARIN" CUISINES

This is the food of the provinces of Hopei (which includes Peking), Shantung, and Honan (not to be confused with Hunan). "Mandarin cuisine," an Occidental term, properly refers to the elaborate and delicate specialties prepared for the elite members of the now-defunct Imperial Court. Mandarin dishes include Bird's Nest Soup, Shark's Fin Soup, and other banquet specialties that originated in various parts of the country before being brought to Peking and refined by the chefs of government officials, the Mandarins.

Everyday Northern cuisine is distinct from China's other

major regional cuisines in a number of ways. Wheat (in the form of noodles, steamed buns, and dumplings) rather than rice is the chief starch staple. Mongolian influence is strongly felt and includes the use of lamb and mutton in such Northern specialties as Mongolian Fire-Pot, Genghis Khan Barbecue, and Jellied Lamb.

Among characteristic Northern flavoring agents are fermented soy bean paste, dark soy sauce, rice wine, and members of the onion family, especially garlic, leeks, scallions, and chives.

The cuisine of Honan and Shantung provinces tends to be a bit sweeter than that of Peking and Hopei Province. Northern cuisine is more heavily seasoned than the cuisines of Canton and Shanghai but less so than those of Szechuan and Hunan. Some Northern specialties are:

Chicken Velvet   A very delicate forcemeat of chicken breast and egg white, often poached and presented with walnuts, poached in soup, or deep-fried.

Moo Shi Pork   Slivers of pork, egg, tiger-lily buds, cloud-ear fungus, and other vegetables that are stir-fried together, combined with a light sauce, and eaten rolled up in Pings, thin flour pancakes. Moo Shi Pork was created by peasants as a dish for using up leftovers.

Peking Duck   This term refers to both the bird (an ancestor of the Long Island duckling) and the cooking process. The chef first pulls the skin away from the flesh with a sharp knife, being careful not to pierce the skin. He then pulls the skin back and seals it over the duck. (Most Chinese restaurants omit this process and, therefore, do not serve authentic Peking Duck). Next, the duck is basted with a honey-and-vinegar mixture and is hung in a hot circular clay oven—the skin puffs away from the flesh, becoming succulently crisp. It is this skin that is the most precious part of the dish. When the Peking Duck is brought to the table, the diner, using an edible scallion brush, smears a sweet bean paste onto a Ping, a thin flour pancake. He then drops the brush on top of the Ping and covers it with cut segments of the duck skin. He then rolls the Ping (as one would a Mexican Taco) and—holding it in his fingers—proceeds to bite into one of the world's culinary masterpieces.

Tea Eggs Hard-boiled eggs, with cracked shells, are marinated in hot spiced tea until a distinctive cracked pattern and flavor is apparent.

SZECHUAN AND HUNAN CUISINES

The cooking of Szechuan Province, an isolated triangular fertile plain enclosed by three massive mountain ranges, is hot, spicy, and relatively oily. The topography helps produce a hot and humid climate that is conducive to Szechuan's most characteristic seasoning, hot chilis. These tongue-scorchers were not introduced into Szechuan until a few hundred years ago, when they were brought over from their New World habitat. The use of chilis is drastically reduced or eliminated in the dishes served at banquets. Even on the peasant level, the people prefer the dishes on the table to have degrees of hotness varying from mild to fiery. This is in contrast to the monotonous everything-as-hot-as-possible approach favored by many non-Chinese Szechuan restaurant-goers. Making one Szechuan dish hotter than another is not a measure of a chef's talent; all it takes is the addition of extra chili, a feat that could be performed by a trained monkey. Epicures judge a Szechuan chef by the subtly complex overtones of his sauces and whether they complement the other ingredients in his dishes.

Besides chilis, major flavoring agents include Szechuan pepper (this gives Szechuan cooking a distinct peppery taste, not burning hotness); the onion family, including garlic and scallions; Five-Spice Powder; mushrooms and other fungi; ginger and fennel. Szechuan cooks strive for "manifold flavor," taste with nuances of heat, bitterness, sweetness, salt, and sharpness.

The primary animal foods are chicken, pork and—to a

lesser extent—game from the mountains. These meats are often smoked or barbecued and sometimes twice-cooked, a method that involves steaming or simmering the meat, then stir-frying or deep-frying it, which gives it a dry and chewy texture much loved by the Szechuanese. Fish plays a minor role, as the province is far from the sea and the local rivers and lakes yield but a light catch. Famous Szechuan dishes include Spiced Meat in Tangerine Sauce, Chicken with Hot Peppers, Szechuan Duck (similar to Peking Duck, but more hotly spiced, eaten with pancakes), Hot and Spicy Carp, Pork with Fish Flavor (cooked with ginger, vinegar, and rice wine), Parchment-Wrapped Chicken, Camphorwood Smoked Duck and:

Ants on the Tree No, not real ants; the dish is a hotly spiced mixture of bits of stir-fried ground beef with cellophane (bean-flour) noodles.

Dry-Fried String Beans The beans are deep-fried until they are leathery and dehydrated, then they are stir-fried with minced meat and hot spices. Dry-Fried Beef Shreds are deep-fried to the same chewy texture.

Hot and Sour Soup Chicken broth spiced with vinegar and pepper and stocked with shreds of pork, bean curd, tiger-lily buds, and cloud ears (a dried tree fungus).

Twice-Cooked Pork Pork is simmered, sliced, then stir-fried with vegetables and a spicy bean-based sauce.

Nearby Hunan Province is somewhat similar to Szechuan in terms of topography, climate, and the hot and spicy nature of its food; but Hunan cooking is usually hotter, earning it, in the minds of some gourmets, a reputation for the most fiery cuisine in China. Hunan specialties include various smoked meats (including ham), Dry Shredded Venison in Hot Sauce, and Kung Pao Chicken, named after an exiled mandarin (cubes of chicken stir-fried with chili paste, bean sauce, and hot peppers). Hunan is also noted (sometimes derisively by other Chinese) for the use of exceptionally long chopsticks, about 50 percent longer than those used elsewhere.

SHANGHAI AND THE CENTRAL COAST

The cuisine of this area is characterized by the liberal use of sugar to sweeten dishes. To many of these dishes, a large dose of the local rice wine vinegar is added, producing sweet-and-sour specialties. On the coast, the red-cooked dishes can be salty and gravy-laden. This regional cuisine makes use of pork and chicken (cooked with rice "wine" in Shanghai, as "drunken chicken"), seafood and fish from the bountiful sea and rivers, and flavorful temperate-climate vegetables. Rice is the chief starch staple.

Compared to Cantonese cooking, the central coastal cuisine is more assertively seasoned and higher in fat content, thus generally higher in calories, but lighter and more mildly seasoned than Peking-Northern cooking. Central coastal chefs tend to cook their ingredients to a degree of doneness that shocks many a Cantonese chef.

The locally produced Shaoshin rice "wine" is renowned, as is Hangchow's Dragon Well tea, which many connoisseurs consider to be the finest green tea in the world.

Specialties from the central coastal region include the Ten Varieties Hot-Pot, a plate of sliced meats and vegetables which the diners cook in a communal pot of steaming broth; Yangchow Fried Rice, leftover rice stir-fried with an especially rich mixture of foods; Eight Precious Rice, a sweet rice pudding with mixed dried fruit, often served in midbanquet; Beggar's Chicken, coated in wet clay, then baked, so that the hardened clay can be chipped away from the tender chicken; Sweet and Sour Pork, which is generally sweeter and more sour than the Cantonese version; and:

Lion's Head   A casserole dish of large steamed pork balls. Casserole dishes in general are popular throughout China during the winter for their warming qualities.

Soused Shrimp   A specialty of Hangchow. Live shrimp are placed in spiced wine; they absorb the wine, become flavorful and inebriated, and are eaten in that condition.

Squirrel Fish   A flattened deep-fried fish (sea bass is a favorite) served whole, smothered in sweet-and-sour sauce. The name comes from the cooked fish's fancied resemblance to a squirrel.

FUKIEN

Fukien is acclaimed for the quality of its soy sauce, and for the red-cooked dishes braised in soy sauce. Other condiments include Hung Chiao (a red paste made from the lees of wine), soy paste, shrimp sauce, and shrimp paste. Fukien clear soups are also famous. The province's location on the southern coast gives access to plenty of fish and seafood.

Provincial specialties include Jou Shun, dried meat "wool" (bits of meat stir-fried with soy sauce, sugar, and Hung Chiao until they become dry and fluffy), Yen Pi (a dumpling dough made of flour and pulverized meat), and Popia. Popia is a party dish of thin pancakes and assorted fillings; the guests choose fillings and roll their own.

Fukien produces what some epicures consider to be the finest black tea in China, if not the world: Iron Goddess of Mercy.

OTHER REGIONS OF CHINA

Yunan Province is famous for its hams, Tibet for its Yak-butter-based cuisine, and Manchuria for its barbecued lamb. Even though a dozen or more regional specialties such as Chicken with Nuts have become national dishes, each area of China modifies such recipes in keeping with its culinary practices and the available ingredients. What is not Chinese are those dishes invented beyond China's borders. These include the fortune cookies and Chop Suey—both American innovations.

THE INDIAN SUBCONTINENT

INDIA

Religion has greatly influenced Indian eating habits. Hindus, who constitute over 80 percent of the population, do not eat beef because the cow is sacred to them. Some Hindus, applying the "reverence-for-life" principle, do not eat meat or fish at all. Some Indian vegetarians abstain from eggs, because they are potential lives. One sect, the Jains, will not even eat root vegetables for fear of killing insects while uprooting the plant.

Moslems, the second largest religious group, eat beef and lamb but not pork. Both the Hindu and Islamic faiths preach abstinence from alcohol. A small percentage—but a fairly large number—of Indians are Christians, with their own food customs.

In the Western world "curry," a term corrupted and popularized by the English but seldom used by Indians, identifies a standardized sauce or powder made of a number of spices. In India so-called curry sauces vary from region to region, dish to dish, cook to cook. They can be mild or hot, thick or watery, yellow or green, prepared from scratch or store-bought, mediocre or inspired. Traditional Indian cooks consider premixed spices inferior to spices freshly ground and mixed for each individual dish. Anise seed, asafetida, chilies, cloves, cardamom, cinnamon, coriander, fenugreek, cumin, ginger, saffron, and turmeric are some of the many spices popular in India. Cooks may use a few or many at a time. Ghee (typically: clarified butter) was once the preferred cooking medium in the north, but it is now being replaced by vegetable oil as an economy measure. The south traditionally prefers coconut oil for cooking.

Classic Indian ingredients such as *murg* (chicken), *machi* (fish), *jingha* (shrimp or prawns), *gosht* (meat—often goat, lamb or mutton), *keema* (chopped meat), *dal* (legumes), *alu* (potatoes), *panir* (fresh curd cheese), *matar* (green peas) or *baingan* (eggplant) can be cooked using many techniques. A Bhartha is a dish of mashed roasted vegetables mixed with spices. Korma dishes are braised, sometimes with Dahi (yogurt). Doh Peeazah dishes are braised with a large volume of onions. Bhuna dishes are sauteed. Kababs are grilled on a skewer.

Each diner is given food in a set of small metal bowls called *katoris*, arranged on a metal tray called the *thali*. The offerings on the *thali* vary from region to region. The diner traditionally eats with the right hand only. Because the left hand is used to clean the body, there is breach of etiquette if it is used at the table.

Wheat grows well in the temperate northern lands, so bread accompanies most meals there. The sauces are made thick so that they can be scooped up with small pieces of bread. Northern cooking includes the rich Moghlai style, in which food is cooked with cream and/or nuts. Some specialties of the north are:

Biryani   A north Indian adaptation of Middle Eastern Pilaf dishes, in which rice is cooked with meat and/or vegetables, fruit and nuts, spices and/or coloring.

Chicken Tandoori   Esteemed by many as India's finest dish. The chicken is marinated for twelve to forty-eight hours in yogurt and spices, then broiled inside the remarkable *tandoor*, a five-foot-deep jar-shaped clay oven, usually sunk vertically in the ground. The intense heat gives the skewered bird a crisp exterior, yet the inner flesh cooks to moist succulence.

Roghan Josh   This deep-red mutton dish, developed by north Indian Moslems, is rich with almonds and toasted spices.

Roti   This general term encompasses several varieties of bread, one of northern India's culinary highlights. Naan, crisp outside, spongy within, is the traditional accompaniment to Chicken Tandoori. It is made of leavened whole wheat flour kneaded into a flat oval shape, then slapped on the inner walls of a hot *tandoor* oven to bake. Paratha is unleavened whole wheat flour dough rolled with Ghee into many layers, then pan-fried. This soft, rich, flaky bread is sometimes stuffed with seasoned mashed potatoes or minced meat. Poori is a soft, puffed, unleavened bread made with whole wheat flour rolled into saucer-sized disks, then deep-fried. Unleavened whole wheat dough is rolled into a pancake shape, then baked on an iron griddle to produce Chapatis. Variations include Chapati Tandoori, baked in a *tandoor* oven, and Phulka, which puffs up after being roasted on top of hot coals. Crisp, brittle Pappadums are made of unleavened seasoned lentil flour dough rolled into tortillalike rounds, then pan-fried.

India's eastern coast relies on rice and fish. Eastern Indian cuisine was once highlighted by the cooking of Bengal. For the specialties of this now-independent area, see the section on Bangladesh.

The south of India is a rice-eating area. Therefore sauces tend to be thin and pungent, flavored with pastes of freshly prepared spices. Southern food is usually simple. The Madras style is characterized by the use of tomatoes and plenty of spice. Though most foreigners equate tea with India, home-grown coffee (with milk and sugar) is south India's breakfast drink.

Idli   A steamed bread of fermented ground legumes and rice. Idli, or a pancake version of the same batter called Dosa, is traditional for breakfast in the south, along with lentils and hot relishes.

Vindaloo A style of cooking. The principal *vindaloo* ingredient—kid, lamb, chicken, or shrimp—is soaked for hours or days in a hot-and-sour marinade made with vinegar and a number of spices including chili pepper, then simmered in the marinade and served with the resulting hot, spicy sauce. Unless you have built up an immunity to fiery spices, it helps to have an asbestos-lined digestive tract.

Residents of Bombay, in the west of India, eat both rice and wheat bread. The rich but not too spicy styles of cooking from the surrounding Maharashtra and Gujarat regions have influenced Bombay's food; so has the distinctive food style of the Parsis, Zoroastrians who migrated to India in search of religious toleration. Although Bombay Duck (a dried fish) is world famous, it is more beloved by Anglo-Indians than by Indians. More significant foods of Bombay and the west coast include:

Dhansak The Parsis prepare this rich (*dhan* means "wealth") mixture of mutton, tripe, several kinds of lentils, and many vegetables. Dhansak is traditional for celebrations and family gatherings.

Khicheri A plain dish of rice and lentils, always accessible to the poor, the ill, and the homesick Indian abroad.

Min Vela Curry A mixed-fish curry (pomfret, mullet, and mackerel are popular) with spices, tamarind, and coconut. The pomfret is an almost boneless fish popular throughout India; here prepared in traditional fisherman's style.

Still on the west coast, 250 miles south of Bombay, is the small state of Goa. Long a Portuguese colony, Goa serves a fascinating amalgam of European and Indian food, including:

Pork Indad Christians make a wet, sweet-and-sour pork curry flavored with vinegar, tamarind, and sweet spices. Pork

Baffat is a dry curry, cooked with a *masala* (blend of spices) but very little liquid.

Sorpotel Cubed pork variety meats simmered with vinegar, sugar, and a spice paste. The flavors mellow for hours or days, then the dish is reheated and served with Sannas, a steamed rice bread flavored and lightened with fermented palm juice.

OTHER INDIAN SUBCONTINENT CUISINES

Bangladesh, once the Bengal state of India, later East Pakistan, is now a separate country. Bengali dishes include Macher Kalihya, Ambal and Rasgulla. Macher Kalihya is fish cooked with yogurt, spices, and vegetables; the amalgam is fried, then simmered with fried onions and Panir. Ambal is sautéed vegetables simmered with spices and tamarind until semiliquid. Rasgulla is a dish made of fresh cheese and nuts poached in a sweet rosewater syrup; there are many similar Indian sweets, based on fresh curd cheese or homemade evaporated milk.

Pakistan shares dozens of India's favorite dishes: Shami Kabab (grilled spiced meatballs), Chicken Tikka (grilled boneless pieces of chicken), and Nargesi Kofta (fried meatballs stuffed with hard-boiled eggs), to name a few. However, in Pakistan there is a greater variety of wild game and meat raised for food. Because Pakistan is predominantly Moslem, there is no strong vegetarian tradition. Chapli Kabab (patties of chopped meat) and Pasanday (strips of spiced beef) are indigenous Pakistani dishes. Pakistani food also resembles Middle Eastern cooking in its accent on grilled lamb, yogurt, and flat breads. Spicing in southern Pakistan is similar to, but milder than, that of nearby northern India, and spicing in northern Pakistan is even milder.

Sri Lanka, once called Ceylon, has one of the hottest cuisines in the world. Chili peppers are used with abandon while making various Sri Lankan curries—most typical are "black curries" based on a mixture of dark-roasted spices. Sri Lankan cooks also prepare "red curries" blazing with red chilis and the comparatively milder, coconut-based "white curries." These curries form part of the everyday Sri Lankan meal, Rice-and-Curry.

Other national specialties include Biththara Appé (Egg Hopper) and Lampries. The Egg Hopper, a raised pancake (made of rice flour and coconut milk) cuddling a shirred egg, is spiked with condiments (sambols) and rolled for eating. Lampries (the name comes from the Dutch) is Sri Lanka's festive dish. It is a complex mixture of rice, hot Sri Lankan curry, sumbols, and perhaps meat, baked together in a banana-leaf envelope. Sri Lanka also makes Dutch-style yeast cakes and Portuguese sweets. Here, as we can see, East has met West for centuries, but the East has prevailed. Because Sri Lanka has both tropical and temperate climates, it is able to produce a broad assortment of fruit. The lengthy coastlines of this island nation also teem with seafood, but it is the shellfish that are particularly delicious. Popular soft beverages include fresh-fruit drinks (including the liquid from Sri Lanka's most important "fruit," the coconut) as well as tea and coffee, the last two major export commodities. Among the alcoholic beverages, Toddy (a coconut-tree product), the more potent Arrack (distilled from a Toddy base), and beer are favorites.

Afghanistan, a remote mountainous nation, has a cuisine bridging south-central Asian and Middle Eastern styles. Palau dishes combine lamb or chicken with rice and vegetables. Traditionally, Afghan men dine first, without women; the same is true in the Middle East and parts of India. An Afghan palau is often accompanied by okra, potatoes, and spinach—vegetables revered in the Middle East and the Indian subcontinent. Aushak is an Afghan dish of lamb, leeks, and tomato sauce baked between noodle layers under a topping of Chaka (garlic-flavored yogurt). Lamb and yogurt are standbys of both Indian subcontinent and Middle Eastern diets.

Equally remote, and equally mountainous, is the Himalayan nation of Nepal. Rice is the major starch staple, but wheat is eaten as well. Most Nepalese are Hindus, but not vegetarians. Wild boar and other game meats are popular. Nepalese food tends to be spicy. Masmas (mixed vegetable curry), Songoor ko Tarkari (pork curry), and even scrambled eggs (Khuras ko Anda) are hot with chilies, coriander, and other spices.

⤳ INDONESIA

OVER 130 MILLION PEOPLE inhabit tropical Indonesia, making it the fifth most populous country in the world. This 13,000-island archipelago stretches several thousand miles along the equator.

The major external culinary influences have been the traders and settlers who came from China, India, and the Arab lands long before the first Europeans arrived. The Chinese introduced their cooking methods, utensils, and ingredients to the islands. From India came the preference for hot curry spices and the second major religion of Indonesia, Hinduism, along with its strictures against beef eating and its tolerance of pork eating. The religion of the majority of the people came from the Middle East: five out of every six Indonesians are Moslems. They may eat beef, but not pork. The Dutch, Portuguese, and other Western colonial powers, who for centuries exploited the profitable nutmeg and clove resources of the Moluccas (or Spice Islands), left only a small mark on today's Indonesian cuisines. Little is known about the culinary influences of the ancient Malays.

Today's most obvious culinary characteristics are the chili-hotness of the foods; the frequent use of peanuts in the sauces; outdoor cooking (especially barbecues); and the use of rice as the principal starch staple. The bare hands are the traditional eating implement.

Popular flavoring agents include coconut milk and cream, shrimp paste (Trasi or Suck), soy sauce, fermented shrimp liquid, rice vinegar, tamarind water, and sago palm sugar. In addition, the following herbs and spices used individually or as part of an Indian-influenced curry also typify Indonesia's cuisine: anise, basil, bay leaf, chili, cinnamon, clove, coriander, cumin, fenugreek, ginger, lemon grass, lime leaf, mace, mustard seed, nutmeg, poppy seed, saffron, sesame seed, and turmeric.

Apart from rice, the most common starch staples include corn, cassava root, sweet potatoes, and sago flour. Bean curd, from the soybean, is another significant food.

A variety of meats is consumed, including the flesh of carabao (a type of water buffalo), cattle, sheep, goat, pig, chicken (and eggs), duck, and pigeon.

Tropical fish is plentiful, but its flavor and texture are unexciting unless the fish is eaten within an hour or two after it is caught. Consequently, fish is a mainstay of coastline inhabitants, but not of inland Indonesians, though the latter do have fishponds and enjoy frying preserved fish. Among the more popular fresh fish from the ocean are garupa (a grouper), mackerel, milk fish, pomfret, and tuna.

Like most tropical and subtropical areas of the world, Indonesia has excellent shellfish. The prawn is popular and relatively inexpensive. Other types of crustaceans such as crab and crayfish are also available, as well as mollusks like oysters and abalone. The eggs of the sea turtle are also prized.

Fruits and vegetables are delicious and well liked. Among the fruits that one is most likely to encounter in the open markets are avocado, banana, breadfruit, carambola, coconut, cucumber, durian, eggplant, jackfruit, java apple, kiwi, lichee, lemon, lime, mango, mangosteen, orange family (mandarins, etc.), papaya, passion fruit, pineapple, pomegranate, pomelo, rambutan, soursop, star fruit, and tomato. Popular vegetables, not previously mentioned, include bamboo shoots, bean sprouts, cabbage, chinese cabbage, corn, mushrooms and other types of fungus such as cloud ears, the onion family (shallot, scallion, garlic, etc.), paté bean, potato, and sugar cane. The kemiri (candlenut), cashew, macadamia, and pistachio are among the nuts that are indispensable to native cooks. Though botanically not nuts, the water chestnut and the peanut are also widely used.

Desserts generally consist of fresh fruit. Sweet preparations made with ingredients such as coconut milk, glutinous rice, and sago palm sugar are enjoyed as between-meal treats.

The most sophisticated cuisine can be found in Bali and the central portions of Java. Balinese cooking is characterized by fiery hotness (even by Indonesian standards) and by the popularity of pork, which may be attributed to the Hindu religion prevailing in the area. Central Javanese cuisine is recognized by its prevailing sweetness. Throughout Indonesia each region possesses its own array of local specialties, but many dishes, like Saté and Soto Ajam, appeal to most inhabitants and can be identified as national dishes.

Though the use of shoddy, mass-made Westernized cooking ware is on the upsurge, the traditional *kuali* or *wajan* is still holding its own; nothing beats iron wok-type utensils for stir-frying. Other mandatory kitchen equipment for the old-fashioned Indonesian kitchen includes a clay pot for cooking dishes containing curry, a mortar and pestle, a stone grinder, a coconut grater, and a small wood-burning outdoor oven.

RIJSTTAFEL

Ask the average sophisticated diner what the national dish of Indonesia is and, chances are, he'll reply, "*Rijsttafel.*" *Rijsttafel* is not a dish; but a full-fledged feast. Neither is *rijsttafel* Indonesian; rather, it is a Dutch invention or, more accurately, an ostentatious Dutch embellishment of the age-old Southeast Asian dining style of serving a variety of dishes to accompany rice. The word *rijsttafel*, however, is Dutch, and means "rice table."

In the colonial era, when Holland controlled most of what is presently Indonesia, the plantation owners and other Dutch settlers staged dramatic dinner parties in an attempt to outdo each other. Out of this pretentious competition developed the *rijsttafel*, usually a Sunday luncheon lasting two to three hours, sometimes longer. Once all invited guests were seated, this extravagance unofficially began with the grand entrance of several dozen or more "boys," each resplendent in flamboyant, pseudo-native costumes and white gloves. Each carried a separate food, such as an elaborately prepared meat dish, a *sambal*, or a plain and simple plate of ripe fruit. The variety was intended to please, sate, and impress. After a heaping scoop of steaming white rice was placed in the center of a special wide-brimmed soup bowl, the servants would march around the table in single file, offering each diner a choice of various foods. Each portion was placed, by the guest or the plate-porter, around the rice or near the bowl's rim, each food being kept separate.

The elaborateness of the *rijsttafels* was judged by the number of food-toting servants; if forty of them were involved, it was known as a forty-boy *rijsttafel*. The Indonesians of today have unpleasant memories of the *rijsttafel* as a degrading sign of servitude imposed on them by Dutch colonialists, but do prepare and serve scaled-down *rijsttafels* to appease tourists who have their hearts set on experiencing a *rijsttafel* during their stay in Indonesia. Do not expect it to be proferred by a small battalion of parading servants; you will probably be serving yourself, buffet-style.

Designing the full-scale *rijsttafel* was no easy task as the chef had to be sure that each main and side dish was in harmonious contrast with all the other dishes. In order to accomplish this, no two flavors, colors, types of meat, vegetable, or cooking methods could be duplicated. For every group of dishes possessing one characteristic, (sweet, spicy, warm, or firm-textured) there had to be a group of dishes with counterbalancing properties (sour, bland, cold, or soft-textured).

Today you'll find the abbreviated *rijsttafel* being offered in Indonesian-style restaurants all over the globe (especially in Holland), but they are mere shadows of the authentic *rijsttafel* in terms of pageantry and food offerings. With the exception of tourist hotels, you will be hard-pressed to find even a scaled-down version in Indonesia, because of its connotations.

FAMOUS INDONESIAN SPECIALTIES

The Indonesian islands have countless specialties; here are brief descriptions of some of the better-known ones.

Atjar   Any of a large variety of pickled relishes.

Bahmi Goreng   Literally, Fried Noodles. Basically the same as Nasi Goreng (see below) except that noodles are substituted for rice.

Gado Gado   An array of raw and parboiled vegetables served with a spicy peanut and coconut-milk dressing.

Gulai   A main ingredient (fish, chicken, etc.) cooked and/or served with a curry and coconut-milk sauce; a popular dish in Sumatra.

Ikan Bambu Bali   Spicy marinated fried fish.

Ketupat and Lontong   Rice rolled and steamed in coconut leaves—or rice cakes steamed and served in woven packets of palm frond.

Krupek   Deep-fried wafers of various colors and sizes, made from shrimp paste and tapioca flour.

Nasi Goreng   Literally, Fried Rice. Cooked rice is stir-fried, then combined with one or more precooked ingredients (chicken, pork, various vegetables, and so on) that have been cut into small portions. The diner sprinkles condiments such as peanuts on his portion. Sometimes the rice is gilded with saffron and/or turmeric, or tinted light brown with soy sauce.

Nasi Kuning   Literally, Yellow Rice. For this special-occasion dish, rice is steam-boiled in a coconut milk with turmeric and saffron, then molded into a cone, garnished with a red flower on top. *Sambals*, *serundeng* (see below), and other preparations are arranged around the bottom of the rice cone to decorate it.

Nasi Tumpeng A cone of white rice (a symbol of purity) garnished with only red, black, and yellow foods (for reasons of religious symbolism).

Opor Ajam Chicken cooked in coconut milk/cream sauce accented with candlenuts and other flavorings.

Rempah Rempah Coconut-meat patties.

Rempeyek Fried wafers made with peanuts and coconut milk. Prawns, grated coconut, or other ingredients may be substituted.

Rendang Beef cooked in a thick, clinging coconut sauce. Popular in Sumatra.

Sambal In its simplest definition, a *sambal* is a chili-hot condiment, relish, or sauce designed to accompany or to be incorporated as part of other preparations. But because there are so many types of *sambals*, the word almost defies definition. *Sambals* may be plain, vegetable, fruit, meat, or seafood with varying compositions. You can have raw or cooked *sambals*; you can have sweet ones or you can have *sambals* that are complete dishes in themselves (these are called *sambalans*). Whatever a given *sambal* may be, its foundation usually comprises these and other ingredients pounded together into a fine paste: chili, lime or other citrus juice, and shallots or other members of the onion family. Some of the more famous *sambals* include Sambal Badjak (a basic hot sauce); Sambal Goreng (literally, Fried Sambal). Derivatives of this *sambal* include Sambal Goreng Kelapa (coconut is the name-giving ingredient): Sambal Ketjap (the root of the Western word ketchup, but the Indonesian preparation is definitely unlike the American tomato-based condiment), usually a fermented seafood concoction, somewhat like soy sauce; Sambal Manis (the best known of the sweet *sambals*); Sambal Telor (egg gives it its second name); Sambal Tomat (now we are getting remotely akin to American tomato ketchup); Sambal Udang (much like shrimp); and

Sambal Ulek (this is one of the simplest *sambals*, finely mashed chili with a touch of acid liquid such as lime or tamarind).

Saté   Small cubes of meat or seafood, such as beef, carabao, pork, lamb, goat, chicken, prawns, or fish, are marinated, threaded on bamboo skewers, then charcoal-grilled. The diner dips the chunks into a fiery sauce comprising (usually) peanuts, chilies, coconut milk, shallots, garlic, and other seasonings. Though *satés* are eaten at mealtime, they are more popular as snacks purchased from curbside stalls and vendors.

Serundeng   Grated coconut is mixed with spices and sometimes peanuts, then fried.

Soto Ajam   A chicken soup that is often spicy and always full-flavored. It usually contains a number of ingredients such as rice noodles and hard-boiled eggs.

BEVERAGES

It is fitting that coffee is popular in Indonesia, because "java" is a one-time American slang term for coffee. Tea is also popular; so are cocoa, sweet fruit drinks, sugar-cane water, and coconut water. The last beverage can be served plain or in the Dutch manner with crushed ice and a liberal lacing of orange-flavored syrup. In some areas (especially Sumatra) the milk of the carabao is a basic drink.

Since most Indonesians are Moslems, the per-capita consumption of alcohol is low. For those who do drink, beer is the favorite alcoholic beverage. Also popular is a rice "wine" called Brom. Some Indonesians make home-brew out of palm sap.

JAPAN ～

JAPANESE COOKS ARE FAMOUS for the beauty of the dishes they prepare. Ingredients are carefully selected, artistically cut, and arranged not merely to please the senses but to conform to elaborate systems of symbolism. Japanese food preparation is intimately related to the Japanese philosophy of human harmony with nature. The arrangement of the finest, freshest foods in peak season, with each flavor distinct, is given higher priority than the concocting of rich sauces and artful melding of flavors.

The roots of Japanese cuisine are largely sixth-to-eighth-century Chinese. Lesser influences include Korean, Portuguese, and post-nineteenth-century Yankee and European. Ironically, the two most famous Japanese dishes, Tempura and Sukiyaki, are of foreign inspiration.

Tempura, one of the few popular fried dishes in Japan, is made with seafood and/or vegetables dipped into light batter and deep-fried. Some food authorities say that the name derives from the Latin *tempora* (meaning "times" and referring to the periods of the year when the visiting Portuguese, as Roman Catholics, could not eat meat and requested seafood for dinner). Following the seventeenth-century expulsion of the Portuguese, the Japanese refined the specialty, using a lighter batter and subtler cooking technique, making the dish truly Japanese.

From the departure of the Portuguese to the mid-nineteenth century, Japan was closed to foreigners. During this period, the Japanese did not eat beef, largely because of fidelity to the tenets of Buddhism, the majority religion. But

since then diplomatic relations with the West and industrial-
ization have produced a Westernization of the traditional diet.
Foods such as beef, bread, butter, and Coca-Cola were
introduced. Sukiyaki, thin slices of beef and vegetables
quick-cooked at the table, was promoted to popularize beef;
it was felt that Western industrial superiority derived in part
from a meat-based diet. There is no longer a religious
abhorrence of beef in Japan, and the beef is often excellent. Its
scarcity on Japanese tables is due to its high price. Most
excellent, and most expensive, is the beef from Kobe,
beer-fed and massaged by hand for tenderness.

The traditional—and still very popular—protein sources in
Japan are fish, shellfish and other seafood, and soybeans. Fish,
shrimp, prawns, octopus, squid, eel, and mollusks, raw or
cooked, are enjoyed throughout Japan. The soybean is
processed into Tofu (bland, nourishing bean curd), Miso (a
fermented seasoning paste), Shoyu (lighter than the typical
Chinese soy sauce), and many other foods. The red *azuki* bean
is popular by itself or as a sweetened paste used in desserts
and confections.

Other popular vegetables include *daikon* (white radish),
spinach, mushrooms, onions, carrots, burdock root, seaweed,
Chinese cabbage, and lotus root. Spicy pickles (Tsukemono)
are considered essential to the Japanese meal; they complement the Gohan (highly honorable rice).

Rice, usually boiled and served at the end of the meal with
pickles, is the main starch staple. Donburi, a bowl of rice
topped with a prepared food such as egg, fish, or cutlets, is a
popular quick lunch. Other fast foods include Udon (wheat
noodles) and Soba (buckwheat noodles), both served with
broth and perhaps some fish, egg or meat.

One of the best ways to understand Japanese food is to
classify dishes according to the method by which they are
prepared. Some of the more important cooking (and
noncooking) methods include:

Agemono   These are fried foods. Famous dishes include
Tempura, Kakiage (a batter-dipped, deep-fried patty of

vegetables and shrimp), and Tonkatsu (a breaded, deep-fried pork cutlet).

Mushimono Steamed foods. The celebrated dish is Chawan Mushi, an egg custard containing chicken and vegetables.

Nimono These foods are boiled. The best known subcategory is *nabemono*, one-pot tabletop cookery in which the ingredients are simmered in a lightly seasoned broth, then usually dipped into a flavorful sauce. *Nabemono's* best-known dishes are Sukiyaki, Shabu Shabu (beef, vegetables, and bean curd), Mizutaki (somewhat like Shabu Shabu, but with chicken instead of beef), Yosenabe (fish, shellfish, and vegetables), and the uncomplicated Yudofo (bean curd).

Sashimi and Sushi Sashimi is a preparation of sliced raw seafood. It is polite to serve Sashimi in pairs; the phrase for "one slice" can also mean "homicide," the phrase for "three slices" can also mean "suicide." Sushi is a class of foods served with cold rice seasoned with vinegar and sugar. Raw fish, fish roe, shrimp, and other seafood are very popular Sushi; egg and seaweed are also popular. Seafoods for Sushi and Sashimi must be absolutely fresh and of the highest quality. Sea bream, tuna, and sea urchin roe are especially prized. Those wishing to play "Japanese roulette" can try Fugu, a blowfish, that can be lethal if improperly cleaned.

Yakimono Foods that are broiled. Some of the best-known dishes are Yakitori (marinated skewer-broiled chicken), Teriyaki (broiled meat or fish first marinated in a sweetened Sake and soy-sauce mixture), Shioyaki (fish salted for an hour or two, then skewer-broiled), and Teppan-Yaki (food cooked on a small tabletop grill).

Cooking varies from region to region. For instance, the Kansai-style cooking (around Kyoto and Osaka in the south) is perceptibly sweeter than the Edo-style cooking (around Tokyo). Even Sushi varies: in Tokyo the fish is pressed onto two-inch oblong rice balls (the style followed by Sushi bars outside Japan), but in Osaka the fish is pressed onto rice in a mold, then usually cut into squares or rectangles.

BEVERAGES

Japan's favorite beverage is O-cha, "honorable tea." Traditional Japanese tea is powdery green tea, brewed with warm water and beaten to a lime-green froth. *Cha-no-yu*, the tea ceremony, is a fundamental and honored part of Japan's cultural life. *Kaiseki*, foods prepared for the tea ceremony, are highly formal and show marked concern for beauty, perfection, and esthetic harmony.

Mugicha, an infusion of burnt barley grains, and Calpis, a sweet lemon-flavored skim-milk beverage, are also popular soft drinks. Sake (really more a beer than a wine because it is brewed) is served warm in small cups. Mirin is a sweet Sake prepared especially for use in cooking. Beer, domestic and imported, is rising in popularity. Imported whiskey (very expensive) and Japanese whiskey (only moderately expensive), enjoyed with meals by Japanese businessmen, are also gaining favor.

KOREA,
SOUTH AND NORTH

JAPANESE AND NORTHERN CHINESE influences can be discerned in Korean cooking; but the "Hermit Kingdom" has evolved a distinctive cuisine. Korean cooking is hearty, which befits a climate that can be cold and windy in winter. Spicing is vigorous; hot peppers, toasted sesame seeds, soy sauce, garlic, ginger, and bean paste are among the commonest flavorings.

Beef is the favorite Korean meat; it appears in many guises ranging from Mandu-Kook, beef broth with pork-and-beef dumplings, to Yook Hae, a Korean version of Steak Tartare, to numerous at-table "barbecues." Pork and chicken are also popular, as are fresh and dried shellfish from Korea's long coastline and cold mountain streams.

Korean cooks show great love and respect for produce. Chinese cabbage, *daikon* (white radish), cucumbers, beans, mushrooms, and bean sprouts are particularly favored. Rice and transparent rice noodles are staples. Some of the many Korean specialties are:

Bul-Gogi A barbecue of thin slices of beef marinated in a soy-and-spice sauce, brushed with sesame seeds, and grilled over charcoal on a table brazier. Bul-Galbi is a similar preparation of chunks of beef short ribs.

Chap Chae Transparent rice noodles pan-fried with minced vegetables and meat in a seasoned sauce.

Kim Chee A hot-spiced mixture of fermented vegetables (Chinese cabbage is especially popular) served as an accompaniment to most Korean meals. Cutting vegetables for Kim

Chee, burying it to ferment, and sampling the finished jars are beloved rituals in Korean homes.

San Juk Marinated beef cubes skewer-broiled, often along with mushrooms, scallions and/or green peppers.

Sinsullo A special treat on a cold wintry night: vegetables and meat simmered in a tabletop, charcoal-heated Mongolian fire-pot.

Desserts are not common in the Korean cuisine, though sometimes fresh fruit is served at the end of a meal.

Herb and spice teas—ginseng, ginger, and cinnamon, for example—are appreciated, as is Sungnyung, toasted rice brewed with hot water. Takju, Yakju, and Soju are alcoholic "home brews" of grain or potatoes, similar to Vodka. The potent Ginseng Cocktail is a sweet-and-sour martinilike concoction flavored with ginseng-root extract.

MALAYSIA ⌐

AS ONE MIGHT EXPECT, Malaysian and Indonesian (especially Sumatran) cuisines share many characteristics, the outgrowth of geographic proximity and somewhat similar ecosystems and histories.

Both tropical nations, for instance, use the same type of cooking utensils and eat with the fingers. They also have a fondness for chili-hot foods, shrimp and/or fish pastes, coconuts, peanuts, and other tropical fruits and vegetables as well as a preference for outdoor cooking and simple, quickly-prepared food from street vendors.

Among the many dishes that Malaysia has in common with Indonesia are Nasi Goreng, Saté, Rendang, Soto Ajam, Gulai, Ketupat, and a limitless variety of *sambals*, which are described in the Indonesian section of this book. Dishes that tend to be slightly more associated with Malaysia than Indonesia, though enjoyed in both countries, include Gula Malacca (sago pudding) and Otak Otak (fish steamed in leaves).

The prime difference between Indonesian and Malaysian cooking is that the latter has been more influenced by Chinese traders and settlers, who introduced their cooking utensils, methods, and flavoring ingredients to the native culinary repertoire. So many Chinese came that today approximately half the blood that runs through the veins of the Malaysian populace has a Chinese heritage.

You will also find stronger Indian and Sri Lankan influences in Malaysia than in Indonesia. This is manifested in the widespread use of curry blends and in the frequent preparation of such Indian dishes as Korma, Pilau, Biryani, and Murg Tandoori.

Unlike the Indonesians and virtually all other Southeast Asian peoples, except the Singaporeans, Malaysians are prone to serve sweet culinary preparations made of glutinous rice and sago palm sugar for dessert.

Most Malaysians are Moslems and therefore abstain from pork and alcoholic beverages, but there are enough nonbelievers in Malaysia to make pork and beer mainstay items in the national diet. Other potent beverages include rice "wine" and fermented palm-tree sap.

Popular nonalcoholic beverages include sweet fruit juices, sugar-cane water, coconut water, and various shaved-ice drinks sold by street vendors. Both tea and coffee are widely sipped, though the latter is more popular despite the strong Chinese heritage in Malaysia.

NEW ZEALAND

NEW ZEALANDERS, LIKE AUSTRALIANS, prefer to prepare their foods in a simple, uncomplicated manner, a cooking trait indicative of their British ancestry. They are also big meat eaters, though lamb rather than beef is the most popular meat in New Zealand. The people share the Australian preoccupation with baking, preserving, and freezing a large portion of the food supplies, and with capturing the natural essence of the home-grown fruits and vegetables and the fresh-caught seafood. Yet despite these common elements, the cuisine of New Zealand maintains a distinctive profile.

The country's majestic snow-capped mountain peaks provide a striking contrast to the vast and perfect pastureland, New Zealand's economic backbone and its most conspicuous physical feature. These verdant, picturesque valleys and rolling hills are dotted with over 50 million sheep (in a country with a population of only 3 million people), not to mention the millions of Jersey dairy and Black Angus beef cattle. Consequently, New Zealand is the world's largest exporter of lamb and dairy products, and one of the leading shippers of wool.

Dairy products such as butter, cream, milk, and ice cream are delicious because of the remarkably high butterfat content of the cow's milk—the direct result of the rich grasslands. Surprisingly, cheese is not as good as it could be, considering the superb raw milk of the land. Sharp Cheddar is probably the best cheese; followed by the semihard British Colby. Both are apt to appear in the cheeseboard assortment, customarily served near, or as the conclusion to, the meal.

The meat of the sheep in New Zealand is generally classified as baby lamb (under three months old), lamb (three to ten months), hogget (ten to fifteen months), and mutton (over fifteen months). Unlike the British, New Zealanders prefer their sheep meat young. If there is a national dish, it would probably be Sunday's traditional Rack of Lamb (or hogget) accompanied by mint sauce and several vegetables. Other popular lamb dishes include Barbecued Lamb, Roast Canterbury Leg of Lamb, and Colonial Goose. This last specialty is actually lamb, not a poultry dish. Domesticated poultry has always been more expensive than lamb, so the economizing cook would stuff a boned leg of lamb as she would a bird, and call it, with tongue in cheek, "Colonial Goose."

Wild game abounds in New Zealand, where you'll find deer, pig, hare, and such game birds as duck and black swan. The most unusual of all game specialties is the mutton bird. It is the young of a shearwater (a sea bird) that, despite its somewhat greasy and fishy taste, can be a delight to an adventurous palate—but only if the bird is quite young, freshly caught, and knowledgeably prepared, preferably by a Maori cook.

The sea surrounding the thousand-mile-long New Zealand nation is one of its principal natural resources. From its ocean waters comes a sizable supply of fish such as the local varieties of tamure snapper, the grouperlike hapuka, the John Dory, and the eel (usually smoked). The inland rivers and lakes provide freshwater fish such as trout (originally imported by British immigrants). Each spring, river mouths yield whitebait, the 1½-inch-long, just-hatched, virtually transparent young of the smelt species. They are coated with egg batter, sautéed, then served hot, perhaps with a light sprinkling of lemon juice.

Shellfish is particularly good in New Zealand. The rarest and most celebrated is the toheroa, a large green-fleshed clam, which to some palates tastes slightly like asparagus. This mollusk is usually transformed into a rich, thick, and quite expensive Cream of Toheroa Soup. Because the bivalve was on the verge of extinction, the government now allows the public to dig for the toheroa only on certain days in the spring.

Digging must be done by hand, as even the wooden shovel is now outlawed. A similar-tasting but more easily come by mollusk is the tua tua, which is also made into a well-known soup.

Rock oysters deserve their fine reputation, especially when served on the half-shell. Good, but not in the same league, is the locally available bluff oyster. Both are served on the half-shell (the best way) and as Oysters Kilpatrick (wrapped in bacon and grilled) and Oysters Mornay (baked with a cheese-infused white sauce).

Nelson scallops, which are normally fried, are also part of the popular New Zealand shellfish treasury, as are kina (sea eggs) and paua (a type of abalone).

Crustaceans are notably excellent and include many species of shrimp, prawns, and "rock lobster" crayfish, the latter being the best of all.

"Kiwi" means several things in New Zealand. First and foremost, it identifies that nocturnal, flightless, grub-and-worm-hunting bird that has become the national symbol. "Kiwi" is also the nickname that New Zealanders affectionately call themselves. Finally, "kiwi" is the name of a delectable fruit with a fuzzy brown exterior and a geometrically patterned, green, juicy, sweet interior. The kiwi (or Chinese gooseberry) fruit is native to China. The bird is strictly indigenous and exclusive to New Zealand.

New Zealand produces a wide variety of fruits and vegetables. The combination of subtropical and temperate regions yields one of the best agricultural climates in the world. The standard assortment includes banana, papaya, mango, orange, lemon, lime, grapefruit, plum, apple, cherry, peach, pear, and apricot. You'll also find the tamarillo, which sometimes looks like a tomato growing on a tree; hence the nickname "tree tomato." This fruit is often cooked with sugar in order to balance its natural tartness.

Among the vegetables is the kumara, a yamlike sweet potato that is frequently found—either roasted or boiled—on dinner tables throughout New Zealand. Unique local pumpkins, of distinctive shapes, colors, and sizes are also popular, as are common European and American vegetables such as potatoes, carrots, and peas.

As in Australia, Pavlova Cake (whipped cream contained in a meringue shell) is the national dessert. The New Zealand version is often topped with kiwi fruit.

BEVERAGES

Tea is the national beverage of New Zealand. As in Great Britain, it is usually black, rather than green or oolong tea, and is served with sugar and/or milk. Tea breaks and teatime are very much part of the New Zealand social fabric. A frequent accompaniment to tea is that baking-powder biscuit, the Scone, which migrated to New Zealand from Scotland (a large percentage of New Zealanders have Scottish ancestors).

Coffee is not a particular favorite except as an ingredient in the popular Irish Coffee.

Beer is one of the justified pride and joys of the country. Like the beers from southern Australia, New Zealand beer and ale are strong and full-bodied.

New Zealand's wine is not outstanding, though some drinkable, moderately priced, everyday red and white wines are produced.

MAORI CUISINE

The first human inhabitants of New Zealand were the Maoris, a Polynesian people who, anthropologists believe, migrated from Tahiti and from some of the other Society Islands somewhere around A.D. 1000.

Their protein mainstay was fish (including eel, a particular favorite) and shellfish (including the toheroa, tua tua, and rock lobster), supplemented by wild pig and various birds caught in traps. Kumara (a sweet potato) was a key starch source.

Just as their Polynesian forebears in the South Pacific cooked in earth ovens (see Polynesian cuisine discussion pp.

189–198), so the Maoris feasted at their earth oven called the *hangi*. An interesting Maori cooking method involved wrapping fish, meat, and vegetables in leaves, placing the packet in a woven flax basket, then submerging it in one of New Zealand's many steaming-hot water pools or geysers.

Today the Maoris represent a small percentage of the total New Zealand population. Despite government intervention, the Maori culture is disappearing. Virtually all Maoris have forsaken their ancestral cooking methods for gas or electric stoves. One thing that has been slow to change, however, is the Maori hospitality—a guest still feels most welcome.

# PACIFIC ISLANDS

THE PACIFIC OCEAN ENCOMPASSES nearly half the world's surface, a vast expanse of water dotted by about a thousand tropical islands, small and widely scattered. Geographers and anthropologists divide this area into three major subunits: Polynesia (Many Islands), Melanesia (Black Islands), and Micronesia (Small Islands).

POLYNESIA, INCLUDING THE HAWAIIAN ISLANDS

Polynesia embraces a massive triangular-shaped body of water, the three terminal points being the Hawaiian Islands in the north, New Zealand in the southwest, and Easter Island in the southeast. Within these parameters lie many island groupings—the best known of which are Society (including Tahiti), Samoa, Tonga, Marquesas, and Cook islands.

Polynesian food, as served in those pseudo-Polynesian restaurants that abound in Western-world cities (including Honolulu), bears as much resemblance to authentic Polynesian cuisine as the moon does to the earth. Pseudo-Polynesian cuisine is largely a bastardization of non-Oceanian influences, such as the sweet-and-sour cooking styles of China and the Tempura (deep-frying) and Teriyaki (marinating) methods of Japan. These alterations were made by immigrants who settled in Hawaii within the last century or so; the cuisine in question should more appropriately be called "Modern Hawaiian."

You are unlikely to find authentic Polynesian food outside the Pacific Islands because Polynesian cuisine consists chiefly

of simply prepared fresh tropical fish, fruits, and vegetables—
once freshness is gone, all is lost. The delicate flavor and
texture of a tropical lagoon fish starts to wane appreciably
within minutes after it is caught. If an unmarinated tropical fish
sits around for even a few hours, you end up with bland and
unexciting food. As for the tropical fruits and vegetables, they
are luscious because each is picked at its ideal time. Those
exported lose much of their potential glory because they are
usually harvested well before reaching proper maturity, when
they have yet to attain their characteristic flavors.

Yet another reason for not being able to find fine
Polynesian fare outside the islands is that the tourists have a
romanticized notion of what Polynesian cuisine is—and the
restaurateurs, being good businessmen, give them what they
want.

Many historians believe that the Polynesian Islands were
initially settled about 2,000 years ago from Melanesia and/or
Micronesia. From islands like Tahiti, Bora Bora, and the
Marquesas, the Polynesians spread out to Hawaii, Easter
Island, and New Zealand. These seafaring migrants carried
aboard their mammoth outrigger canoes a limited, but
well-selected, variety of foodstuffs including pigs, poultry,
taro root, coconuts, breadfruit, sweet potatoes, and bananas.
Without most of these items, the settlers (or at least their
descendants) would not have survived, because uninhabited
lands—including Hawaii—usually lacked a sufficient base of
life-supporting plants and animals. The two saving graces were
the abundance of protein-rich fish and shellfish that could be
found along most island shorelines and the fertile soil and
mild tropical climate ideally suited for growing the transported plants.

The next major wave of introduced foods came when
sixteenth-through-nineteenth-century explorers, plantation
owners, merchants, and missionaries linked Polynesia with the
rest of the world. This phenomenon occurred especially in the
Hawaiian Islands when Japanese, Chinese, Filipinos, Koreans,
Indians, Caribbeans, Scots, Polynesians, and other ethnic
groups settled, bringing with them their cooking methods and

ingredients. Today Hawaii has the most cosmopolitan admixture of cuisines, races, and cultural institutions in the world (only about 1 percent of Hawaii's population is pure-blooded Polynesian). Most of these ethnic groups still follow at least some of their ancestral cuisine heritages. To illustrate, the Korean-Hawaiian eats more beef than pork, while the opposite is true for the Chinese-Hawaiian.

The non-Hawaiian Polynesian Islands offer a more genuine, less adulterated Polynesian cuisine—though the influence of the colonizing powers is evident. For example, the food in Pago Pago in Samoa has been somewhat altered by the Americans, while contemporary Tahitian cuisine has a strong French imprint. One sees native Tahitian delivery boys placing freshly baked French bread loaves in the mailboxes strung along the tropical road. But there will be no mistake when you visit the bustling, colorful Tahitian marketplace in downtown Papeete, whose many stalls teem with fish, vegetables, and fruits, including the coconut.

Coconuts are one of the major pillars of Polynesian cuisine—and the more remote the village or island, the more they are used. Their white flesh is eaten plain or used to make those two flavoring agents called coconut milk and coconut cream (not to be confused with the coconut water, the refreshing liquid drink sloshing inside the fruit). The flesh is also used to make coconut oil, the prime frying medium of Polynesia. Even the shells and husks are not wasted: the first is made into drinking cups, the second is used as fuel in the cooking pits.

Other major foods and cooking ingredients found in Polynesian marketplaces include a wide variety of tropical and subtropical fruits including avocado, banana, breadfruit, custard apple, durian, granadilla, guava, jackfruit, lemon, lichee, lime, mango, mangosteen, melon, orange, papaya, passion fruit, pineapple, pomelo, rambutan, star fruit, soursop, tamarind, tangerine, and even watermelon. And some of these fruits come in many varieties. There are hundreds of distinct types of edible bananas, for example, some of which can be eaten raw while others must be cooked.

Among the most popular vegetables are the taro root and its leaves, varieties of the sweet potato, and the yam.

Pork is by far the leading meat. The pig, which can thrive in rich tropical islands without much attention, reaches its highest culinary pinnacle when roasted whole in a *luau*-type fire-pit. If that pig is a wild one, all the better. If that pig is old and tough, papaya juice or pulp can be used because the enzymes in that fruit chemically tenderize the meat. Beef and lamb, because of the climate and lack of suitable pasture, are largely imported and mainly consumed by visitors to the island. In the past, dog meat was considered a treat.

Seafood has always been the chief source of animal protein for the Polynesians. While both fish and shellfish are abundant, the latter is the epicurean joy of the islands. Tropical shellfish is superb—and that includes the local crayfish, prawns, shrimp, crabs, octopus, squid, cuttlefish, sea slugs, univalves such as the abalone, and bivalves like the various clams. The eggs of the sea urchin and other roe are also delicious, though often rare and expensive.

Tropical fish is never as flavorful and fine-textured as the fish netted in the cooler temperate-zone waters, but it can be heavenly if eaten raw or cooked simply, if consumed soon after it is caught and not drowned in a rich sauce. Most Polynesians prefer to grill their fish, or fry it in coconut oil, or serve it raw and marinated. Among the several hundred species are the much-appreciated squirrel and parrot fishes that are netted or spear-gunned in the lagoons. Also popular are the mahimahi and others that are generally caught beyond the reef.

Today many Polynesians cook with modern Western-style kitchen equipment; but in other islands one still finds the old-fashioned simple cooking methods such as broiling or barbecuing meat, roasting breadfruit, or wrapping food in ti-leaves, placing it under embers or hot volcanic stones. Outdoor cooking is very much a part of Polynesian cuisine. Most of the islands lack proper clay for making fireproof cooking pots; early Polynesians, like the Neolithic man, learned to boil or simmer food by dropping hot volcanic stones into a calabash gourd containing a cooking liquid.

Of course, the most famous Polynesian cooking method is the *luau* (a Hawaiian term; others include *tamaaraa* in Tahiti and *hangi* in New Zealand).

Essentially, *luau*-style cooking involves digging a pit several feet deep, lining the bottom with wood and coconut husks, topping the fuel with volcanic stones, then lighting the fire. When the flames die down to form embers, the red-hot stones are covered with a layer of leaves (often banana leaves). On top of this layer is placed the food to be cooked: the whole pig, breadfruit, taro root, yam, sweet potato, fish, shellfish, and whole chicken, in addition to such preparations as Chicken Luau and Haupia (discussed later). Some items are wrapped in leaves; each is placed according to its individual cooking properties. The food is then covered with another layer of leaves and perhaps a thick layer of sand to help retain the earth-oven's heat.

While the food is cooked in the *imu* (as the Hawaiians call the earth-oven), the guests relax. Several hours later, the guests reassemble for that glorious moment when the earth-oven is opened, yielding its aromatic treasure. In accordance with Polynesian custom, the food is usually removed and put aside to cool to at least a tepid state.

The guests sit on the ground under the coconut trees and eat off banana leaves and drink out of primitive bowls such as empty coconut-shell halves. Fingers are used rather than cutlery and there are no courses: all dishes are offered simultaneously. In ancient times women were not allowed to cook the *luau* food or to eat with the men. This taboo was annulled in Hawaii in the nineteenth century.

Surprisingly, each food tends to retain its own individual characteristics despite steam-roasting with other foods. The foods do develop a common smoked flavor, a characteristic that is savored by the Polynesians.

As for beverages at a modern-day *luau*, beer is the most common, though you will also encounter other liquid refreshments such as fruit juices (both fresh and fermented), coconut water, and punches and cocktails of both the alcoholic and nonalcoholic variety. In days of old, Kava was also very popular (see Polynesian Beverage section below).

These feasts were given for both religious and secular reasons, such as celebrating a birth, anniversary, or completion of a new outrigger. *Luaus* played an important social role because they provided an opportunity for families and friends to meet and reinforce their bonds. If you were a stranger, it would not have been that difficult to wangle an invitation because Polynesians are generous people—especially when it comes to sharing food. But when it came time to carve the pig, strict social protocol usually existed: the more honored a guest or the higher he was in rank or seniority, the better the piece of meat he could expect to receive.

Since full-fledged *luaus* require much preparation, Polynesians generally opt for "mini*luaus*" or "*poi*-suppers," where everyone assembles at a suitable beach, gathers wild edibles such as coconuts, catches lagoon fish, then settles down for a beach party, singing and all. These occasions, though small in scope, are infinitely more joyous and more true in spirit to the original feasts than organized tourist *luaus*.

FAMOUS POLYNESIAN SPECIALTIES

Below are some of Polynesia's most famous culinary specialties. Unless otherwise indicated, the names are Hawaiian (each island group has its own name and preparation variations, too many to cover in a book of this size).

Chicken Luau Chicken combined with chopped taro leaves and coconut cream, traditionally steam-roasted in a *luau* earth-oven. The Tahitian equivalent is Chicken Fafa.

Fafaru To make this much-talked-about Tahitian specialty, soak fish in seawater for several days outdoors, then discard the fish. After straining the resulting malodorous liquid, marinate a fresh bath of fish chunks in it for four to ten hours—then drain and serve.

Haupia   A sweet mixture of coconut and arrowroot that is traditionally wrapped in ti-leaves, then steam-roasted in a *luau* earth-oven until firm. Usually served as a dessert.

Kalua (Baked) Pig   This is an all-important component of any full-fledged *luau*. The pig can weigh anywhere from eight pounds (for a suckling) to over one hundred pounds (for a young pig). While the suckling variety is the best tasting, the larger pig is the type generally served in large-scale *luaus*. To ensure that all parts of the pig cook evenly in the earth-oven, hot volcanic stones can be placed inside the abdominal and throat cavities, cooking the pig from the inside as well as from the outside.

Laulau   A combination of pork and taro leaves wrapped in ti-leaves, then (traditionally) steam-roasted in a *luau* earth-oven.

Lomi Lomi   Chopped or shredded salmon (raw, salted, or smoked) that is marinated with minced scallions and tomatoes. Often served on crushed ice as a salad.

Mahimahi   Dolphin filets or steaks, usually fried, grilled, or eaten raw. Environmentalists take note: The dolphin is the fish, not the mammal.

Poi   In Hawaii, Poi almost always refers to boiled taro root that has been pounded into a starchy paste, which is the traditional starch staple of the people. The consistency of this preparation is rated on a scale of one to five fingers: one-finger Poi is sufficiently thick and sticky to be picked up with your index finger, while five-finger Poi is so liquid that you need to make a scooping cup out of your entire hand. Hawaiian-style Poi varies in taste from bland (if freshly made) to slightly sour (if allowed to ferment for two or three days).
Elsewhere in the Pacific, such as in Tahiti, Poi (or Poe) refers to a sweet puddinglike concoction made from pounding one or more fruits such as papaya, pineapple, banana, breadfruit, or guava into a pulp.

Poisson Cru   Though most South Pacific islanders eat raw fish marinated in citrus juice and coconut cream, it is the Tahitians who are most noted for it. In Tahiti this culinary creation is called both I'a Ota and Poisson Cru. L'a Ota refers to the authentic native version as defined above, while Poisson Cru (which means "raw fish" in French) is a more involved mixture with European-influenced additions such as chopped onions and tomatoes.

You'll also find in Hawaiian households countless other dishes, such as Butterfly Shrimp, Glazed Ham Steak and Pineapple, Barbecued Sweet-and-Sour Spareribs, and Jerked Beef—but these were introduced or created by Hawaii's Oriental and European immigrants.

POLYNESIAN BEVERAGES

As with the food of the country, there is a great misconception perpetuated by some foreigners as to what legitimately constitutes Polynesian beverages. Virtually all those mixed tropical cocktails with catchy names are recent inventions.

Ancient Polynesians got their "high" principally through Kava, or Ava as this drink is called on some of the islands. To prepare this beverage, you chew the fibrous root of the kava pepper plant, spitting the resulting pulp and saliva into a community bowl, which contains a little water. After a few hours fermentation, you and your friends sip it.

Of more recent popularity, though still ancient in concept, are drinks made by allowing fruit juices to ferment in a bottle for a few days. Another approach is to cut off the top of a pineapple while still attached to its plant, sprinkle sugar on the exposed flesh, replace the top, then leave it to ferment for several hours in the hot sun.

Today the most popular alcoholic beverage on most of the islands is beer. Some places like Tahiti brew excellent beers (Hinano, Vahine, and Manuia) because the superb local drinking water ranks among the best in the world. Wines are also drunk, especially on the French-influenced islands, but the price is usually too high considering quality, selection, and storage practices. In any event, wine does not combine well with Polynesian food. Most of the hard-liquor consumption occurs on the densely populated islands; on some of the other islands, citizens are forbidden to drink liquor.

One of the most popular nonalcoholic beverages on the remote islands is coconut water. The water (or juice) is the liquid that sloshes inside the coconut; coconut milk (or cream) is the liquid that you get by squeezing the coconut flesh in a cloth. Polynesians learned long ago that the best coconut water was from the green (slightly unripe) coconut that has not yet fallen to the ground. Consequently, one must shimmy up the tree to dislodge the fruit in order to get the coconut water and flesh at their sweetest and most delicious stage.

MELANESIA AND MICRONESIA

Melanesia lies immediately west of Polynesia, yet the peoples of these two areas are racially different. While the Polynesians have brown skin with straight hair, the Melanesians—who are classified as Oceanic Negroid—have dark skin and frizzy hair.

Nonetheless, these peoples are ethnic cousins, especially when it comes to food. The cuisines of Polynesia and Micronesia, as well as that of Melanesia, bear a rough resemblance to one another because the food staples that can be most efficiently gathered and cultivated in the Pacific tropical islands are more or less the same: taro root, coconuts, lagoon fish, pig.

And because there has been contact among the various island groups dating back a thousand or more years, there has been an interchange of cooking styles. The principal difference between the cuisine of one island group and the other is due to outside influences. Thus, you will find French overtones in places like New Hebrides and New Caledonia, a

British touch in the Fiji Islands, a Yankee imprint on Guam and American Samoa, and a light trace of Dutch and German culinary practice in Papua/New Guinea. Other outside influences drifted in with the Indians who came as indentured workers, the Chinese who came as merchants, and the Japanese who came in vast numbers as invaders during World War II. Still other influences came with migrants from Indonesia, Vietnam, and other nearby Asian lands.

Since World War II, the trend toward the Westernization of the Pacific Island cuisines has been accelerating at an alarming pace, especially in the larger island towns, where the can opener is now used more often than the coconut scraper. Stone Age cookery is still being practiced by isolated tribes on Papua/New Guinea and other relatively untouched Melanesian Islands. Basically, it is a direct cooking style that makes good use of the open fire for roasting. Another feature of Melanesian Stone Age cooking is the frequent use of the clay pot.

Modern-day beverage preferences are much the same throughout most of the Pacific Islands. Beer (followed by various fermented fruit juices and Kava) is the most popular alcoholic refreshment, while coconut water, fruit juices, and just plain water are the ranking nonalcoholic drinks. Hard liquor and wine are generally too expensive for the ordinary person's budget.

⟿ PHILIPPINES

THE CUISINE OF THE Philippines has been fashioned more by distant foreign influences than by its original inhabitants and that to a greater extent than in other countries of similar size. To illustrate, the Philippine Lumpia and Ginataan specialties were inspired by, respectively, the early Chinese and Malay traders and settlers. Starting several centuries ago, the Spanish (who undoubtedly made the biggest culinary impact) introduced a wide assortment of Iberian specialties, including Flan. The most recent contributors were the Americans, who introduced Coca-Cola, the modern supermarket, and various mass-oriented culinary practices to the Filipino.

Another notable characteristic of Philippine cooking is the liberal use of salt (usually imparted by means of pungent fish or shrimp paste called Bagoong and/or the amber-hued liquid fish seasoning Patis). Philippine cooking also has a noticeable sour flavor, the result of adding acid ingredients such as vinegar, and limelike calamansi, or tamarind.

Philippine cooks also enjoy using ample portions of garlic. However, not all responsibility for seasoning lies in the hands of the cook. It is customary for the diner to flavor many of the foods at the table with a variety of dipping sauces, collectively called Sawsawan.

Still other characteristics include the practice of mixing diverse main ingredients such as meat, fish, seafood, and/or vegetables in the same dish. Frying in oil, the use of dried fish, and eating with the hands also typify the country's cuisine and traditional eating style. Plain boiled rice is the common starch staple, eaten morning, noon, and night.

Significant regional differences are obvious in the diet, especially when one compares the north to the south. Though the majority of the nation's population is Roman Catholic, the southern lands, such as the island of Mindanao, are predominately Moslem. Consequently, pork eating is at a minimum. Another characteristic of southern cuisine is its hot and spicy nature, a style borrowed from neighboring Indonesia. Most other Philippine cooks use comparatively few spices.

The most famous dishes of this nation of over 40 million people and 7,000 islands include:

Adobo   Along with Lechon, this specialty comes closest to being the national dish. Adobo is (usually) pork or chicken that is sautéed, then simmered with vinegar, garlic, and soy sauce. Other possible ingredients include beef and seafood. In some regions, coconut milk is used.

Lechon   Barbecued whole pig featuring crisp skin and juicy flesh. A vinegar-spiked liver dipping sauce is the traditional accompaniment.

Pancit   Cantonese-style noodles sautéed and served with a virtually unlimited combination of flavorful ingredients such as shrimp, colorful vegetables, and garlic.

Sinigang   One of the most typical dishes of the Philippines—it is a sour, salty medley of many ingredients, which may include meat, fowl, seafood, and vegetables.

Other well-known Philippine specialties include Balut (boiled duck egg complete with the embryo), Dinuguan (a flavorful pork stew served in a dark, blood-thickened sauce), Ginataan (most often a sweet concoction of fruits and vegetables like the sweet potato prepared with coconut milk), Kari-Kari (an ox-tail and vegetable stew), Lumpia (the Chinese egg roll, though this version is usually served wrapped in lettuce leaves), Morcon (rolled beef flank steak stuffed with a variety of ingredients such as boiled eggs and sausages), Rellenong Bangus (stuffed whole milk fish), Rellenong Alimango (deep-fried crab shells stuffed with crab meat), Rellenong Manok (whole chicken stuffed with minced pork and other ingredients), and Ukoy (a deep-fried shrimp and bean-sprout patty).

Popular desserts include Flan and Halo-Halo, a mixture of ingredients such as preserved fruits, crushed ice, and milk.

The best-selling alcoholic beverage is beer, the finest brand being San Miguel. Outside the towns the homemade Tuba spirit, made from the sap of the palm tree, is popular. Carbonated soft drinks have become very popular.

SINGAPORE ⌒

SINGAPORE, THE TINY INDEPENDENT nation whose name means "lion city," is a powerful banking and shipping center, owing partially to its strategic location on the Strait of Malacca, the maritime gateway between the Indian Ocean and the South China Sea.

The principal external culinary influences are Chinese (three-quarters of Singaporean blood is Chinese), Malayan, Indonesian, Indian, Singhalese, Japanese, and European. In Singapore you will find the cuisines of those lands in their near-original form—or an amalgamation of two or more of these cooking styles.

By far the most interesting of these cuisines is *nonya* or, as it is often called, Straits Chinese. It began back in the early nineteenth century when a large number of Chinese men came to Singapore for employment, settled down and married native Malayan women, and insisted that their mates cook Chinese-style. A compromise resulted: whenever possible, the Malay-born spouse used Chinese cooking utensils, methods, and ingredients such as pork (the forbidden meat of Moslem Malaysians), but she also used some local ingredients, unknown in China, out of necessity. Most important of all, she gave the food a definite spicy touch, not as much as enjoyed by the native Malayans but far more than the Chinese immigrant was used to back home. *Nonya* (the word also defines a Straits Chinese housewife) cooking slowly evolved into a rather complex cuisine of great distinction. Unfortunately today it is endangered because the modern Straits Chinese housewife—unlike her grandmother—doesn't have the time and/or inclination to invest hours in the kitchen preparing each meal, as true *nonya* cooking usually demands. This is a victory for the women's liberation movement but a setback for fine eating.

Practically all the dishes mentioned or described in the Indonesian and Malaysian section of this book are also popular in Singapore—and that includes Saté, Nasi Goreng, and the various Sambals. The same is true for cooking methods, ingredients, and utensils. Two dishes, however, are especially associated with Singapore:

Chili Crabs   Local crabs cooked and served in a spicy sauce.

Rojak   A medley of vegetables (such as cucumber) and fruits (pineapple, for instance) that are stir-fried in a sweet-and-sour shrimp-based sauce.

The most exciting culinary highlight of Singapore is the famous Orchard Street Car Park. By day it is a nondescript parking lot, by night a tightly packed, quickly set-up array of temporary cooking stalls and tables where hundreds of enterprising vendors prepare, vociferously promote, and serve their particular specialties into the wee hours. Normally a sultry tropical evening is not conducive to a hearty appetite, but here the inviting odors of Malaysian, Chinese, Indonesian, Indian, and other ethnic foods are almost guaranteed to start your gastric juices flowing. Should you not be near the Car Park, don't fret; alfresco eating stalls and foot-borne vendors can be found everywhere in Singapore, especially after the setting of the hot equatorial sun.

Should the sun still be up, you may wish to amble over to the legendary Raffles Hotel and order a cooling Singapore Sling, a concoction of gin, cherry brandy, and lemon juice that was a favorite—it has been told—with Somerset Maugham as well as with many a tourist who relished playing the (now outdated, we hope) "Great White Man" role while ensconced in an oversized wicker chair. The other Singaporean beverages, whether alcoholic or not, are generally much like those found in Malaysia or Indonesia.

THAILAND

THE FREE USE OF the hot chili pepper is one of the major characteristics of Thai cooking.

As with most other parts of tropical and semitropical Asia, meals in Thailand center on rice. The customary bowl of rice is accompanied by a number of dishes, some of the better-known possibilities being:

Kaeng   These "liquid" dishes are soups, curries, or stews that complement rice. Kaeng Chud is a Chinese-inspired soup of broth, varied meats, and vegetables. Tom Yam is a Thai soup of one kind of meat or seafood in broth, often spiced with lemon grass. Kaeng Kari, Kaeng Phed, and Kaeng Kao Wan are Thai curries cooked in coconut milk. Kaeng Kari, with a yellow sauce, is comparatively mild; red Kaeng Phed is hotter, and green Kaeng Kao Wan is hottest. The colors come from the chilies and other spices in the curry paste. Fish and seafood are very popular Kaeng ingredients; beef, chicken, and pork are used less extensively.

Mee Krob   A classic celebration dish of rice noodles in a sweetened pork-and-crustacean sauce. Traditionally it is served in a mound with an elaborate, colorful garnish.

Nam Prik   A term used both for the beloved Thai hot sauce and for dishes of raw or cooked vegetables, eggs, fish, or meat served with rice and a sauce. There are many variations of Nam Prik sauce; most include chilies, garlic, fish sauce, and shrimp paste, with other ingredients to the taste of the cook.

Yam   A Yam (literally, Mixed with the Hands) is a Thai salad. But the salad is not restricted to raw vegetables: cooked vegetables, meat, fish, even flowers can be used. Pork and oranges, and beef and roses make up the bases of two popular Yams.

The Thais enjoy fish in other forms besides the Kaeng. Pla Tu (small fried mackerel) are popular; so are Tot Num Pla (fish dumplings) and Luk Chin (fishballs for soup).

Your meal will also include *krueng kieng,* "side dishes," which are not mere condiments. A *krueng kieng* is a seafood, meat, or vegetable dish cooked with little or no sauce; the "main dishes" have plenty of liquid to flavor the rice. To top off the meal, there is a selection of luscious, exotic tropical fruits including rambutans, longans, mangosteens, mangoes, sapodillas, guavas, and custard apples.

Thai cooks are particularly fond of herbs such as lemon grass and coriander leaves. Other popular flavoring agents include Nam Pla (fish sauce), Kapi (shrimp paste), java root, and the previously discussed chilies.

OTHER ASIAN CUISINES

THE FOUR LANDS OF Burma, Vietnam, Laos, and Cambodia have culinary affinities. In each country, rice, fish, shellfish, pork, and poultry are common cooking ingredients; beef is rare. Fish sauce and shrimp paste are favored condiments.

BURMA

The Burmese enjoy Hin, light, clear soups, often made with a fish stock; "sour curries" cooked in sesame or peanut oil (prawn curry is a favorite); lightly cooked fresh leafy greens, and assorted condiments called Tolee Molee, or "bits and pieces." Blachan, also called Ngapi and Balachaung, is a dried prawn paste used very often in the Burmese kitchen for flavoring and as a condiment. Two very popular dishes are:

Mohingha A meal-in-a-bowl of curried fish, fish stock, rice vermicelli, and circlets cut from the heart of a banana tree.

Kaukse-Hin A bowl of thin noodles, topped with curried meat, gravy, and assorted side dishes and condiments. The curry base is likely to be chicken, lamb, prawns, or fish. The side dishes are such things as chopped hard-boiled eggs, crabmeat, mushrooms, and even dried flowers. Garlic and herbs are served so that the diner can season the curry to taste. The popularity of curries in Burma is understandable considering the country's proximity to India.

VIETNAM

Nuoc Mam (fish sauce), alone or spiced up into Nuoc Cham (hot sauce), is the characteristic Vietnamese flavoring. Lemon grass as well as a delicate-tasting native mint are other popular seasonings. Vietnamese cooking reveals a Chinese influence, but Vietnamese cooking is lighter and less oily because many foods are boiled rather than fried. Unlike its neighboring countries, Vietnam relishes beef dishes, for example Bo Bay Mon, a buffet of seven beef dishes prepared in different styles; Bun Bo, a mixture of beef, rice vermicelli, peanuts, and vegetables—and:

Cha Gio An appetizer or snack of fine-chopped vegetables, meat, and/or seafood, wrapped in edible rice paper or dough and deep-fried. To eat Cha Gio, you sprinkle the fine-chopped ingredients with fresh herbs, roll the food in green salad-type leaves, and dip the package into Nuoc Cham.

Pho A beef-and-noodle soup. Pho is seldom prepared at home; instead, the Vietnamese go to the innumerable food stalls to enjoy bowls of beef broth, with quick-cooked rice vermicelli, bean sprouts, and scallions, often with a few drops of Nuoc Mam for zest.

Generally speaking, the cuisine of the north is subtler and more refined than the cooking of the south, which is comparatively assertive.

LAOS

The Laotians, especially the northerners, favor glutinous rice for daily use. Glutinous rice, which becomes sticky when cooked, is known throughout Asia, but usually reserved for desserts. However, the Laotians steam this rice in cylindrical molds, then slice it and serve it with hot sauce as a savory dish. The Laotians relish soups such as Khao Poun, spicy fish or chicken stock with rice vermicelli and vegetables, and Furr, a breakfast specialty of broth, noodles, pork, and marijuana leaves.

Lap, also called Koy, is a traditional Sunday lunch. It consists of fine slivers of raw venison flesh and liver, served with broth, steamed glutinous rice, green vegetables, and hot sauce.

CAMBODIA

Cambodian cooking exhibits Thai, Laotian, and Chinese influences. The Cambodians share the Southeast Asian predilection for noodle soup for breakfast. Pigeons, sparrows, and water-buffalo meat are part of the Cambodian larder. Fish dishes such as Trei Aing, charcoal-grilled fish served with raw vegetables, herbs, ground peanuts, and hot sauce, are popular. Fish roe and milt are considered delicacies. Phoat Khsat is stir-fried rice mixed with meat, seafood, and egg—with fish sauce, of course.

PART IV
The New World

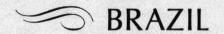 # BRAZIL

THE PORTUGUESE COLONISTS WHO settled in Brazil in the early sixteenth century found a sparse Indian population. Fish, land game, jungle fruit, and manioc were the staples of the rather limited, somewhat monotonous Indian diet. This cuisine was subsequently broadened by the many newcomers including the conquering Portuguese and the enslaved Africans. From the Portuguese heritage came, for example, the popularity of salt cod.

Brazil, ranking fifth in area among the world's nations, has three major culinary styles. The Bahian style comes from the midnorth along the east coast; the Cariocan, from Rio de Janeiro in the midsouth; and the Paulista from São Paulo some 200 miles farther south.

BAHIAN CUISINE

Bahia's style is the one most influenced by the African slaves who were imported to work the plantations. The classic Bahian dish is Vatapá de Camarão e Peixe, fresh shrimps and fish in a thick sauce made with dried shrimp, coconut milk, nuts, and *dendê*, the palm-nut cooking oil. All these ingredients are West African in origin or spirit, which is not surprising considering that Bahia resembles West Africa in geography and climate.

CARIOCAN CUISINE

Rio de Janeiro-style Cariocan cooking has been more influenced by the Portuguese than Bahian cooking is, but the most famous regional dish has little connection with the colonizing mother country. Feijoada Completa is an assortment of meats such as smoked tongue, jerked and fresh beef, pork, smoked and fresh sausages, and pigs' feet and ears arranged on a platter and accompanied by side dishes of black beans, rice, shredded kale, hot pepper sauce, and orange slices. In addition, manioc (cassava root) meal is sprinkled over practically everything, as it is with many other Brazilian specialties.

Tutú de Feijoa is a plainer Cariocan dish: whole cooked black beans served with puréed black beans. A variant is Tutu a Mineira, puréed black beans mixed with eggs, pork, and Portuguese-style *linguiça* sausage.

PAULISTA CUISINE

São Paulo-style cooking is the most subtle and delicate of Brazilian cooking styles. Besides owing some of its character to the Portuguese, West Africans, and Aborigines, it has been influenced by the Italians, Germans, and other Europeans who settled in southern Brazil in great numbers. An interesting local dish is Cuscuz Paulista, cornmeal steamed and molded with meats and vegetables, somewhat like the famous cracked-wheat Couscous of North Africa.

NATIONAL CHARACTERISTICS

Throughout the most populated regions of Brazil, black beans and rice sprinkled with Farinha de Mandioca (manioc meal) are the staff of life. Also quite common is the lime-spiked hot sauce Môlho de Pimenta e Limão, as well as Palmitos (hearts of palm used in salads, soups and main dishes) and fruit pastes, made from guava, banana, quince, peach, mango, or coconut. Desserts, and cooking in general, tend to be sweet, a fact indicative of the Iberian heritage.

BEVERAGES

Brazil's coffee industry began in 1727, when a Brazilian military man and diplomat, Melo Palheta, brought coffee seedlings from French Guiana. Following the abolition of slavery in 1850, coffee replaced sugar cane as the major cash crop. Today Brazil grows approximately one-third of the world's coffee. While most Brazilian coffees are somewhat harsh, falling short of true greatness, the small, curled Bourbon Santos coffee bean can produce a worthy cup.

Yet, while small cups of sweet, strong black coffee are popular in Brazil, coffee is not the universal beverage one might expect. The people also relish the uniquely Brazilian Guaraná, a soft drink produced from dried berries, water (or carbonated water), and sugar. Its admirers claim it gives them increased energy and endurance. Brazilians, like Paraguayans and Argentinians, also enjoy Yerba Maté, the herb tea.

For those wanting something a little stronger, there are Brazilian wines—but don't expect quality. Far more interesting is the potent Cachaça, a clear sugar-cane brandy that is the traditional accompaniment of Feijoada Completa; its incendiary properties allow the happy diner to eat a little more. Adding lemon juice and sugar turns straight Cachaça into the renowned Batida Paulista cocktail.

CANADA ⁓

THE NATION OF CANADA spans vast diversity: fishing villages in the Maritime Provinces, cosmopolitan cities in the south, rough pioneer life in the Northwest Territories, all of this Canada. Two main cultural zones exist: Québec Province speaks French and cooks in the Gallic style, while most of the rest of the country communicates in English. In addition, Canada has a substantial Native American population including Cree and Inuktituk. Canada's extensive area embraces several varieties of climate and soil conditions, so analysis of several regions is a good way to gain insight into Canada's eating habits.

THE MARITIME PROVINCES

The cooking of the four provinces of Atlantic Canada (New Brunswick, Prince Edward Island, Nova Scotia, and Newfoundland) is not unlike that of coastal New England. The climate is similar (though somewhat colder) and fishing is a major industry (both groups of fishermen work the same waters). Furthermore, numerous Loyalists left the United States after the Revolutionary War, taking their recipes with them, and settled in this area. Specialties like Brown Bread and Baked Beans, therefore, are traditional for Saturday night supper. Dishes that are more closely associated with the Maritime Provinces include:

Hugger-in-Buff A salt-cod dish, prepared with potatoes, onions, salt-pork cracklings (Scrunchions), and a little milk.

This dish is also called Fish and Scrunchions and House Bankin'. When the German Canadians in Lunenburg County, Nova Scotia, enrich this dish with sour cream, their neighbors call the result Dutch Mess. Fish and Brewis is salt cod stewed with hardtack (a hard, dried biscuit), fried onions, and Scrunchions.

Jiggs Dinner   A boiled dinner of salt ribs, or in the New England fashion, corned beef, cooked with potatoes and root vegetables. The traditional accompaniment is Pease Pudding, made of dried split peas (a Canadian staple).

Pâté Rapé   This baked potato-pudding, also called Chiard, is a specialty of the Acadian fishermen of New Brunswick and Nova Scotia. The grated potatoes are combined with fish, meat or poultry, and broth. Poutine Rapée is a large dumpling made of the same mixture, but boiled rather than baked.

QUÉBEC PROVINCE

French Canadian food comprises both the *haute cuisine* found in fine restaurants in large cities like Montreal, and hearty home cooking, marked by a heavy use of herbs and a love for pork. Typical French Canadian dishes include:

Cipâte   This mixed-meat and vegetable pie layered with pastry enjoys a variety of spellings, from Cipaille to Six-Pâtes to Sea-Pie. A Cipâte aux Bleuets is a blueberry pie (blueberries are much appreciated in Canada) with a top, a bottom, and a middle crust.

Cretons (Grattons) du Québec   Spiced pork bits are sautéed in lard, then puréed and cooled to make this very popular spread for canapés and sandwiches.

Tourtière   A meat pie, traditionally served on Christmas Eve after Midnight Mass. The first Tourtières were made of passenger pigeons (tourtes); today fresh pork is most popular, though other meats may be used.

THE NORTHWEST TERRITORIES

The recipes followed in this area are not unusual: steaks, pot roast, meatloaf, baked fish filets. The surprises come from the ingredients. Canada's Arctic North is not conducive to farming, but it is a hunter's paradise. Big-game animals include deer, bear, buffalo, caribou, Dall sheep, elk, and moose. Beaver, muskrat, rabbit, and squirrel provide meat with less sporting challenge. Ptarmigan, snow goose, wild duck, grouse, and partridge are only some of the game birds available. The waters yield seal (Seal Flipper Pie is a specialty), whale, Arctic char (a delicate fish which tastes something like both salmon and trout), grayling, and inconnu (a large river fish with rich flesh).

CANADA'S MELTING POT

Most Canadians are of English or French descent, but a sizable number, especially in the Western prairies, are immigrants or the descendants of recent immigrants from many European or Asian countries. New dishes have been developed that are truly ethnic-Canadian.

The Mennonites, a religious group which is also well established in America's midwest and Pennsylvania Dutch country, settled in Manitoba and Ontario; the Hutterites, a communal fundamentalist group, settled in Alberta. Both sects share a German and Central-European heritage of hearty foods such as potato soup, dumplings, fried spareribs, fruit soup, doughnuts, and sweet buns.

Winnipeg is home to Icelandic and Ukrainian colonies. Vinaterta, a seven-layer cake filled with prune compote and topped with almond icing, is a popular Icelandic dish. Ukrainians call their noodles stuffed with cheese or sauerkraut Varenyky or Pyrohy; their neighbors avoid pronunciation problems by ordering Perogies.

The Scots in the Maritime Provinces perform many variations on the themes of herring and oats. Vancouver has a large Asian Indian colony. From Fish and Brewis to Biryani, it all adds up to Canadian food.

If there is one pan-Canadian culinary trait, it probably is the availability of a variety of fresh- and salt-water fish (Canada has the longest coastline in the world, not to mention innumerable lakes and rivers). Also popular throughout Canada are maple syrup, pea soup, and berries.

CARIBBEAN ISLANDS

WHILE THE FOOD OF the Caribbean islands, covering a 2,000-mile arc from Florida to South America, has some aboriginal Arawak and Carib Indian traces, the major influence is foreign. West Africa's culinary heritage entered this area when slaves were shipped across the ocean to work on sugar-cane plantations. Migrants from India made traditional Indian food commonplace on certain islands such as Trinidad. And the colonizing European countries left their mark. A distinct French imprint is apparent in Martinique and Haiti, an English touch in Jamaica and Barbados, and a Spanish overlay in Puerto Rico and Cuba. Tourists are also responsible for affecting the cuisine, demanding and receiving dishes to accord with their ideas of what tropical-island food should be like.

All these foreign influences, though important, have been limited by what the islands and the sea could produce. In Martinique, for example, a French-inspired dish is more likely to be made with fish than beef. Even an authentically prepared French fish dish will taste different from one in Paris because fish from tropical waters are less flavorful than those from northern seas. This phenomenon helps explain the popularity of salt cod on tropical islands surrounded by fresh fish. Definitely worth seeking out in the Caribbean, however, is shellfish, especially the spiny lobster and the conch, the latter an enticing salad, soup, and stew ingredient. The meat of the conch must be marinated or well pounded to tenderize it. Conch must not be overcooked, or it toughens again.

The food of diverse cultures stretching over 2,000 watery

miles cannot be reduced to a few pages of description. Here, however, is an alphabetical sweep through some of the islands and their foods, beginning appropriately with:

THE "A B C" ISLANDS

Aruba, Bonaire, and Curaçao, also known as the Netherlands Antilles, share a Dutch heritage and linked cuisines. Keshy Yena is a cheese ball stuffed with chopped vegetables, shrimp, meat or chicken, and then baked. The name may derive from the Spanish Queso Relleno (Stuffed Cheese). The cheese, as befits the once-Dutch area, is Edam.

Another Antillean dish is the lamb or goat stew called Stobá. The meat is stewed with celery, cucumbers, sweet and hot peppers, and olives, and is spiced with capers, cumin, garlic, ginger, and lime.

Sopito is a fish chowder made with coconut milk and cow's cream, salt pork or corned beef, onions, and tomatoes added to any available fresh local fish.

CUBA

Cuba is famous for its Black Bean Soup. The dark beans also appear with white rice under the tongue-in-cheek name of Moros y Cristianos—literally, Moors and Christians.

Two Hispanic dishes in this Spanish-speaking island are Picadillo, made of chopped or shredded beef, olives, raisins, tomatoes, and peppers; and Ropa Vieja (Old Clothes), made of shredded beef, tomatoes, and peppers, this time spiced with bright-orange annatto.

GUADELOUPE AND MARTINIQUE

These islands combine a base of Carib Indian cooking with African, Asian Indian, and French elements to provide a delicate yet spicy cuisine.

Acras l'en Mori are very light salt-codfish fritters seasoned with chives and shallots. Land crabs are served stuffed with boiled crabmeat, breadcrumbs, and spices. Fresh fish or sea urchins can be served as Blaff: plain poached seafood served with its lime-, clove-, and allspice-scented broth.

The Indian influence is revealed in the now-common colombo dishes. Colombo is a powder containing coriander, turmeric, mustard, garlic, hot peppers, and other spices. The word can also be used—as the word *curry* is—to refer to a dish cooked with the powder.

HAITI

This French-speaking republic shares the island of Hispaniola with the Spanish-speaking Dominican Republic. Haiti's modification of French cooking can be seen in Court Bouillon—here, the name refers to the finished dish and not merely, as in France, to the poaching broth.

Rice and beans, and rice and "red peas" (kidney beans) are popular dishes. Riz au Djon-Djon is rice simmered with garlic, cloves, bacon, hot peppers, and dried Haitian mushrooms that exude an inky juice as they cook. The plantain, fried or boiled, is another starchy staple.

Griots are spicy bits of pork loin basted with lime sauce and/or Piment Boucar hot sauce. Raw rum called Clairin can be added to the basting sauce or to the diner.

JAMAICA

The yellow, bland ackee fruit is so common in Jamaica that it is called "free food." It is a basic ingredient for one of the national dishes, Salt Fish and Ackee. Salt codfish also appears in the form of fritters called Stamp and Go. Another island classic is Jamaican Pepper Pot, which can be a soup or stew of pork and beef with tropical vegetables, often including okra, plantains, cassava root, and dasheen (a potatolike tuber). Red

Pea Soup is made from the kidney beans beloved in Jamaica.

Goat and mutton are the most popular meats of Jamaica's poorer classes. Curried Goat (the dish can also be made with lamb) is a traditional celebration dish.

Fried fish sauced with peppers, onions, and vinegar is called Escovitch in Jamaica. The name and method seem to be derived from the Spanish *en escabeche*: food with a vinegar sauce.

PUERTO RICO

Like most of the Caribbean, the Commonwealth of Puerto Rico (part of the United States) enjoys rice, beans, chicken, and salt cod. Rice and beans are frequently served together as a meal or a side dish. Gandules—green pigeon peas—are relished with or without rice, or in the form of soup. Chicken and rice appear together in the popular Asopao, a soup-stew flavored with ham, peas, peppers, garlic, oregano, olives, and capers. The olive-caper combination, called *alcaparrado*, frequently is used to give zest to Puerto Rican cooking. Annatto (here called *achiote*) and cilantro (fresh coriander) are common seasonings. Many recipes start with Sofrito: onions, peppers, ham, and seasonings simmered in lard or oil.

No discussion of Puerto Rican cooking is complete without mentioning the plantain. Fried plantain, mashed with pork cracklings—*chicharrones*—and garlic make the *pâté*-textured Mofongo. A stuffing of ham, beef, tomatoes, and onion, and a swim in boiling oil, turn plantain slices into Piononos. A similar stuffing, enriched with raisins, pork, *alcaparrado*, and mashed plantains or squash is steamed in a plantain leaf and served up as Pasteles. Boiled plantains are mashed to thicken broths of fish or chicken. Green plantains are boiled and served with the popular codfish in a dish called Guineos. Finger bananas, *guineitos*, a related species, are used for main dishes and desserts.

A religious or secular celebration is likely to feature Pernil—rolled pork shoulder roasted or pot-roasted with lots of garlic, onions, and *alcaparrado*. Mondongo is a stew of tripe, chickpeas, and tropical vegetables. Turnovers (Pastelillos) with meat or cheese fillings are relished as between-meal snacks.

Puddings are popular desserts: Tembleque, or coconut pudding; Pudin de Pan, or bread pudding, for example. Guava paste and Cascos de Guayaba, or guava shells, are also favorite desserts.

ST. MARTIN/ST.MAARTEN

This small island (thirty-seven square miles) is divided into two parts and two heritages: French and Dutch. The Dutch side—which uses the "St. Maarten" spelling—has naturalized *rijsttafel*, and serves its local lobster in salad and its land crabs with stuffing. Peanut-butter soup is another St. Maarten delicacy. Saba Spice is a drink of rum and local spices. Over on the other side, food of the French persuasion prevails on restaurant menus.

TRINIDAD AND TOBAGO

Pudding is an Anglo-Saxon contribution to the cooking of Trinidad and Tobago. Pudding, also enjoyed in Barbados, means blood sausage. Its usual partner is Souse, pig's head, feet, and tongue marinated in lime juice. The combination often appears at Sunday brunches and afternoon parties.

A small number of Asian Indian immigrants contributed a large influence to the diet of Trinidad. Deep-fried Indian vegetable fritters are popular during carnival time. Pelau, a combination of pigeon peas, rice, chicken or meat, raisins, tomatoes, and saffron, is a Trinidadian national dish.

THE VIRGIN ISLANDS

Many flags have flown over the Virgin Islands, so there has been a rich mixture of cooking styles. This eclectic cuisine keeps changing; an important influence today is the large-scale arrival of Puerto Rican immigrants. A large percentage of the population of St. Croix is now of Puerto Rican descent, so Puerto-Rican-style dishes are gaining in popularity.

Callaloo, fish-and-crab chowder, is enjoyed in the Virgin Islands. Most Caribbean Callaloos are made with taro leaves, but the Virgin Islanders prefer to use spinach. The traditional accompaniment to a Virginian Callaloo is Funchi, or cornmeal dumplings. Gundi is a common St. Croix dish; it's a cold salad mold of fish or lobster, potatoes, onions, and beets. Maufé is another Crucian dish: chopped salted meats and fresh fish combined and cooked in a cornmeal gruel.

OTHER CARIBBEAN ISLANDS

Grenada, Barbados, the Bahamas, and Bermuda share a British heritage, which is reflected in customs such as tea drinking. All these islands share a love of pigeon peas and rice, conch, and coconuts. Oil Down is a Grenadan stew of breadfruit, green bananas, and pig's tails cooked with coconut oil. The bright-scarlet fruit-based syrup Grenadine is originally from this island. Flying fish are extremely common on Barbadian tables in April and May. Jug-Jug, a national dish of Barbados, is a molded meat, cornmeal, and pigeon-pea pudding. Though not technically part of the Caribbean, Bermuda offers comparable delights to sand-loving visitors. It also offers similar foods: fish; turtle and conch soups; lobster; codfish and bananas—the last two sometimes combined for breakfast.

The Dominican Republic, Haiti's Spanish-speaking neighbor, uses the fruits of the sea in Pescado Santo Domingo, a cold appetizer of sea bass, and in Sopa Hamaca, a soup-stew of fish, lobster, rice, potatoes, and vegetables.

GENERAL CARIBBEAN CHARACTERISTICS

Well-seasoned soup-stews made with the tropical fruits and vegetables that grow so abundantly are enormously popular. The principal nonvegetarian ingredient in these soup-stews is seafood, with pork and chicken next in popularity. Two of the best-known soup-stews are Callaloo, normally made with young taro leaves and crab, and the vegetable and meat Sancocho.

Hot chili peppers are frequently employed to season foods. Bananas, plantains, yams, cassava root, taro root, rice, and breadfruit are day-to-day staples and contribute to making the diet of the islands exceedingly starchy, a Caribbean culinary characteristic.

Numerous tropical fruits grow on the Caribbean islands, among them the plentiful coconuts, mangoes and bananas. The sapodilla is about the size of a plum, with brown skin and yellow flesh. The soursop, used in soft drinks and ices, is a green, spiny fruit with tangy white flesh. The Jamaican ugli fruit—which looks like a grapefruit that has been on the losing end of a barroom fight—is bred by crossing grapefruit, orange, and tangerine. Fortunately it tastes better than it looks.

BEVERAGES

Rum is the principal spirit of the Caribbean and tends to be light in the Spanish-speaking islands, such as Puerto Rico, and dark in such former English colonies as Jamaica. Derived from sugar cane, it is the base of Caribbean-invented alcoholic drinks that are known the world over: Daiquiri, Rum and Coca-Cola, Piña Colada, and Planter's Punch. Today Planter's Punch can mean any drink of rum and fruit juice. The traditional formula is "one of sour (lime juice), two of sweet (sugar or sugar syrup), three of strong (rum), and four of weak (water or ice)." That's a two-fisted drink. Tamer are the nonalcoholic Batidos, tropical-fruit milkshakes.

Though its people are not really big coffee drinkers, the Caribbean produces one of the greatest (some say *the* greatest) coffees in the world: Jamaican Blue Mountain. It is expensive and rare and therefore often counterfeited by profiteering coffeemongers.

MEXICO

THE COMBINATION PLATES (Tacos, Enchiladas, Tamales, Tostados, Refried Beans, Tortillas, etc.) served in restaurants outside Mexico are not typically mainstream Mexican. First, these platters are laden with foods prepared in the culinary style of Mexico's arid and thinly populated northern states; thus, they do not represent the cuisine of Mexico's more fertile and heavily populated southern heartland. Furthermore, popular adaptations like Tex-Mex and Cal-Mex cooking further distort the typical Mexican cuisine by adapting it to foreign tastes. This is done by substituting different or inferior cooking ingredients because authentic ones are unavailable, and by fabricating new dishes—as was the case when Chili con Carne was invented in Texas. Third, to many Mexicans, dishes like Tostados and Enchiladas are considered *antojitos* ("little whims"), and more appropriate as appetizers or snacks, not serious eating.

For more characteristic Mexican food, one must travel at least several hundred miles south of the Rio Grande, where different climates yield different raw ingredients that in turn yield different cuisines. Let's explore several of the most important ones.

THE COASTAL CUISINE

The coastal areas—such as those around Acapulco on the Pacific and Veracruz on the Caribbean side of the country—rely more on the natural goodness of their fresh ingredients, especially the seafood and tropical fruits, than on a sophisticated cooking style.

Huachinango a la Veracruzana, a typical coastal recipe, is red snapper marinated in lime juice and baked with chilies, tomato purée, olives, and capers. Another Veracruz seafood dish is Jaibas en Chilpachole—crabs simmered in a thin, spicy tomato broth flavored with the oft-used Mexican herb epazote, sometimes called Mexican tea, Jerusalem oak pazote or wormseed in America.

THE MEXICO CITY AREA

The inland semitemperate plateaus, such as the Mexico City area, feature relatively more sophisticated cooking and a broader array of ingredients. One notable creation is Mole Poblano de Guajolote—turkey cooked in a complex sauce incorporating dozens of ingredients, including various chilies and chocolate, though you shouldn't taste more than a hint of the chocolate. It has definite pre-Columbian origins, but most cookbooks and the dish's own name link it to sixteenth-century nuns in a convent in Puebla, a town about 100 miles southeast of Mexico City. About 100 miles south of Puebla is the town of Oaxaca, whose residents believe its hotter Mole Negro is far superior.

YUCATÁN

Yucatán's unique dishes include Pollo Pibil (chicken marinated with reddish annato spice, rolled in banana leaves, and steamed in an outdoor pit), Sopa de Lima (lime-infused chicken soup garnished with sizzling tortilla fragments), and Papatzul (rolled and stuffed tortillas smothered with a pumpkin-seed sauce).

The inhabitants of this ancient Mayan region also enjoy Panuchos, a casserole of chicken breasts, black beans, and eggs, and Muk-Bil Pollo, a chicken pie baked beneath a crust of cornmeal.

JALISCO

Fiery Pozole is a Mexican staple originating from Jalisco, a state located in the middle of Mexico's west coast. One way to make Pozole is to simmer chicken stock, pork butt, and a pig's foot with hominy, oregano, and a great deal of dried chili.

NATIONAL CHARACTERISTICS

Mexican cooking wouldn't be the same without its variety of chilies—not all of which are hot. The Chile Poblano is large, green, and mild. The chipotle, pequin, and jalapeño are examples of the hot chilies.

Certain herbs, spices, and flavoring agents are equally popular: cumin, cinnamon, cloves, coriander, oregano, onions, garlic, and lemon or lime juice. Red and green tomatoes, avocados, plantains, bananas, and other fruits play a prominent role in Mexico's cooking. The chayote (christophine) is a large, sweet squash served as a fruit. Nopales are edible cactus leaves. Jicamas are starchy vegetables that look a lot like turnips and taste a little like water chestnuts. The cherimoya is a fruit related to the Caribbean custard-apple, eaten raw with cinnamon and lime juice.

Mexico's main starchy staples are maize, rice, and beans. The principal meats are beef in the cattle-grazing lands in the north and pork, kid, chicken, and turkey in the central and southern areas. Fish and shellfish—especially shrimp—are popular along the coasts.

Tortillas, which can be made of wheat or corn, are the bread of Mexico. In the northern states, where rainfall is insufficient for growing reliable corn crops, the Tortilla is often made with wheat flour. The rest of Mexico uses the corn-based Tortilla, just as the Aztecs did more than a half-millennium ago.

Tortillas appear in almost every traditional Mexican meal—from *desayuno* (breakfast) to *comida*, the midday dinner, to *cena* (light supper) served somewhere between 8 and 10 o'clock. A traditional *comida* has many courses: soup, *sopa seca* (dry soup), poultry, fish, and/or a meat main dish, dessert, and siesta. The *sopa seca* is a starchy food—perhaps rice or leftover Tortillas—cooked in a little broth.

In Mexico as a whole, sauces are very popular. Almost every meal is served accompanied by Salsa Cruda, a freshly-made condiment of chopped tomatoes, onions, chilies, and coriander leaves.

Many desserts originated in the convents established by the Spanish. Mexico's preference for sweet desserts, such as Flan, can also be traced to Spain, which originally gained its sweet tooth from the Middle East via the Moors. Street vendors throughout Mexico sell candies, sometimes made of sweet-potato-and-sugar paste, and rich cakes.

BEVERAGES

Mexico is well-known for its frothy hot chocolate, traditionally whipped up in the cup with a *molinillo*, a carved wooden stick. The Aztecs restricted this drink to royalty; the Spanish added sugar and cinnamon and democratized the beverage.

Mexico is becoming a major coffee producer—the Altura Coatepec is its best. A favorite way to serve the brew is with hot milk and cinnamon.

The sap of the maguey plant is fermented into Pulque, a twelve-proof drink enjoyed by many Mexicans and few foreigners. Visitors are, in general, fonder of Tequila, a strong, colorless drink distilled from the cactuslike agave plant. For the best, look for the darker-colored, aged product.

But the best accompaniment to a spicy Mexican meal is an icy bottle of excellent Mexican beer: the light Carta Blanca, Superior, or Bohemia, the dark Dos Equis or Leon Negro.

PERU AND ECUADOR

THESE TWO COUNTRIES, ALONG with parts of Bolivia and northern Chile, share a rich Inca heritage. Today the cooking styles of both nations are mainly creole, a combination of the deeply rooted Indian and Spanish cuisines.

Rather than thinking in terms of Peruvian vs. Ecuadorian cuisines, it makes more sense to categorize the cuisines into two distinct geographic areas that Peru and Ecuador share: the coastal lowlands and the Andean mountains.

The coastal lowland creole cuisine is lighter (mainly because of the warmer weather) and more sophisticated (principally because of the greater range of available cooking ingredients and the relatively higher standard of living) than the mountain cuisine. The cook certainly has a wide choice of semitropical and, from the irrigated river valleys, temperate-climate fruits and vegetables. Coastal inhabitants also enjoy excellent fish and shellfish, thanks to the plankton-rich Peru Current. The fresh waters yield a fine harvest, too, including the large, highly regarded crayfish named the camarone. Basic staples include maize (corn), bananas and plantains (especially in Ecuador and northern Peru), avocados, peanuts, beans, rice (found in many dishes, often with beans), and the potato.

It is in the Andean highlands, however, that the potato comes into its own. This indigenous tuber is ideally suited (and just about the only vegetable suited) for this chilly climate. Because the weather is cold, hearty soups and stews are regular table offerings, even if it means merely a simple potato soup for the poor family. These peasants also boil the potatoes, perking them up with hot peppers, salt, available herbs and perhaps cheese. Some potatoes are preserved by the ancient Incan freeze-dried method.

Both the lowland and mountain cuisines share a fondness for spicing their foods with the ají, a variety of hot chili which can be scorchingly hot or merely tingling to the palate, depending on the species. Both regions love coloring their foods red-orange with the annatto seed.

The more famous Peruvian/Ecuadorian specialties include:

Anticuchos Chunks of beef heart marinated in vinegar, then skewered and grilled with hot sauce; a popular hors d'oeuvre and street snack.

Ceviche Sometimes spelled *Seviche*, it consists of chunks of raw fish and/or shellfish marinated in lime or lemon juice and, if you like, chopped onion and ají pepper flavoring.

Guinea Pig This rodent can be roasted, grilled, stewed, or sautéed much as you would rabbit or chicken.

Llapingachos Potato-and-cheese croquettes, much loved in Ecuador.

Locro A thick, beef-broth-based potato-and-cheese soup, sometimes served with a garnish of avocado slices, especially popular in Ecuador.

Pachamanca A special occasion, cook-in-a-pit affair that resembles the Hawaiian *luau*. It can include whole piglet or kid, chicken, guinea pig, and accompanying vegetables, all steam-roasted over hot stones in a pit, lined and covered with sweet-smelling leaves.

Papas a la Huancaina Potatoes with a spicy cheese sauce.

Of course, the nearly ubiquitous Latin American Tamale or Humita is a major treat in Peru and Ecuador, as are other dishes such as Escabeche ("pickled" meat).

East of the Andes lies the thinly populated tropical rain forest. Here most inhabitants—except those residing in the rare Amazonian towns, like the Iquitos—live a primitive existence, gathering and eating whatever the untamed jungle can provide, be it iguanas, snakes, monkeys, bird eggs, river fish, edible roots, or tropical fruits like the banana.

BEVERAGES

Pisco Brandy is the base of Peru's famous cocktail, the Pisco Sour, made with lemon or lime juice, bitters, frothy egg white, and sweet syrup. Chica de Maíz Morada is a soft beverage made from purple corn, among other ingredients. Its potent cousin is Chicha de Jora, again concocted from purple corn, but this time fermented into a beerlike drink. Soda pop, vendor-sold fresh-fruit drinks, and coffee are basics, too, as is beer, which can be rather good.

⌒ UNITED STATES

GENERAL AMERICAN CHARACTERISTICS

To understand American food we must contemplate *abundance*: vast tracts of land blessed with fertility and tilled with the aid of modern technology. For the sake of illustration, let's examine one particular culinary facet that is very much associated with America: meat. While hungry immigrants tasted it infrequently in their homelands, today most of their sons and grandsons are "meat-and-potatoes men" who eat this protein-rich food twice or three times a day.

Pork was the most popular meat in the colonial, federal, and antebellum periods in the United States, because any farmer (and many town-dwellers) could keep a few hogs. The independent porkers could fend for themselves and, come slaughtering time, furnish plenty of fresh meat, cooking fat, and smoked hams and sausage that would keep without refrigeration.

Nowadays beef is America's favorite meat, the result of its good quality and, by worldwide standards, relatively low price. This can be largely attributed to the great amount of "surplus" productive land that is allocated for grazing acreage and fodder raising as opposed to growing foods such as fruits, vegetables, and dairy products for direct human consumption. We also should not underestimate the invaluable contribution made by the midnineteenth-century development of the railroads. Before the iron horse came, cattle had to be driven to market, foraging en route. In this age, grain is shipped by railroad to fatten cattle, and the cattle themselves are shipped (thus eliminating a long walk for the cattle, which toughens the meat) or the meat is shipped while it is still fresh. Many of the American beef steaks, chops, and roasts are tender enough to be eaten after a quick high-heat cooking—this, too, is a rarity in most other parts of the world.

Another culinary characteristic mainly pioneered by Americans is the scientific production of foodstuffs. To illustrate, most chickens, which appear in the supermarkets, are raised in indoor farm factories that spew forth less expensive, and less flavorful, poultry—it is a mixed blessing.

The same cost-efficiency methods have been applied to grains, vegetables, and fruits. Advances in canning, freezing, transportation, and processing make it possible for Americans to eat almost any food grown anywhere in any season. This accessibility has added variety and broken down provincialism; but it has also suppressed rich traditions of regional cuisine. At one time, fruits and vegetables were available only in season, and only if they were produced locally. This was not as limiting as it seems because local growers supplied many varieties of fresh produce—apples, for example, came in dozens of tasty varieties. Now fewer varieties are available, because a vast mechanized farm must specialize in a particular apple, potato, or tomato. The varieties grown are often chosen more for appearance, longevity, and ease of processing than for flavor.

In early America commercial food processing was minimal. Either homegrown food was prepared from scratch, or lightly processed foods such as flour were bought and turned into finished dishes. The nineteenth century introduced canned foods, prepared yeast, and baking powder; the twentieth century, an increasing tendency toward the purchase of fully prepared foods. Canned, boxed, or frozen meals must be standardized; and subtlety and individuality must be sacrificed to bacterial safety, shelf-life, and mass appeal.

An American-inspired custom that is slowly being transmitted to the world is the hurried meal. Tons of "fast foods"—items that can be prepared en masse and served quickly—are consumed every year. The Hamburger, grilled ground beef on a soft bun, and the Hotdog, a rather bland sausage served on an elongated bun, are popular examples.

Heroes, Grinders, Submarines, and Poor-boys are some of the names given to hot or cold sandwiches, often vaguely Italian in inspiration, served inside long, thin loaves of bread. Fried chicken, fried fish, Mexican- and Italian-style foods are also common fast-food items. Ice cream and a multiplicity of doughnuts satiate the sweet tooth on the run.

To many Americans no meal is enjoyable without a dessert. Most American desserts are less sweet than, say, Middle Eastern pastries and confections—but American desserts are eaten once or twice a day, every day, not reserved for occasional indulgences. Sugar also finds its way into many entrées—Americans collectively have a sweet tooth.

Certain fabled horrors of the American table—"casseroles" made from desiccated leftovers or canned tuna, interspersed with layers of limp macaroni and laved with canned soups, for example, are mercifully disappearing, at least among a small but growing faction. As food prices and consciousness rise, there is a trend toward reviving the cooking of America's immigrant ancestors and the traditional regional cooking of America: economical dishes lovingly prepared with fresh, high-quality ingredients.

NEW ENGLAND

The English settlers experienced terrible hardships for the first few years in New England, which was less like the old than the name, hopefully given, suggests. The English encountered a raw land with huge forests and rough seas, settled only by relatively few Indians. The settlers, who were basically city dwellers, were unfamiliar with farming, fishing, and hunting. The English wheat they planted failed miserably, so they had to resort to corn, introduced to them by the Indians, in addition to many other unfamiliar plants, such as squash, beans, and berries.

Once the initial awkwardness was overcome, the New Englanders reaped the bounty of the land, compounding a cuisine that was hearty and basically English. The Puritans had no objection to bright colors, drinking per se, and good food;

they were hampered more by lack of materials than by doctrine.

The early New England housewife would probably do all her cooking over and in front of the fireplace that also provided heat, light, and hot water. An elaborate fireplace would have a panoply of hooks, cranes, brick ovens, spits, and reflectors; a simple fireplace, nothing but a hearth and a wooden lug-pole to suspend a caldron. The cook might possess cast-iron spiders (three-legged frying pans), Dutch ovens (in this case large three-legged covered iron pots for cooking in hot ashes), and drip pans; or she might have nothing more than a large iron caldron or two. In any event she would want slow-cooking foods that needed little tending as she went about her other work. She would use the foods easily available to her to produce typical New England dishes such as:

Baked Beans Dried beans, salt pork, molasses or maple sugar, and an onion, heaped into a bean pot, could bake in hot ashes at home, or in a communal oven. Some early New England settlers took a hard line on the Sabbath and, to avoid lighting a fire on the day of rest, would bake the beans and steam the accompanying corn-rye Brown Bread in the retained heat of an oven "turned off" on Saturday night. The beans were served after church. With less strict observance, Baked Beans became a traditional economical Saturday night supper.

Boiled Dinner This combination of salt pork, corned beef, or salt cod (all readily available, long-keeping foodstuffs) with potatoes, onions, cabbage, turnips, carrots, and beets required little attention from the cook. Hungry family members could get a hot meal from the caldron at any time of day; and leftovers could be chopped into Red-Flannel Hash.

Clam Chowder The clams swim in a stock of milk, salt pork, pilot crackers, and potatoes. Rhode Islanders and Manhattanites skip the milk and include tomatoes; such goings-on are deplored in Massachusetts and Maine.

Codfish Balls Fishing, especially cod fishing, was and is a mainstay of the New England table and economy. One popular use for dried cod was the fabrication of fish cakes, often savored on Sunday morning with leftover beans, Brown Bread, and Dropped Eggs (elsewhere called poached).

Indian Pudding A milk, molasses, and cornmeal (Indian meal) pudding that could be wrapped in a cloth and steamed over a cooking pot or laundry boiler. Hasty Pudding is similar: cornmeal mush served with a sweet sauce often based on molasses.

Other New England products include lobsters, clams, blueberries, and cranberries. The shellfish are often steamed; the berries are preserved or go into muffins, grunts, and slumps. The latter two alarming names refer to desserts of stewed fruit topped with biscuits.

THE MIDDLE ATLANTIC STATES

This populous region houses a variety of cooking styles. The Pennsylvania Dutch are descendants of German Pietists. New York is the home of millions of second- and third-generation Americans of immigrant descent, so fascinating culinary styles have evolved, which are discussed below. Maryland's cooking stems from the gifts of the sea.

The Pennsylvania Dutch, (including the Amish and Mennonites) believe in hard work and a simple life without modern conveniences. They also believe in a profusion of food—soups, meat dishes, relishes, and sweets, served buffet-style at every meal. A Pennsylvania Dutch table might feature:

Potpies The Pennsylvania Dutch name for large, flat noodles. Meat or chicken, vegetables, and broth are cooked with the potpies.

Schnitz und Knepp Dried apples (*schnitz*) and dumplings *(knepp)* cooked with ham broth or bits of ham.

Scrapple   Cooked pork scraps mixed with seasoned cornmeal and packed into loaves. Scrapple is sliced and broiled or fried for breakfast, or used like sausage in main dishes.

Seven Sweets and Seven Sours   Each meal has a selection of the cook's own homemade relishes and side dishes: pies, cakes, pudding, apple butter, home-canned pickles, chow-chow, piccalilli, and other relishes.

Shoofly Pie   A crumb pie with a molasses filling. There are two schools of shoofly-pie bakers: dry for dunking, wet for spooning. Other Pennsylvania Dutch pies include Funeral Pie (made with raisins), Preaching Pie (small dried-fruit turnovers for restive children to munch during sermons), and Schnitz Pie (filled with dried apples).

Two famous Pennsylvanian preparations that are not Pennsylvania Dutch in origin are:

Fish House Punch   One of the countless "authentic" recipes calls for a mixture of rum, cognac, peach brandy, and sweetened lime or lemon juice.

Pepper Pot   A tripe soup seasoned with lots of peppercorns (one of the few popular American dishes to use tripe).

Maryland is famous for its seafood: crab cakes and other dishes of crabmeat, Terrapin Stew (turtle cooked with cream, eggs, and sherry), and sociable oyster roasts, where the bivalves open over hot coals and are served with butter or hot sauce.

THE SOUTH (AND SOUL FOOD)

The southern economy has always revolved around cash crops—cotton and tobacco—rather than food crops. Rich planter, poor white, and black slave had the same basic diet: pork, corn, greens, peas, game, and fish. The planters got the sweet smoked ham, the rich Spoonbread, the delicate fish; the poor (black and white) existed on the jowls, salt pork, coarse cornbreads, and the homely—in both senses of the word—catfish.

Beaten Biscuits   These are made of soft white flour; so are Baking-Powder Biscuits. Beaten Biscuits contain no leavening, and are lightened by repeated beating.

Burgoo   A Kentucky stew of beef, chicken, and/or game (usually squirrel) with fresh vegetables. Brunswick Stew is similar.

Chitlins   Well-scrubbed hog intestines—a Soul specialty—boiled or fried; in either case, served with lots of hot sauce.

Cornbread   White and yellow cornbread appear in many forms in the southern kitchen. The traditional cornbread is unsweetened and baked in an iron skillet. Corn Sticks are baked in iron molds shaped like ears of corn. Spoonbread is rich, light, eggy, and puffy. Hush Puppies are fried morsels sometimes used to quiet importunate canines (or humans) until the fish or chicken is properly fried.

Country Ham   Fine southern hams come from grain- or peanut-fed hogs, and are salt-cured, sometimes rubbed with molasses, always smoked carefully over hardwood fires and well aged. The celebrated Smithfield Hams come from peanut-eating razorback hogs. Country Ham is served cold with biscuits, or sliced and frizzled for breakfast with Red-Eye Gravy, made by deglazing the frying pan with water or black coffee.

Fried Chicken   A controversial topic. Some cooks marinate the chicken in vinegar, buttermilk, or sweet milk; some do no marinating. The chicken can be floured or dipped in a flour-egg-milk batter. Sometimes the chicken is deep-fried; sometimes browned in fat, then finished in a frying pan with a little water, or baked. The time-honored way to do the original frying is in an uncovered skillet. This keeps the cook occupied the next day—scraping the grease off the kitchen walls.

Grits   Hominy Grits are ground, lye-treated corn kernels cooked into a thick porridge, which can be served for breakfast, lunch, or dinner.

Hoppin' John   Black-eyed peas and rice. A traditional Soul Food for New Year's day, for luck throughout the year.

She-Crab Soup   A Charleston, South Carolina, specialty involving the meat and eggs of the female crab.

Other Soul Food specialties include Barbecued Spareribs, Smothered Chicken (sautéed, then cooked slowly with onions and liquid), Greens and Pot Likker (the juice produced by boiling greens with salt pork), Hog Maw (stuffed pig's stomach), and Sweet Potato Pie. Wild foods such as fried catfish, roast opossum, beaver, and raccoon are part of the Soul Food legacy; slaves were allowed to capture small "worthless" game to supplement their diet at no cost to the master.

Bourbon is an indigenous American drink. Scottish and Irish immigrants in Pennsylvania, Maryland, and Virginia comforted themselves with flacons, at first made with their accustomed rye, then with rye mixed with the indigenous corn, then with corn alone. By the late eighteenth century they had developed Bourbon. The Mint Julep is a cocktail of sweetened Bourbon and water flavored with mint; Southern Comfort is a proprietary blend of a sweet peach-flavored Bourbon.

NEW ORLEANS

Two of the major contributors to this unique cuisine are the Creoles and the Cajuns. The first are descendants of the French colonists; the Cajuns (Acadians) are an isolated group descended from the French who migrated via New Brunswick, Canada. Creoles and Cajuns share an appreciation for seafood, *charcuterie*, and spicy tomato sauce. They cook with *roux,* a mixture of butter or olive oil and flour, and decorate seafood with High Holy Mayonnaise. (It's not a religious slur—just a Louisiana version of Aïoli.) Other New Orleans favorites include:

Calas   Rice fritters especially savored during the hungry interval between Sunday Mass and breakfast. After the Civil War, many freedwomen earned a living selling Calas door to door and outside the churches.

Dirty Rice   A pilaf of rice and chicken giblets, which gives the rice its "dirty" appearance.

Grillades and Grits   A hearty New Orleans breakfast of veal or beef steak braised with Creole Sauce (tomatoes, onions, green peppers, celery, garlic) served on a bed of bland and porous Hominy Grits.

Gumbo   A mixture of seafood and/or chicken and/or ham, vegetables, and liquid served over rice. There are two kinds of Gumbo thickener: okra and filé (crumbled or powdered sassafras leaves). The two are never used together. Gumbo z'Herbes, made of vegetables only, is prescribed on Good Friday for a lucky year.

Jambalaya   A Cajun stew of crawfish, shrimp, chicken, sausage, and ham, in proportions dictated by availability and inspiration; all with rice. Rather like an uninhibited Paella.

La Médiatrice   An aristocratic poor-boy sandwich: French bread stuffed with fried oysters.

Oysters Rockefeller   Oysters on the half-shell, smothered with an anise-flavored sauce, then baked and served on a bed of rock salt.

New Orleans is also famous for its mud bugs (crawfish) which can be visualized as one-ounce freshwater lobsters, served boiled or *étouffée* (smothered). Crabs, oysters, and shrimp are also local mainstays.

Café Brulôt is an elaborate hot drink of coffee and spices

flamed with Brandy. The Sazerac and Suissesse are anise-flavored New Orleans cocktails.

FLORIDA

Florida's food bounty comes from its subtropical climate and its waters. The tough but delectable conch is made into chowder, fritters, and salad. Sea crayfish (spiny lobsters) are served boiled. The delicately flavored pompano fish is presented broiled or en *papillote*, steamed in a package of parchment paper or foil, while turtles are usually reincarnated in soup. Stone crabs can be literally recycled: one claw is broken off the live crab, which is returned to the sea, where it regenerates a new claw to provide further crabmeat.

Tons of Florida oranges are squeezed for juice. The key lime, whose juice flavors Key Lime Pie, is a tropical fruit growing in Florida; so are bananas, coconuts, pineapples, mangoes, and tamarinds. Palm trees also flourish in this climate; palm hearts are the focus of Millionaire's Salad.

Expatriate New Yorkers have brought the delicatessen to Florida; Greek fishermen and Cuban refugees have also contributed their favorite foods to the Florida cuisine.

THE MIDWEST

This is farming country, the breadbasket not only of the United States but also of many foreign countries. Although immigrants, especially those from Central and Eastern Europe, had their impact on the midwestern table (see the section on Immigrant Cuisines below), midwestern food tends to be simple, classic American, and lightly seasoned. Steak and french fries is a popular meal. Fried or stewed chicken, pork chops, and pot roast are also typically midwestern. The accent is on hearty, filling meals with a sweet dessert—say, gingerbread, apple pie, pumpkin pie, or brownies—at the end.

Food and fellowship are traditionally combined in midwestern pot-lucks and church suppers, sponsored by women's clubs for fund-raising, enjoyment, or as a showcase for each woman's favorite and tastiest recipe.

State fairs blend education and trade with good times. Much pride goes into the production of livestock and foods for judging. (Too often, however, the blue ribbon rewards superficial beauty or size, not flavor and texture). Farm wives still enter their best home-canned food and preserves for judging.

TEX-MEX COOKING

The Texans (and their fellow southwesterners) join the Mexicans in their love and admiration for the chili pepper. But Texas cooks scorn all the South-of-the-Border tricks for stretching a little meat a long way, or for serving meatless meals. Plenty of meat is available, and they love to eat it as well as serve it to their guests. "Meat" usually means beef, though an occasional sparerib or baby goat (*cabrito*) finds its way into the barbecue pit. The cattlemen called lamb "wool on a handle"; this expression is not entirely outdated. Beefsteaks can be broiled or "chicken-fried"—pounded, batter-dipped, and fried. Texans like Enchiladas (meatier and less spicy than its Mexican counterpart), Tacos, Pepper Cornbread studded with chili peppers, and Barbecue; they also like (and discuss):

Chili The "bowl of red" has many enthusiasts in and out of Texas. Eastern cooks seize on it as a bean-filled, inexpensive meal, stretched with tomato sauce. Midwesterners serve their chili over spaghetti, sometimes studded with frankfurters. Texans are divided into several schools of thought about chili, each school fiercely defending its orthodoxy. It is generally agreed that ground beef makes inferior chili; chopped or scissor-cut steak is felt to have the correct texture. Commercial chili powders are scorned, and beans are taboo. Most Texans exclude tomatoes from their chili—but Lyndon Baines

Johnson, a patriotic Texan, insisted on tomatoes. Border Buttermilk—Tequila and lime juice—is a deceptively cooling accompaniment to properly fiery chili.

CALIFORNIA

The most characteristic attribute of Californian cooks is the willingness to experiment—centuries-old tradition be damned. While most of the trial-and-error escapades have created culinary monstrosities, some commendable dishes have resulted. One of the best-known innovations is the Caesar Salad, a mixture of romaine, garlic croutons, and raw or coddled eggs. A host of other salads are made with California oranges, dates, avocados, and other fresh produce.

California is also noted for its seafood—abalone, rex sole, Dungeness crab, among other species.

PIONEER AND COWBOY COOKING

Pioneers on the move, or cowboys on a cattle drive, had to eat what they could carry, catch, or harvest on the way. Cooking had to be done over an open fire, with simple metal skillets, caldrons, and baking sheets. The Wild West cook's biggest asset was the Dutch oven, which could be nestled in the coals, with more coals piled on its heavy concave lid for baking.

The cowboys had plenty of beef available. They had lots of beans ("Mexican strawberries"), biscuits, and coffee, but not much else. As a special treat, the chuck-wagon "cooky" might bake dried-apple pie with biscuit dough. When a young calf was killed, there would be Son of a Bitch Stew made with the calf's internal organs. The marrow gut—an infantile digestive organ—was prized for the flavor it gave the stew.

The pioneers had less access to fresh meat, though some carried lambs in their wagon trains. Most of their meat was salt pork, bacon or ham. The diet was monotonous and starchy—pork, biscuits, cornbread, and coffee—relieved by game, fish, and fruit encountered en route. The wagons usually carried some dried fruit. Dried-Apple Pie was served frequently, greeted by all the enthusiasm with which a modern politician faces his ten-thousandth plate of Chicken à la King.

NATIVE AMERICAN (INDIAN) COOKING

The food of diverse American Indian tribes, with their individual resources and cultures, cannot be described in a few words. The following is just a brief summary.

Much Indian agriculture was based on the "Indian triad" of corn, beans, and squash. The Indians taught the English settlers to grow corn in hills, fertilizing each mound with fish. Fresh or dried corn and beans, sometimes stewed with meat, made Succotash, an Indian dish adopted by the settlers. The Indians also taught the newcomers to make Hominy by treating corn kernels with lye, and Popcorn by heating dried corn kernels.

The Indian diet relied heavily on meat. The Indians relished turkey, deer, squirrel, bear, and many other kinds of game. The flesh and fat of game animals, pounded with berries, made Pemmican, a nutritious long-keeping food adopted by the European newcomers. Sun-dried meat called Jerky was another Indian contribution to the American diet.

The Indians were skilled foragers, providing many nuts, vegetables, and fruit to vary their diet and ensure good nutrition. They used cranberries, pine-needle and other herb teas to prevent scurvy.

The diet of the Plains Indians, and their culture as a whole, centered on the buffalo. They ate the meat, clothed themselves with buffalo skins, carved utensils out of buffalo bones; nothing was wasted. The white man's destruction of the buffalo also destroyed the Plains Indian culture. The destruction of other Indian cultures was less dramatic, but no less real.

IMMIGRANT CUISINES

When Italians, Jews, Scandinavians, Irish, Germans, and other immigrants entered the United States, they found climate and available food ingredients somewhat alien. Sometimes they used old recipes, but more often they used new ingredients in the old style or invented completely new dishes.

Frequently, a man would come to America alone to work for his family's passage money. These temporary bachelors often ate in restaurants established by their compatriots. The food was not subtle. In the case of Italian food, for instance, it exaggerated Sicilian and Neapolitan tendencies to produce cheap, filling meals redolent of garlic and roseate with tomato sauce. Soon Americans of non-Italian backgrounds would be patronizing the "red ink joints," decorated with red-checked tablecloths and candles in straw-covered Chianti bottles. You could get a bottle of wine and dishes like:

Cioppino This hearty mixed-fish soup-stew has cousins in Italy, but was born and raised in San Francisco.

Pizza Italy has a simple snack of bits of bread dough with garnishes. The American version is a gargantuan wheel of dough, tomato sauce, and cheese garnished with mushroom, sausage, cheese, anchovies, peppers, meatballs, or whatever cook and customer can agree on. After World War II, this style of "American" Pizza was transported to Italy.

Spaghetti and Meatballs Italy, of course, has spaghetti, lots of it, and meatballs, some of them; but the combination became a famous dish in America where meat, especially chopped meat, was comparatively cheap.

Italian-American and Italian foods such as Calzone (fried Ricotta cheese and sausage turnovers), Zeppole (irregularly

shaped doughnuts), Tortoni (frozen almond mousse), Spu-
moni (multiflavored ice cream), and Espresso and Capuccino
coffees are very popular in the United States. Bologna's
Mortadella sausage is a very remote ancestor of the American
Baloney.

Generations of comedians and writers have publicized
Jewish food to such an extent that even many Kansan gentiles
are familiar enough to joke about Lox and Bagels.

Not many Jews keep kosher, but most maintain an
occasional nostalgia for foods like:

Chicken Soup "Jewish penicillin," prescribed for all
illnesses and every Friday-night dinner. The chicken broth
usually has Lokshen (noodles), Knaidlach (matzo-meal
dumplings), Kreplach (meat-filled noodle dough), or something starchy floating in it.

"Deli" The range of goodies available at the delicatessen,
which, in Jewish parlance, is a kind of restaurant rather than a
kind of grocery store. Corned beef, pastrami, garlic salami,
among other meats, are stacked up on rye bread with dark
mustard. Cole slaw, potato salad, sauerkraut, garlic-flavored
pickles, and celery tonic (a sweetish carbonated drink) are
some traditional accompaniments. For those Jews who do
keep kosher, some delis also feature "dairy" (meatless) dishes
like: Blintzes (pancakes stuffed with cottage cheese or fruit
and anointed with sour cream), "Mock Chopped Liver"
(string beans or mushrooms and hard-boiled eggs), Chopped
Liver (made of chicken livers, chicken fat, and onions). The
traditional Sunday brunch stars some kind of fish—herring in
manifold guises, smoked whitefish, or Lox (salt-cured salmon)
with cream cheese and Bagels (doughnut-shaped rolls
parboiled, then baked) or Bialies (chewy, flat, onion-flavored
rolls).

Gefilte Fish The traditional second course of the Sabbath
dinner. Gefilte Fish is a forcemeat of fish (carp, whitefish, and

pike are especially popular) formed into large patties and poached in fish stock, then served cold in the jellied stock.

The opening of restaurants serving authentic Chinese foods is a fairly recent development in the United States, although restaurants serving so-called Chinese food have been popular for over a century. These Americanized Chinese restaurants were the birthplaces of pseudo-Oriental specialties like Fortune Cookies and Chop Suey.

German, Austrian, Czech, Hungarian, and Polish immigrants, many of whom settled in the midwest, brought their love for pork (including garlic sausages such as Kielbasa), rich meat stews like Gulyas, cabbage (as sauerkraut or stuffed with meat), and rich pastries filled with jam, cheese, or poppy seeds. Noodles and dumplings are much relished; so is the flavor of caraway.

The Scandinavians, many of whom settled in the upper midwest, also enjoy caraway in their rye breads and cakes. They gave America foods like Lutfisk (cod preserved with lye) and Skyr (a kind of yogurt), though most Americans associate Scandinavians with the *smörgåsbord*.

Vichyssoise (cold leek and potato purée soup) and Chicken à la King (creamed chicken with pimientos) were invented in America, not France, as some people think. France's strong culinary influence is most evident in the cosmopolitan United States cities.

More recent immigrants include Cubans and Puerto Ricans, who now serve *comidas criollas* ("home cooking") in many of the large cities of the United States. Cuchifritos (fried pork snacks) have joined Pizza, Knishes, Kielbasa, Tacos and Egg Rolls in the politician's diet.

POT-LUCK

There are many outdoor feasts native to the United States. New Englanders get together for clambakes, where clams, lobsters, and corn steam in seaweed and are set over hot stones in a pit. Marylanders hold oyster roasts. Southerners barbecue pork with spicy sauce. Easterners barbecue steaks, hamburgers, and hotdogs over small portable grills. Texans barbecue beef and kid on a gargantuan scale—huge fire-pits and huge cuts of meat.

Americans celebrate with food at fairs, church suppers, and bean fests. A pot-luck supper, or covered-dish party, is a meal where everyone contributes a dish to the meal. The donations at your table can be luscious or inedible, varied or monotonous. It's a legal form of gambling and as American as apple pie.

Apple pies aren't strictly American, of course; but Americans have developed a wide range of fruit pies, from two-crust numbers to deep-dish pies or cobblers of stewed fruit topped with biscuits. There are custard and cream pies, and one-crust pies topped with meringue. Pie appeared on many nineteenth-century American tables three times a day. Today its dessert dominance is challenged by ice cream, cake, fudgy Brownies, and cookies, including the chocolate-chip *Toll House* Cookie.

BEVERAGES

Americans drink coffee, milk, fruit juice, milk shakes, carbonated soft drinks (called soda, pop, tonic, or soda pop, depending on where you live), tea, iced coffee, and iced tea. In some places, a hot cup of coffee is handed to you with, or before, a restaurant menu. Adult Americans drink milk, and even water, deviations which horrify the averge Frenchman. Americans put ice cubes in most beverages; iced coffee and iced tea are American innovations, largely because wide-spread domestic refrigeration began in the United States. The national sweet tooth is expressed in carbonated drinks, whether sugared or artificially sweetened, and in milk shakes, malts, and other fountain concoctions. Milk shakes and malts used to contain milk, cream, and ice cream (which in turn contained milk and cream); today they often contain skim milk or nondairy products. How the mighty are fallen.

Of course, not every liquid sliding down an American throat is nonalcoholic. Beer, usually mild and very cold, and hard liquor are consumed. Vodka is the most popular hard liquor. Scotch, Bourbon and Gin are also standard. Rum and Tequila are gaining in popularity. The preeminence of Vodka may be due, in part, to its absence of taste; it mixes well with orange juice (Screwdriver), tomato juice (Bloody Mary) or well-nigh anything else (read a Vodka ad). The cocktail (and the cocktail lounge) is in large part an American phenomenon; straight liquor is more popular elsewhere.

Wine drinking is increasing in America, especially in the metropolitan areas, but the average American still consumes far less wine than the average Italian or French person. This is not due to the unavailability of drinkable domestic wine; excellent wines are produced in the United States, the best of them from California. Besides making a unique and noteworthy red wine called Zinfandel, the state produces red Cabernet Sauvignon and white Chardonnay wines that can rival all but France's rare and great wines such as Le Montrachet and Château Lafite-Rothschild. Where California is unquestionably superior to France is in the making of *vin ordinaire*, the inexpensive day-to-day table wine, the mainstay of any wine-drinking nation.

Prohibition's effect on American wine-drinking habits was ambiguous. The American wine industry, then in its infancy, was literally uprooted. But wine, cleverly disguised as grape juice or gingerale, could be obtained in certain restaurants and speakeasies. Sometimes it was less caustic than needled beer or bootleg booze. The habit of drinking wine became established—but the wine was "red ink," not Château Latour, or even fine California Zinfandel. After Repeal, some Americans switched to liquor; some stayed with low-quality wines (their descendants now drink sweet "pop" wines); some learned to love and appreciate good wines. America has wine snobs, who debate the proper Burgundy to drink with a liverwurst sandwich; it also has wine connoisseurs who love to accent a fine meal with the appropriate wine.

⤳ OTHER
NEW WORLD CUISINES

ARGENTINA AND URUGUAY

Argentina is fortunate in sharing with Uruguay the fertile, temperate plains of the pampas where grass grows freely, making cattle raising economical. Naturally, both countries consume a great deal of gaucho-reared beef at modest prices—though by United States standards the meat tends to be a little tough and overcooked. One noticeable difference between these countries is that while Uruguay is also a substantial producer of beef, it does favor lamb and mutton more than its neighbor Argentina.

Some famous beef specialties include:

Carbonada A stew of beef, squash, corn, and peaches baked and served in a hollowed pumpkin or squash shell.

Parrillada A mixed grill of steaks, sausages, and variety meats—few parts of the animal's anatomy are overlooked.

Other popular beef-based specialties include Asados (spit-roasted beef), Bifes a Caballo (steak topped with fried eggs), Matambre (marinated, stuffed, and rolled flank steak), Empanadas (chopped-meat turnovers), Puchero (beef stew), and Churrasco (grilled steak). The national dessert is Dulce de Leche, a sweet custard.

Virtually all Argentine and Uruguayan ancestry can be traced to Europe, including Spain, Italy, England, Ireland, Germany, and Switzerland. Though these bloods have been diffused, you will still find distinct ethnic enclaves with cuisines to match. For instance, you may think you are in Italy when you dine in a restaurant in the La Boca district of Buenos

Aires—or in Switzerland when you eat in some of the homes in the Argentine lake district in the south.

Although Argentina is the fourth-largest wine producer in the world (after France, Italy, the United States, and Spain), little of the wine deserves praise. Argentina and Uruguay's most famous nonalcoholic beverage is the tealike Yerba Maté, made by steeping the leaves of a holly bush in boiling water. This infusion, which can be consumed hot or cold, plain or sweetened, is traditionally sipped through a special tube protruding from a small, hand-held gourd.

BOLIVIA

Body-warming soups and stews such as the various Chupes are logical products of the kitchen stove in this country with its cold climate due to its high altitude.

Despite the fact that Bolivia is landlocked, fish is a component of the diet, provided by icy mountain streams. Also popular are Empanada Salteña (meat turnovers), Lomo Montado (steak topped with fried eggs), Chuno (freeze-dried potatoes, an Inca invention) and the chicken dish Picante de Pollo, spicy in nature, as is much of the Bolivian fare.

Pisco Brandy is widely enjoyed, as is beer, a beverage that manages to produce an enormous head when poured into a glass because of the low atmospheric pressure that exists in these altitudes. Whatever the alcoholic beverage, you are likely to get a quick high in the rarefied air.

CENTRAL AMERICA

From north to south, the seven countries of Central America are Belize, Guatemala, Honduras, El Salvador, Nicaragua, Costa Rica, and Panama. Throughout this necklace of nations, you'll notice definite Spanish influence in the cuisine, with such pan-Latin American favorites as Ceviche, Arroz con Pollo, and the Tamale. You will also notice distinct

Mexican-style dishes, such as Tacos and Enchiladas, particularly in the four northernmost countries. This quartet also reveals traces of Mayan cuisine, since it was once part of the ancient Mayan civilization. In Belize, a touch of the British also exists. The cuisines of the southernmost countries—Nicaragua, Costa Rica, and especially Panama—bear some resemblance to the cooking style of northern Colombia.

All seven countries produce a wealth of tropical fruits (bananas and plantains being the two most prominent examples) that are much employed in the cuisine. The lengthy coasts yield ample fish and shellfish, but it is the latter that wins the epicure's prize. The three principal bulk staples among the peasantry are corn, beans, and rice—the latter two are often served together.

Each nation has its own specialties—or, at least, dishes to which it has some claim for ownership. For instance, Gallo en Chicha (chicken cooked in a ciderlike beverage) is a national favorite in El Salvador and Guatemala. This latter country is also known for Carne en Jocon, a spicy beef stew thickened with crumbled Tortillas. Nicaragua is renowned for its tripe-and-vegetable soup-stew Mondongo, though other Central American republics also readily prepare it. Panama is known for its meat stew Sancocho—but, again, this dish is known in a number of other countries.

The two principal alcoholic beverages of Central America are beer and rum, the latter being the base for a long list of mixed drinks. Tiste is Nicaragua's popular corn-and-cocoa beverage. Coffee is popular—some of the world's finest is grown in Central America, notably in Guatemala and Costa Rica.

CHILE

Chile has three climates: arid in the north, cold and rainy in the south, and fertile and temperate in the middle. There is a minimum of good grazing land, so beef is not a major element in the Chilean diet. Most of the protein comes from the bountiful seafood harvest from Chile's 2,600-mile-long coast-line, enriched by the cool-water Peru Current. Particularly noteworthy are the eels, the oversized sea urchins called erizos, and the congrio (a fish, although its name means "eel" in Spanish). Vegetable mainstays are beans, corn, and squash.

Among the most famous Chilean specialties are:

Caldillo de Congrio   A soup-stew of congrio steaks, potatoes, tomatoes, and onions.

Pastel de Choclo   A deep-dish pie usually made with beef and/or chicken, baked under a topping of chopped corn kernels.

Porotos Granados   A well-seasoned vitamin-filled stew made from fresh beans, corn kernels, squash, and tomatoes.

Other popular treats include Empanadas (pastry turnovers of chopped beef, eggs, onions, raisins, and olives), Humitas (Chile's version of the Hot Tamale), and Chupe de Mariscos (shellfish chowder).

While Chile does not produce anywhere near the quantity of wine its neighbor Argentina does, the wines of Chile are generally of much better quality. Favorite potent drinks include the Pisco and the often slightly bitter Aguardiente brandies, and beer.

COLOMBIA AND VENEZUELA

The majority of the populations of these two countries reside in the inland areas where a comfortable temperate climate prevails. Fittingly the staple foods include corn, potatoes, and beans—yet coastal tropical fruits and vegetables such as the banana, plantain, pineapple, and avocado readily find their way into the kitchens of the upland citizens. Rice and, depending on the region, yucca and coconuts are also mainstays.

Seafood plays a major culinary role along the coasts, while

chicken, pork, lamb, goat, and beef rule inland; beef tends to be tough, requiring slow-cooking techniques.

The two most famous specialties are:

Arepa Ground corn is mixed with salt and water, shaped into small round cakes, and either pan- or deep-fried—it is the peasant's daily bread. Arepas can also be stuffed with fillings such as cheese or seasoned chopped meat.

Hallacas A well-seasoned meat mixture, stuffed inside ground-corn dough, wrapped in banana leaves, and boiled— this is certainly one of Latin America's best versions of the Tamale.

Other well-known dishes include Papas Chorreadas (potatoes smothered in a cheese-and-onion sauce), Pabellon Criollo (shredded beef with rice, black beans, and plantains), Sancocho (a meat or fish and vegetable soup-stew), Ajiaco (a thick potato-and-chicken soup), and Sobrebarriga (stuffed, rolled, and breaded flank steak).

Coffee is widely grown and consumed, particularly in Colombia, which produces some of the world's finest. Hot chocolate and beer are also popular drinks, but if you want something more on the potent side, try the sugar-cane based Guarapo and Aguardiente drinks.

PARAGUAY

This landlocked South American country has adopted many of the culinary traditions of its neighbors, especially those of Argentina. Distinct national dishes include the chopped beef and vegetable soup-stew Soyo-Sopy and the cheese-laden cornbread Sopa Paraguaya. Beef is popular, as are the various delicate-flavored river fishes such as the cherished surubi. Corn, cassava, beans, and oranges figure prominently in the average person's daily diet. The rumlike Caña is Paraguay's premier distilled beverage. Beer, coffee, and Yerba Maté (see Argentina and Uruguay section, above) are also well liked, as is wine, partially the result of the large number of Paraguayans of Italian descent.

GUYANA, SURINAM, AND GUIANA

Guyana's culinary heritage is a mixed bag. You have the influence of the American Indians (the original inhabitants), the British (who came as colonists and settlers), and the Asian Indians, Indonesians, and West Africans (who arrived in great numbers as plantation workers). Still other immigrants included the Chinese, Portuguese, Germans, and Americans, all of whom brought with them their own cooking prejudices and philosophies. Reflecting that cultural variety is a variety of Creole dishes as well as distinct ethnic specialties from around the world. For instance, from India come the many curry-type dishes, from Indonesia comes Nasi Goreng, from Portugal comes garlic pork, and from West Africa come the plantain balls, Foo Foo. Of Guyana's many specialties, it is probably the Pepper Pot (a spicy, long-cooked meat-and-vegetable soup-stew) that is considered the national dish, at least among the townfolk. Pepper Pot is often invigorated with Cassareep, a pre-Columbian condiment made from bitter cassava and various spices. In the more remote inland areas the inhabitants survive on a more or less primitive diet, gaining most of their foods from the surrounding uncultivated lands.

The cuisines of Surinam and French Guiana are in ways similar to that of Guyana, but in these lands Dutch and French influences replace the British influence. In Surinam, for example, the Dutch-Indonesian *rijsttafel* is popular, while in French Guiana, dishes of Gallic persuasion appear on restaurant menus and in private homes.

In all three lands the national hard beverages are rum and beer. The latter is particularly refreshing considering the hot tropical climate.

BIBLIOGRAPHY

EUROPE

Alfredo Viazzi's Italian Cooking by Alfredo Viazzi (Random House, 1979).

Antoine Gilly's Feast of France by Antoine Gilly and Jack Denton Scott (Cassell & Company 1974).

Apicius Cookery and Dining in Imperial Rome edited and translated by Joseph Dommers Vehling (Dover Publications, 1977).

The Art of Belgian Cooking by Sarah Miles Watts and René Colau (Doubleday, 1971).

The Art of Cuisine by Henri de Toulouse-Lautrec and Maurice Joyant (Crescent, 1966).

The Art of Dutch Cooking by Countess van Limburg Stirum (Doubleday, 1965).

The Art of French Cooking by Fernande Garvin (Bantam, 1969).

The Art of Hungarian Cooking by Paula Pogany Bennett and Velma R. Clark (Doubleday, 1954).

The Art of Italian Cooking by Maria Lo Pinto and Milo Miloradovich (Bantam, 1972).

Art of Polish Cooking by Alina Żerańska (Doubleday, 1968).

The Art of Russian Cooking by Nina Nicolareff and Nancy Phelan (Galahad, 1969).

The Art of Scandinavian Cooking by Nika Standen Hazelton (Macmillan, 1965).

The Art of Spanish Cooking by Betty Wason (Doubleday, 1963).

The Belgian Cookbook by Nika Standen Hazelton (Atheneum, 1977).

The Best Foods of Russia by Sonia Uvezian (Harcourt Brace Jovanovich, 1976).

The Best of French Cooking (Larousse, 1977).

British and Irish Cooking by Sally Morris (Garland, 1972).

Charles Virion's French Country Cookbook by Charles Virion (Hawthorn, 1972).

Classic French Cooking by Craig Claiborne and Pierre Franey (Time-Life Books, 1970).

The Complete Book of Pasta by Enrica Jarratt and Vernon Jarratt (Dover Publications, 1977).

The Complete Book of Pasta by Jack Denton Scott (Bantam, 1970).

Cooking à la Cordon Bleu by Alma Lach (Harper & Row, 1970).

Cooking from the Heart of Europe by Robin Howe (David & Charles, 1975).

The Cooking of Germany by Nika Standen Hazelton (Time-Life Books, 1969).

The Cooking of Italy by Waverly Root (Time-Life Books, 1968).

The Cooking of Provincial France by M.F.K. Fisher (Time-Life Books, 1968).

The Cooking of Scandinavia by Dale Brown (Time-Life Books, 1968).

The Cooking of Spain and Portugal by Peter S. Feibleman (Time-Life Books, 1969).

The Cooking of the British Isles by Adrian Bailey (Time-Life Books, 1969).

The Cooking of Vienna's Empire by Joseph Wechsberg (Time-Life Books, 1974).

Cooking the Spanish Way by Elsa Behrens (Spring Books, 1972).

Cooking with a French Touch by Gerald Maurois (Doubleday, 1951).

The Cuisine of Hungary by George Lang (Bonanza, 1971).

The Cuisine of Venice & Surrounding Northern Regions by Hedy Giusti-Lanham and Andrea Dodi (Barron's, 1978).

Customs and Cookery in the Périgord and Quercy by Anne Penton (David & Charles, 1973).

Dinner with Tom Jones by Lorna J. Sass (The Metropolitan Museum of Art, 1977).

Dutch and Belgian Cooking by Heleen A. M. Halverhout (Garland, 1973).

The Eastern European Cookbook by Kay Shaw Nelson (Dover Publications, 1977).

Eating in Italy by Richard Hammond and George Martin (Charles Scribner's Sons, 1957).

Eat Russian by Sofka Skipwith (David & Charles, 1973).

The Estonian Cookbook edited by Viivi Piirisild (Estonian Women's Club of Los Angeles, 1976).

Everyday French Cooking by Henri-Paul Pellaprat (New American Library, 1970).

Finlandia Gastronomica by Matti Viherjuuri et al. Otava, 1974).

The Finnish Cookbook by Beatrice A. Ojakangas (Crown, 1975).

Flavors of Hungary by Charlotte Biro (101 Productions, 1973).

Food & Festivals Swedish Style by Kristina Carheden (Dillon Press, 1968).

France: a Food and Wine Guide by Pamela Vandyke Price (Hastings House, 1966).

French Cook Book by the Editors of Sunset Books (Lane Publishing Co., 1976).

French Cookbook by Suzanne Gibbs (Tradewinds, 1974).

French Cooking by the Staff of 'La Bonne Cuisine', (Garland, 1973).

French Cooking for Americans by Louis Diat (Paperback Library, 1967).

French Country Cooking by Elizabeth David (Penguin, 1966).

French Favorites by Nathalie Le Foll (Determined Productions, 1969).

French Gourmet Vegetarian Cookbook by Rosine Claire (Celestial Arts, 1975).

The French Provincial Cookbook by Colette Black (Collier, 1969).

French Provincial Cooking by Elizabeth David (Penguin, 1969).

French Provincial Cuisine by Christian Délu (Barron's 1977).

The German Cookbook by Mimi Sheraton (Random House, 1965).

German Cookery by Elizabeth Schuler (Crown, 1978).

German Cooking by Arne Krüger (Garland, 1973).

The German Pastry Bakebook by Margit Stoll Dutton (Chilton, 1977).

The Grand Masters of French Cuisine by Céline Vence and Robert Courtine (G.P. Putnam's Sons, 1978).

Great Chefs of France by Anthony Blake and Quentin Crewe (Harry N. Abrams, 1978).

Home Book of Italian Cooking by Angela Catanzaro (Fawcett, 1970).

The Hundred Glories of French Cooking by Robert Courtine (Farrar, Straus & Giroux, 1973).

Italian Cookbook by the staff of the Culinary Arts Institute (New York: Consolidated Book Publishers, 1977).

Italian Cook Book by the Editors of Sunset Books (Lane Books, 1975).

Italian Cooking by Luisa de Ruggiere (Garland, 1973).

Italian Cooking for Pleasure by Mary Reynolds (Hamlyn, 1972).

Italian Cooking Made Easy by Ted and Jean Kaufman (Paperback Library, 1974).

Italian Food by Elizabeth David (Penguin, 1972).

Italian Regional Cooking by Ada Boni (Bonanza, 1969).

La Cuisine by Raymond Oliver (Tudor, 1969).

Larousse Gastronomique by Prosper Montagné (Crown, 1961).

Luchow's German Cookbook by Jan Mitchell (Doubleday, 1962).

Mama D's Homestyle Italian Cookbook by Giovanna D'Agostino (Golden Press, 1975).

Mastering the Art of French Cooking, Volume 1 by Julia Child et al (Knopf, 1977).

Mastering the Art of French Cooking Volume 2 by Julia Child and Simone Beck (Knopf, 1977).

Masterpieces of French Cuisine edited by Francis Amunategue (Macmillan, 1971).

McCall's Introduction to British Cooking edited by Linda Wolfe (Saturday Review Press, 1972).

McCall's Introduction to French Cooking edited by Linda Wolfe (Dell, 1971).

McCall's Introduction to German Cooking edited by Linda Wolfe (Saturday Review Press, 1972).

McCall's Introduction to Scandinavian Cooking edited by Linda Wolfe (Saturday Review Press, 1971).

Michel Guerard's Cuisine Minceur (William Morrow, 1976).

Natural Cooking the Finnish Way by Ulla Käkönen (Quadrangle, 1974).

The Northern Italian Cookbook by Teresa Gilardi Candler (McGraw-Hill, 1977).

Northern Italian Cooking by Francesco Ghedini (Hawthorn, 1973).

The Nouvelle Cuisine of Jean & Pierre Troisgros translated by Roberta Wolfe Smoler (William Morrow, 1978).

Ola's Norwegian Cookbook by Lucie Keyser Frölich (Modern Printing Co., 1951).

Paul Bocuse's French Cooking translated by Colette Rossant edited by Lorraine Davis (Pantheon Books, 1977).

Polish Cookbook by the Staff of the Culinary Arts Institute (Consolidated Book Publishers, 1976).

Polish Cook Book (Creative Composition, 1977).

Popular French Cookery by Mary Berry (Octopus, 1972).

Portrait of Pasta by Anna del Conte (Paddington Press Ltd., 1976).

Recipes of Old England compiled by Bernard N. Bessunger (David & Charles, 1973).

Regional French Cookery by Kenneth Toyé (International Wine and Food Publishing Co./David & Charles, 1973).

The Regional Italian Kitchen by Nika Hazelton (M. Evans, 1978).

Revolutionizing French Cooking by Roy Andries de Groot (McGraw-Hill, 1976).

The Romagnolis' Meatless Cookbook by Margaret and G. Franco Romagnoli (Little, Brown, 1976).

The Romagnolis' Table by Margaret and G. Franco Romagnoli (Bantam, 1977).

Russian Cooking by Helen and George Papashvily (Time-Life Books, 1969).

Sallets Humbles and Shrewsbery Cakes by Ruth Anne Beebe (David R. Godine, 1976).

Scandinavian Cookbook by the Editors of Sunset Books (Lane Publishing Co., 1975).

Scandinavian Cooking (Crown, 1976).

Scandinavian Cooking by Gunnevi Bonekamp (Garland, 1973).

Scandinavian Recipes compiled by Julia Peterson Tufford (Tufford, 1973).

Simple French Food by Richard Olney (Atheneum, 1977).

Smörgåsbord and Scandinavian Cookery by Florence Brobeck and Monika Kjellberg (Grosset & Dunlap, 1948).

The Spanish Cookbook by Barbara Norman (Bantam, 1971).

A Taste of Ireland by Theodora FitzGibbon (Pan Books Ltd., 1971).

To The King's Taste by Lorna J. Sass (The Metropolitan Museum of Art, 1975).

To The Queen's Taste by Lorna J. Sass (The Metropolitan Museum of Art, 1976).

Traditional British Cookery by Maggie Malpas Pearse (International Wine & Food Publishing Co., 1972).

Treasure Trove of Hungarian Cookery by Mariska Vizvári (Branden Press, 1961).

What's Cooking in Portugal by Saul Krieg (Macmillan, 1974).

When French Women Cook by Madeleine Kamman (Atheneum, 1976).

MIDDLE EAST AND AFRICA

The African Cookbook by Bea Sandler (World Publishing, 1972).

African Cooking by Laurens van der Post et al. (Time-Life Books,1970).

The Art of Greek Cookery by The Women of St. Paul's Greek Orthodox Church (Doubleday, 1963).

The Art of Syrian Cookery by Helen Corey (Doubleday, 1962).

A Book of Middle Eastern Food by Claudia Roden (Vintage, 1972).

The Complete Greek Cookbook by Theresa Karas Yianilos (Avenel Books, 1970).

Cooking and Baking the Greek Way by Anne Theoharous (Holt Rinehart and Winston, 1977).

Eastern Mediterranean Cooking by Roger Debasque (Galahad,1973).

First Catch Your Eland by Laurens van der Post (William Morrow, 1978).

The Flavor of Jerusalem by Joan Nathan and Judy Stacey Goldman (Little, Brown 1975).

The Greek Cook Book by Sophia Skoura (Crown, 1977).

Greek Cooking for the Gods by Eva Zane (101 Productions, 1976).

In a Persian Kitchen by Maideh Mazda (Charles E. Tuttle, 1960).

The Israeli Cook Book by Molly Lyons Bar-David (Crown, 1977).

Kitchen Safari by Harva Hachten (Atheneum, 1970).

Middle Eastern Cookery by Eva Zane (101 Productions, 1974).

Middle Eastern Cooking by Harry G. Nickles (Time-Life Books, 1969).

The Moroccan Cookbook by Irene F. Day (Quick Fox, 1975).

Rayess' Art of Lebanese Cooking by George N. Rayess (Librairie du Liban, 1966).

The South African Culinary Tradition by Renata Coetzee (C. Struik, 1977).

A West African Cookbook by Ellen Gibson Wilson (Avon, 1971).

ASIA AND THE PACIFIC

Adventures in Indian Cooking by Mary Atwood (Jaico, 1975).

Afghan Cookery compiled and edited by Doris McKellar (Afghan Book, 1972).

The Art of Indian Cooking by Monica Dutt (Bantam, 1972).

The Art of Indian Cuisine by Pranati Sen Gupta (Hawthorn, 1974).

The Australian Hostess Cookbook edited by Hanna Pan (Thomas Nelson Ltd., undated).

The Bengal Lancers Indian Cookbook by Mohan Chablani and Brahm N. Dixit (Henry Regnery, 1976).

The Book of Tofu by William Shurtleff and Akiko Aoyagi (Autumn Press, 1975).

Ceylon Cookery by Chandra Dissanayake (Metro Printers, 1976).

The Chinese Cookbook compiled and edited by M. Sing Au (Culinary Arts Press, 1970).

The Chinese Cookbook by Craig Claiborne and Virginia Lee (Lippincott, 1972).

The Chinese Cookbook by Lydia Wang (Kamakura Shobo Publishing Co. Ltd., 1971).

Chinese Cookery by Ella-Mei Wong (Arco, 1976).

Chinese Cooking by Lee To Chun (Garland, 1973).

Chinese Cooking for Pleasure by Helen Burke and Fu Tong (Hamlyn, 1965).

Chinese Gastronomy by Hsiang Ju Lin and Tsuifeng Lin (Pyramid, 1969).

The Chinese Menu Cookbook by Joanne Hush and Peter Wong (Holt, Rinehart and Winston, 1976).

Chinese Tasty Tales Cookbook by Gary Lee (Chinese Treasure Productions, 1974).

Classic Chinese Cook Book by Mai Leung (Harper & Row, 1976).

The Complete Asian Cookbook by Charmaine Solomon (McGraw-Hill, 1976).

The Complete Book of Japanese Cooking by Elizabeth Lambert Ortiz with Mitsuko Endo (M. Evans & Co., 1976).

The Complete Book of Oriental Cooking by Myra Waldo (Bantam, 1960).

Cooking Hunan Style by Louise Stallard (Drake, 1973).

The Cooking of China by Emily Hahn (Time-Life Books, 1968).

The Cooking of India by Santha Rama Rau (Time-Life Books, 1969).

The Cooking of Japan by Rafael Steinberg (Time-Life Books, 1969).

Cooking of the Maharajas by Shivaji Rao and Shalini Devi Holkar (Viking, 1975).

Cooking Szechuan-Style by Louise Stallard (Drake, 1973).

Cooking the Indian Way by Attia Hosarn and Sita Pasricha (Spring Books, 1962).

Cook Japanese by Masaru Doi (Kodansha International Ltd., 1970).

The Culinary Culture of the Philippines edited by Gilda Cordero-Fernando (Vera-Reyes Inc., 1976).

The Easy Way to Chinese Cooking by Beverly Lee (New American Library, 1971).

Eight Immortal Flavors by Johnny Kan and Charles L. Leong (Howell-North Books, 1963).

Eighty Precious Chinese Recipes by May Wong Trent (Macmillan, 1973).

An Encyclopedia of Chinese Food and Cooking by Wonona W. Chang et al. (Crown, 1970).

Far Eastern Cookery by Robin Howe (Drake, 1971).

Far Eastern Cooking for Pleasure by Nina Froud (Hamlyn, 1971).

The Fine Art of Chinese Cooking by Dr. Lee Su Jan and May Lee (Gramercy Publishing, 1957).

Five Treasures of Chinese Cuisine by Flora L. Chang and Gaynell M. Fuchs (Oriental Publishing, 1975).

Flavors of India by Shanta Nimbark Sacharoff (101 Productions, 1972).

Florence Lin's Chinese One-Dish Meals by Florence Lin (Hawthorn, 1978).

Florence Lin's Chinese Regional Cookbook by Florence Lin (Hawthorn, 1975).

Florence Lin's Chinese Vegetarian Cookbook by Florence Lin (Hawthorn, 1976).

Good Food From India by Shanti Rangarao (Jaico, 1977).

Henry Chung's Hunan Style Chinese Cookbook by Henry Chung (Harmony Books, 1978).

Himalayan Mountain Cookery by Mrs. Rudolph M. Ballentine, Sr. (Himalayan International Institute of Yoga Science and Philosophy, 1976).

The Home Book of Indonesian Cookery by Sri Owen (Faber and Faber, 1976).

How to Cook and Eat in Chinese by Buwei Yang Chao (Random House, 1945).

How to Order and Eat in Chinese by Buwei Yang Chao (Vintage, 1974).

Illustrated Step-by-Step Chinese Cookbook by Paul C. Huang (Simon and Schuster, 1975).

Indian Cookery by Surjeet Malhan (Jaico Publishing House, 1969).

Indian Cookery by Mrs. Balbir Singh (Weathervane Books, 1973).

Indian Cooking by Dharamjit Singh (Penguin, 1970).

Indian Cooking for Pleasure by Premila Lal (Hamlyn, 1970).

Indian Meat & Fish Cookery by Jack Santa Maria (Rider, 1977).

Introducing Chinese Casserole Cookery by Lilah Kan (Workman Publishing, 1978).

An Invitation to Indian Cooking by Madhur Jaffrey (Vintage Books, 1975).

Japanese Cooking by Sadako Kohno (Shufunotomo Co., 1968).

Japanese Cooking by Peter and Joan Martin (New American Library, 1970).

Japanese Country Cookbook by Russ Rudzinski (Nitty Gritty, 1969).

Japanese Food and Cooking by Stuart Griffin (Charles E. Tuttle, 1971).

The Joy of Chinese Cooking by Doreen Yen Hung Feng (Grosset & Dunlap, undated).

The Key to Chinese Cooking by Irene Kuo (Knopf, 1977).

The Long and the Short of Chinese Cooking by James Rollband (Crossing Press, 1977).

The Love of Chinese Cooking by Kenneth Lo (Octopus, 1977).

Madame Chu's Chinese Cooking School by Grace Zia Chu (Simon and Schuster, 1975).

Mrs. Chiang's Szechwan Cookbook by Ellen Schrecker and John Schrecker (Harper & Row, 1976).

Mrs. Ma's Chinese Cookbook by Nancy Chih Ma (Charles E. Tuttle, 1960).

Mrs. Ma's Favorite Chinese Recipes by Nancy Chih Ma (Kodansha International Ltd., 1970).

Naturally Chinese by Ruth Rodale Spira (Rodale Press, 1974).

Oriental Cook Book by the Editors of Sunset Books (Lane Publishing Co., 1977).

Oriental Cooking the Fast Wok Way by Jacqueline Hériteau (New American Library, 1971).

Pacific and Southeast Asian Cooking by Rafael Steinberg (Time-Life Books, 1970).

Philippine Cooking in America by Marilyn Ranada Donato (Circulation Service Inc., 1977).

The Pleasures of Chinese Cooking by Grace Zia Chu (Pocket Books, 1977).

The Pleasures of Japanese Cooking by Heihachi Tanaka and Betty A. Nichols (Cornerstone Library, 1971).

The Polynesian Cookbook by Victor Bennett (Galahad, undated).

Recipes of the Philippines compiled and edited by Enriqueta David-Perez (DM Press, 1968).

Regional Cooking of China by Margaret Gin and Alfred E. Castle (101 Productions, 1975).

The Science of Philippine Foods by P.T. Arroyo (Abaniko Enterprises, 1974).

The Scrutable Feast by Dorothy Farris Lapidus (Dodd, Mead, 1977).

Simple Japanese Cooking compiled by the Japanese Cooking Companions (Nippon Kodo, 1967).

South East Asian Food by Rosemary Brissenden (Penguin, 1972).

A Taste of Bali by Thelma Peck (P.T. Bap, 1975).

A Taste of India by Mary S. Atwood (Avon, 1969).

Tempura and Sukiyaki compiled by the Japanese Cooking Companions (Japan Publications, 1961).

The Thousand Recipe Chinese Cookbook by Gloria Bley Miller (Grosset & Dunlap, 1970).

Typical Japanese Cooking edited by the Japanese Cooking Companions (Japan Publications, 1970).

The Wok by Gary Lee (Nitty Gritty, 1970).

NEW WORLD

American Cooking by Dale Brown (Time-Life Books 1968).

American Cooking by Irena Kirshman (Galahad, 1973).

American Cooking: Creole and Acadian by Peter S. Feibleman (Time-Life Books, 1971).

American Cooking: New England by Jonathan Norton Leonard (Time-Life Books, 1970).

American Cooking: Southern Style by Eugene Walter (Time-Life Books, 1971).

American Cooking: The Eastern Heartland by José Wilson (Time-Life Books, 1971).

American Cooking: The Great West by Jonathan Norton Leonard (Time-Life Books, 1971).

American Cooking: The Melting Pot by James P. Shenton et al. (Time-Life Books, 1971).

American Cooking: The Northwest by Dale Brown (Time-Life Books, 1970).

American Food by Evan Jones (Dutton, 1975).

American Gastronomy by Louis Szathmáry (Arno, 1974).

The American Regional Cookbook by Nancy and Arthur Hawkins (Prentice-Hall, 1976).

Authentic Mexican Cooking by Betty A. Blue (Prentice-Hall, 1977).

The California Heritage Cookbook by The Junior League of Pasadena (Doubleday, 1976).

Caribbean Cooking for Pleasure by Mary Slater (Hamlyn, 1970).

The Carter Family Favorites Cookbook by Ceil Dyer (Delacorte, 1977).

The Complete Book of Mexican Cooking by Elizabeth Lambert Ortiz (Bantam, 1976).

Cooking American by Sidney W. Dean (Hill and Wang, 1975).

The Cooking of the Caribbean Islands by Linda Wolfe (Time-Life Books 1970).

Cooking the Caribbean Way by Mary Slater (Novelty Trading, 1974).

The Cuisines of Mexico by Diana Kennedy (Harper & Row, 1972).

Eating in America by Waverly Root and Richard de Rochemont (William Morrow, 1976).

Favorite American Recipes (USDA, 1974).

Favorite Regional Recipes of America edited by Marian Tracy (Grosset & Dunlap, 1952).

The Florida Cookbook by George S. Fichter (E.A. Seemann Publishing, 1973).

Foods from Harvest Festivals and Folk Fairs by Anita Borghese (Thomas Y. Crowell, 1977).

Foods of the Frontier by Gertrude Harris (101 Productions, 1972).

The Frugal Colonial Housewife by Susannah Carter (Dolphin Books, 1976).

Geoffrey Holder's Caribbean Cookbook by Geoffrey Holder (Viking, 1973).

Good Food from Mexico by Ruth Watt Mulvey and Luisa Maria Alvarez (Collier, 1962).

Gourmet's Guide to New Orleans by Natalie V. Scott and Caroline Merrick Jones (Pelican, 1975).

Grace Hartley's Southern Cookbook by Grace Hartley (Doubleday, 1976).

Grandmother's Country Cookbook by Ted and Jean Kaufman (Warner, 1966).

Harvest of American Cooking by Mary Margaret McBride (Putnam, 1957).

June Platt's New England Cook Book by June Platt (Atheneum, 1971).

Justin Wilson Cook Book by Justin Wilson (Pelican, 1975).

The Ladies' Aid Cookbook by Beatrice Vaughan (Stephen Greene Press, 1971).

Latin American Cooking by Susan Bensusan (Galahad, 1973).

Latin American Cooking by Jonathan Norton Leonard (Time-Life Books, 1968).

McCall's Introduction to Mexican Cooking edited by Linda Wolfe (Dell, 1971).

The Melting Pot by Maria Gitin (The Crossing Press, 1977).

The Mexican Cook Book by George and Inger Wallace (Nitty Gritty, 1971).

Mexican Cookbook by the Editors of Sunset Books (Lane Books, 1972).

Mexican Cookbook by Erna Fergusson (Doubleday, 1965).

Mexican Cookbook by the Staff of the Culinary Arts Institute (Consolidated Book Publishers, 1976).

The Mexican Stove by Richard Condon (Doubleday, 1973).

Nantucket and Other New England Cooking by Nancy Hawkins, et al. (Hastings House, 1976).

National Treasury of Cookery compiled by Helen Duprey Bullock (Heirloom, 1967).

The New York Times New England Heritage Cookbook by Jean Hewitt (G.P. Putnam's Sons, 1977).

On the Town in New York by Michael and Ariane Batterberry (Charles Scribner's Sons, 1973).

Original Boston Cooking-School Cook Book 1896 by Fannie Farmer (New American Library, 1974).

Pennsylvania Dutch Cook Book by J. George Frederick (Dover, 1971).

Pennsylvania Dutch Cookbook edited by Claire S. Davidow (Culinary Arts Press, 1961).

Pennsylvania Dutch People's Cookbook edited by Lillie S. Lustig (Culinary Arts Press, 1968).

Plain Cooking by Bill Randle (Quadrangle, 1974).

Princess Pamela's Soul Food Cookbook (New American Library, 1969).

Pueblo & Navajo Cookery by Marcia Keegan (Earth Books, 1977).

Puerto Rican Cookery by Carmen Aboy Valldejuli (Alpine Press, 1975).

Recipes from America's Restored Villages by Jean Anderson (Doubleday, 1975).

Recipes from the Regional Cooks of Mexico by Diana Kennedy (Harper & Row, 1978).

A Salute to American Cooking by Stephen and Ethel Longstreet (Hawthorn, 1968).

The Saturday Evening Post All-American Cookbook by Charlotte Turgeon and Frederic A. Birmingham (Thomas Nelson, Inc., 1976).

Soul Food Cookbook by Jimmy Lee (Award, 1970).

Soul to Soul by Mary Burgess (Woodbridge Press, 1976).

The South American Cook Book by Cora Brown et al. (Dover, 1971).

Southwestern Cookery compiled by Louis Szathmáry (Promontory Press, 1974).

Spoonbread and Strawberry Wine by Norma Jean and Carole Darden (Anchor Press, 1978).

The Taste of America by John L. Hess and Karen Hess (Grossman, 1977).

The Tortilla Book by Diana Kennedy (Harper & Row, 1975).

The World of Mexican Cooking by Mary Margaret Curry (Nash Publishing, 1971).

Yukon Cookbook by Leona Kananen (J.J. Douglas Ltd., 1975).

BEVERAGES

Alexis Lichine's Encyclopedia of Wines & Spirits by Alexis Lichine et al. (Knopf, 1967).

The Book of Drinking by John Doxat (Triune Books, 1973).

Cheers by Francesca White (Paddington Press, 1977).

Coffee by Charles and Violet Schafer (Yerba Buena Press, 1976).

The Diner's Guide to Wines by Howard Hillman (Hawthorn, 1978).

Frank Schoonmaker's Encyclopedia of Wine by Frank Schoonmaker (Hastings House, 1975).

The Game of Wine by Forrest Wallace and Gilbert Cross (Doubleday, 1976).

Gods, Men and Wine by William Younger (Wine and Food Society, 1966).

The Great Book of Wine by Edita Lausanne (World, 1970).

The Great Wines of Italy by Philip Dallas (Doubleday, 1974).

Grossman's Guide to Wines, Spirits and Beers by Harold J. Grossman and revised by Harriet Lembeck (Charles Scribner's Sons, 1977).

A History of Brewing by H.S. Corran (David & Charles, 1975).

Larousse Dictionary of Wines of the World by Gérard Debuigne (Larousse, 1970).

The New York Times Book of Wine by Terry Robards (Quadrangle, 1976).

The Signet Book of American Wine by Peter Quimme (New American Library, 1975).

The Signet Book of Coffee and Tea by Peter Quimme (New American Library, 1976).

The Signet Book of Wine by Alexis Bespaloff (New American Library, 1971).

The Taste of Wine by Pamela Vandyke Price (Random House, 1975).

The Taster's Guide to Beer by Michael A. Weiner (Collier Books, 1977).

Tea by Milane Christiansen (Ventures International, 1972).

The Vintage Wine Book by William S. Leedom (Vintage, 1963).

Wine by Hugh Johnson (Simon & Schuster, 1966).

Wine Talk by Frank J. Prial (Times Books, 1979).

A Wine Tour of France by Frederick S. Wildman Jr. (William Morrow, 1972).

Wines and Spirits by Alec Waugh (Time-Life Books, 1968).

The Wines of America by Leon D. Adams (McGraw-Hill, 1978).

Wines of California by Robert L. Balzer (Harry N. Abrams, 1978).

Wines of France by Alexis Lichine and William E. Massee (Knopf, 1965).

The Wines of Germany by Heinrich Meinhard (Stein and Day, 1976).

The Wines of Italy by Cyril Ray (Octopus, 1966).

The Wines of Italy by Sheldon Wasserman (Stein and Day, 1976).

Wines of the World edited by Andre L. Simon (McGraw-Hill, 1967).

World Atlas of Wine by Hugh Johnson (Mitchell Beazley Publishers, 1971).

World of Drinks and Drinking by John Doxat (Drake, 1971).

World Wine Almanac and Wine Atlas by Grace Treber (International Wine Society, 1976).

GENERAL

The Art of Jewish Cooking by Jenny Grossinger (Bantam, 1972).

The Cookbook of the United Nations compiled and edited by Barbara Kraus (Simon and Schuster, 1970).

Correspondent's Choice edited by Lee Foster (Quadrangle, 1974).

Dictionary of Gastronomy by Andre L. Simon and Robin Howe (The Overlook Press, 1978).

Dictionary of International Food & Cooking Terms by Myra Waldo (Macmillan, 1967).

Exotic Food by Rupert Cruft-Cooke (Herder & Herder, 1971).

Famous Dishes of the World by Wina Born (Macmillan, 1973).

Fine Art of Food by Reay Tannahill (A.S. Barnes, 1970).

Food in History by Reay Tannahill (Stein and Day, 1973).

The Food of the Western World by Theodora FitzGibbon (Quadrangle, 1976).

Gastronomy by Jay Jacobs (Newsweek Books, 1975).

Good Housekeeping International Cookbook edited by Dorothy B. Marsh (Good Housekeeping Book Division, 1964).

Grand Diplôme Cooking Course (20 volumes) edited by Anne Willan (Danbury Press, 1972).

Hering's Dictionary of Classical and Modern Cookery translated by Walter Bickel (Virtue & Company, 1974).

The Horizon Cookbook by William Harlan Hale, et al. (Doubleday, 1968).

Jewish Cookery by Leah W. Leonard (Crown, 1977).

Jewish Cookery from Boston to Baghdad by Malvina W. Liebman (E.A. Seemann Publishing, 1975).

Jewish Cooking for Pleasure by Molly Lyons Bar-David (Hamlyn, 1965).

The Jewish Festival Cookbook by Fannie Engle and Gertrude Blair (Warner, 1975).

The Joy of Eating by Katie Stewart (Stemmer House, 1977).

Love and Knishes by Sara Kasdan (Fawcett, 1956).

Molly Goldberg Jewish Cookbook by Gertrude Berg and Myra Waldo (Pyramid, 1971).

A Quintet of Cuisines by Michael and Frances Field (Time-Life Books, 1970).

Seven Wonders of the Cooking World by Myra Waldo (Dodd, Mead, 1971).

Woman's Day Encyclopedia of Cookery (12 volumes) by the Editors of Woman's Day (Fawcett, 1966).

The World Atlas of Food contributing editor, Jane Grigson (Mitchell Beazley Publishers, 1974).

You Don't Have to be Jewish to be a Good Cook Book by Lois Levine and Kathryn Winer (Apollo, 1971).

INDEX

For a complete list of books available from Penguin in the United States, write to Dept. DG, Penguin Books, 299 Murray Hill Parkway, East Rutherford, New Jersey 07073.

For a complete list of books available from Penguin in Canada, write to Penguin Books Canada Limited, 2801 John Street, Markham, Ontario L3R 1B4.

THE TASTE OF AMERICA

John L. Hess and Karen Hess

American food has been drained of flavor and nourishment, crammed with additives, and disguised by fancy packaging. Our cookbooks are full of nonsense, and our finest restaurants serve frozen foods with French names at intolerable prices. Worst of all, our so-called experts encourage food-snobbery and promote ignorance and error. This is an angry and a much-needed book; it is also a hopeful one, for John L. Hess and Karen Hess celebrate the richness of what used to be and tell us that we can once again enjoy good food if only we resist the forces of bad taste and bad nutrition. "A passionate and sweeping philippic...a spectacular collection of faults found, chances missed"—*The New York Times Book Review*.

THE WHOLE-WORLD WINE CATALOG

William I. Kaufman

Wine labels contain, says William I. Kaufman, much more information than most people suspect—information that wine-shoppers could put to good use and profit if only they understood the meanings of the words and the symbols. In this easy reference guide to the world of wines, wine labels, and tastings, Kaufman shows us how to interpret the labels on hundreds of wines ranging from Amontillado to Tokay, from vineyards in countries as diverse as Algeria, Argentina, Denmark, France, the United States, Japan, and South Africa. Using this remarkable book, you can be sure of getting exactly the wine you want, within any price range.